DEATH IN THE WEST

DEATH IN THE WEST

Fatal Stories from America's Last Frontiers

Chris Becker

NORTHLAND
PUBLISHING

www.northlandbooks.com

Composed in the United States of America
Printed in Canada

Edited by Claudine J. Randazzo
Art Directed by Sunny H. Yang
Designed by David J. Alston

First Impression 2007
ISBN 10: 0-87358-893-2
ISBN 13: 978-0-87358-893-5

10   09   08   07   4   3   2   1

Library of Congress Cataloging-in-Publication Data:

Becker, Chris
Death in the West / by Chris Becker.
        p. cm.
Includes bibliographical references and index.
ISBN-13: 978-0-87358-893-5 (sc : alk. paper)
ISBN-10: 0-87358-893-2 (sc : alk. paper)
1. West (U.S.)—History—Anecdotes. 2. West (U.S.)—Description and travel—Anecdotes. 3. Death—West (U.S.)—History—Anecdotes. 4. Violent deaths—West (U.S.)—History—Anecdotes. 5. Accidents—West (U.S.)—History—Anecdotes. 6. Disasters—West (U.S,)—History—Anecdotes. 7. Wilderness area users—West (U.S.)—Biography—Anecdotes. 8. West (U.S.)—Biography—Anecdotes. I. Title.
F591.B38 2007
917.8—dc22

                        2006102213

To the victims herein and their families,
let this sharing of stories serve not to bring more pain,
but to inform the steps of those who follow them.

And to Danielle and Evie,
who spent many nights milling around the bookstore
waiting for me to finish writing this book. I love you.

CONTENT

Introduction
It Can Happen To You

A man diving for abalone off the coast of California never sees the great white shark that has targeted him. His head washes up on the beach a week later.

Two visitors looking for a little taste of the desert head into the backcountry above New Mexico's Carlsbad Caverns. They plan to spend one night and hike a mile into the sands. They are found four days later, one having stabbed the other to death. According to the survivor, he was putting his friend out of his thirsty, sunbaked misery.

In that same New Mexico desert, a psychotic handyman builds a torture chamber in a nondescript white trailer on his barren property. He continues torturing and murdering women for close to a decade before getting caught.

Meanwhile, on one of America's busiest ski mountains, primordial gasses from the Earth's inner reaches kill five skiers inside of a minute.

And in southern California, torrential rains detach a mountainside that proceeds to bury an entire town under a thick mantle of mud and rock.

None of these things will happen to you in Ohio, or South Carolina, or Vermont. Every one, however, can happen in the American West. In fact, each one did.

More than any region of the United States, the West connotes an air of danger—of gunfights and natural catastrophes, punishing weather extremes, and a somewhat shadier, stranger element than the rest of the country would likely put up with. (Name a town in New England that would accept being called Tombstone, or Truth or Consequences, the little New Mexico town monikered after a 1950s game show.) In addition, the natural pitfalls westerners face make the very landscape a threat when conditions degenerate. Yellowstone National Park, for example, rests upon one of the largest cauldrons of volcanic activity in the entire world; if a major eruption happened there, people from Los Angeles to Jackson Hole would know about it, though only for a couple of minutes.

Yet the West's population continues to grow by huge leaps, fed by people from America and abroad seeking a piece of a mystique as expansive as the region's geography. California holds a sacred place as the geographic embodiment of opportunity, from the Gold Rush up through the Silicon Valley and the current influx of Latino immigrants. Phoenix and Las Vegas are the latest American boomtowns, places where buying low and selling high attract fortune seekers from the more predictable, staid cities of the East. Colorado, Washington, Oregon—all these states evoke images of beautiful landscape, clean and healthy communities, and outdoor adventure of the most wholesome and picturesque kind. Among many other things, perceptions like these bring people westward in search of the land their forebears have flocked to for the last two centuries.

That place exists, certainly. But so does the Wild West (not the Wild West with the cowboys—but a whole new breed of wild). And sometimes, it ain't pretty. Despite sparkling P.R. from John Muir on down through Ansel Adams and Edward Abbey, despite continued growth and modernization, despite the sheer population boom the West has seen over the last twenty years, its ornery streak still persists. Those immigrants seeking their fortunes across the border die by the hundreds every summer, succumbing to merciless heat in one of America's most lethal places. People setting out for relaxing hikes and bike rides find their days rudely ended by predatory creatures with mouths full of sharp teeth. Perhaps most disturbingly, in a perverse side effect of its "land of opportunity" attraction, deranged men and women from the rest of the country migrate to the West in order to ply their murderous trades, staining benign places like Yosemite and Malibu with fear and paranoia.

Despite our best efforts to tame and domesticate this Wild West, despite every attempt to bring it under our sway with air conditioning, paved hiking trails, and tourist-trappy visitor centers, the project never quite finished up.

From an environmental point of view, there are excellent and multiple reasons to consider the western United States a hostile landscape. Average summertime temperatures in Arizona and inland southern California regularly top out at one hundred twenty degrees, as high as temperatures in the Sahara Desert and perfectly capable of boiling your insides within hours without proper hydration and exit strategy. The Pacific roils off our western shore, with all its temper and force, and periodically storms batter California until large pieces of the place slide off as muddy chunks into the ocean. The so-called Red Triangle off San Francisco, home to the world's highest concentration of great white sharks, is the most dangerous patch of ocean in North America. Towering mountains dot the landscape, beckoning climbers both skilled and otherwise to maroon themselves on massive rock faces, while the simple predominance of wide-open, uninhabited space makes many outdoor destinations very lonely places to find yourself out of luck. To say nothing of the geologic commotion underfoot; California's San Andreas Fault may be the shakiest section of real estate in the world, already responsible for tens of thousands of quakes over the last century, some of them truly titanic. And let's not forget those primal forces resting—for now—under Yellowstone. The idea of a major catastrophe there fits the phrase "doomsday scenario" better than just about anything else you can think of. Our land animals occasionally make human beings part of their food chain, and attacks from some such beasts are on the rise as we insinuate ourselves ever deeper into their natural habitats. Trust me when I say that every one of these factors has made someone regret ever thinking about following that westward train, often in his or her final minutes on this planet.

Death in the West provides firsthand proof that, despite all the building and taming we've done over the last century or so, every one of these factors still presents a danger, albeit a thankfully small one in most cases.

Other stories here demonstrate the terrible things human beings can do to each other, either out of perceived necessity, terrible malice, or simple recklessness. Murderers foul the air all over this country, as they do the world. The killers included here, however, all have a certain connection with the West's defining characteristics—Cary Stayner conducted his savage business in and around Yosemite, one of the world's most beautiful places; William Bonin and his various accomplices prowled the legendary highways of California, the birthplace of American road culture, turning that heritage into a bloody nightmare; and the wide, punishing southwestern desert played host to David Parker Ray and his demented "fun house," swallowing the screams of his victims with its isolation.

Stories of murder and mayhem never make sense to sane people, and the murderous tales here are no different in that respect. But many of the tales involving nature and its vagaries do add up; despite nature's capriciousness (and she can certainly be that at times), few of these stories involve calamity dropping out of a clear blue sky. Instead, luck, decision, and circumstance intersect at the worst possible moment, and somebody ends up dead.

Above all else, really, *Death in the West* stands as a monument to rotten luck—being in the wrong place when the rockslide loosens, or the boat passes too close, or the plane falls from the sky. Even when the fatal event is precipitated by human errors, the fatal outcome is by no means the only one possible. Other people have performed most of the stupid acts in these stories; they simply lived to tell about it, being far luckier. From small judgment lapses to colossal, idiotic mistakes, very few errors are fatal in and of themselves. But when abetted by an environment that refuses, particularly in moments of greatest distress, to cooperate, mistakes large and small can, and sometimes will, kill you. The West, at its worst moments, is an unforgiving environment, one of the harshest considering how much we've already put into taming it.

So maybe we can afford to be a tad flip at times in the face of what are, to be sure, terrible events. Many of these stories, perhaps even most of them, could have been avoided had someone brought the map, kept their hands to themselves, or otherwise prepared for the situation they suddenly faced. The Wild West simply helps calamity along most of the time. The truly unlucky among these victims encounter such long odds that worrying about them would be akin to keeping track of how you'll spend your lottery dollars when you win. As terrible as being attacked by a shark, or bear, or psychotic human being might be, it just doesn't make sense to sweat about it, even if you spend every day of your life on the left side of the country.

The moral is this: respect the West, keep mistakes to a minimum, and it probably won't kill you. In fact, it probably won't even if you screw up royally.

But it could happen. Here's how.

CHAPTER ONE

Death Deep In
Mishandling the Backcountry

Everyone who dies out there dies of confusion.

—LAURENCE GONZALES,
Deep Survival: Who Lives, Who Dies, and Why

Hiking, skiing, biking—none of these activities immediately strikes the danger chord. In fact, they make up the relatively tame end of the outdoor sports spectrum; your grandmother can participate in every one of them, and a lot of grandmothers, including mine, do. Or did—though some might consider her tooling, miles-long strolls around New York City something less than a real hike.

But as in the world of real estate, the truest test of an outdoor excursion's threat level is location, location, location. A brisk walk through the East Village may be a hike, but get thirsty and you're fine, provided you have a few bucks. The same logic applies in the well-traveled zones of state and national parks—you stand a pretty small chance of getting into trouble if you stick to the paths, and if something does happen, a friendly ranger will almost certainly bail you out.

Once you leave the trail, though, you're on your own, which is one reason so many people take to the backcountry in the first place. Wilderness journeys derive much of their appeal from solitude, along with the satisfaction inherent in taking care of yourself—from wake up and roll up to campfire dinner. You aren't *supposed* to see anybody out there; you want to get as close as you can to a one-on-one with the natural world, a worthy goal provided you are ready for the implications of that powwow.

Hitting the western backcountry and doing it successfully is no picnic. The amenities get a whole lot leaner, for one thing; throughout much of the West, nature is something less than hospitable. In some places, the only comforts of home to be found are the ones you bring along in your backpack. And the backcountry, by definition, doesn't feature well-traveled routes along which you're bound to find help if things go badly. The deserts of Arizona, New Mexico, and southern California don't forgive mistakes, period. The same could be said of the high mountain crags of the Rockies, or the waters of the West's numerous lakes and rivers. If things spiral away beyond your ability to fix them, the backup from the bench is quite shallow in all these places.

Even the boundaries of our best-known national parks contain worlds in which human beings have none of the advantages that civilization confers. To the contrary—these parks sometimes set up an expectation of ease that just isn't there. Yellowstone National Park, for example, takes up as much space as Delaware and Rhode Island combined; much of that space is unpaved, unpathed, and untouched. Get too far away from the walkways and gift shops without proper preparation, and that friendly park with all the steam and mud can start to look like another hot place where the lakes boil.

Out in the wild, alone or even in groups, people are a lot more vulnerable than they think they are, no matter how experienced in outdoor recreation or survival they might be. Not acknowledging that reality—in other words, not giving the backcountry the respect it deserves—may be the number-one error people make on the road to real disaster.

The ultimate causes of most hiking fatalities are pretty easy to figure out—people fall, or they get lost and starve, or run out of water, or animals attack them. But these tragedies generally happen away from civilization's prying eyes, in areas sparsely populated with potential witnesses. Under such conditions, knowing *exactly* what happened in a hiker's or climber's final moments becomes an exercise in conjecture, if not flat-out speculation. Great books aplenty have addressed the possibilities of those last clock ticks, their authors wondering, and often guessing at, what really happened back there. *The Perfect Storm, Journal of the Dead,* and a hundred other works of conjecture do a bang-up job of trying to answer the big questions, and probably get quite a lot of it right.

Regardless of the exact circumstances and what we know (or don't know) of them, backcountry calamity usually reveals one thing above all others:

the consequences of not following the simple rules of the wilderness. Don't push on when the sky is going black with clouds; don't head into the desert without enough water; don't travel anywhere without a map, even if you think you know where you are. It's not too much to say that following such rules will keep you out of trouble when it comes knocking, plain and simple. It's also quite clear that, given the books mentioned above along with a truckload more, people don't follow the rules as much as they probably should, for any number of reasons.

In the forested backcountry of the West's national parks, the rules boil down to a fairly simple few. First off, people hiking alone are a lot more vulnerable to dying than people in groups are. So are those who travel too lightly, forgetting (or losing) essentials like matches, first aid gear, food, and water. Traveling at night is a fairly bad idea, too, though this changes a bit when the landscape in question is a blazing desert in July. Break any of these rules, along with a few other ones, and the chances for trouble increase exponentially, no matter who you are and how much experience you have.

This is true even if you happen to be a park ranger like Jeff Christensen. Christensen worked in Rocky Mountain National Park, located just outside of Estes Park in Colorado. A broad track of wilderness laced through with vistas and valleys, Rocky Mountain National Park isn't for the faint of heart; it boasts more than 355 miles of trail, much of it through remote backcountry, and high altitudes make those trails tougher than they would be on lower ground. More than sixty named peaks shoot up over 12,000 feet, and even the park's "low-elevation" hikes are located from 7,500 feet on up. Long's Peak, the tallest mountain in the park, hits 14,259 feet. If you don't normally operate in altitudes like these, you could be in for some trouble, particularly if dehydration sets in and your head starts to swim and pound. Throw in the potential for avalanches, rockslides, hypothermia, and hair-trigger changes in the weather, and Rocky Mountain National Park can become a pretty forbidding place in short order. Approximately fifty climbers have lost their lives on Long's Peak alone, as the margin of error on that big peak is even skinnier than it is on the rest of them.

Christensen, however, wasn't in the backcountry during the tricky early spring months, when avalanches are the worst, nor was he on Long's Peak. He didn't lack for experience, either—2005 marked Jeff's fourth season as a ranger at Rocky Mountain National Park. He was, according to his co-workers, an accomplished skier and hiker, spending his winters on the ski patrol at the Winter Park Resort, one of Colorado's finest wintertime hills. He scored high on his physical fitness tests, and even qualified for "Arduous Duty" during his Wildland Fire Fighter training. In every respect, Christensen knew what he was doing, and the people who knew him best verified that ability in the wake of his accident.

On July 29, Christensen set out into the backcountry for a routine patrol. He set off alone, as park rangers often do, around 11:00 a.m. for a thirteen-mile hike through the Mummy and Hague ranges. A fellow ranger dropped him off near Chapin Pass, an entry trail to the backcountry tundra of the Mummy Range. The sun shone and there were only light winds all day, making for excellent hiking conditions among the peaks. Christensen planned on being at the Lawn Lake trailhead around 6:30 or so, in order to get out that night and look for a new car. He had only hiked the area once before, though he gave no indication that he didn't know exactly where he was going.

Things proceeded quietly enough for the first few miles; a pair of hikers from Oklahoma saw the ranger between noon and 12:30 p.m., while another hiker from Minneapolis saw him around 2:30. That hiker would be the last person to see Jeff Christensen alive.

What happened next will never be fully known. We do know that if a few small things had worked out differently, Jeff Christensen would have been found in short order, or might never have fallen at all. Apparently he had deviated from the route he had discussed before setting out, possibly to take pictures with the camera he carried; he'd taken some photos of bighorn sheep that day, prior to becoming injured. The source of his injury isn't clear, either—falling rocks may have struck him on the head, causing a fall, or he may have lost his footing and went down. Whatever brought it on, the fall he eventually took bruised Christensen's hip and cut him up all over. It also landed the *coup de grace*: a massive fracture on the left side of his skull that caused internal bleeding along the brain.

Whatever the cause, the head injuries he sustained were so profound that they could have rendered him unable to follow emergency procedures. He may have tried to call for help with his radio—in the subsequent official report, one ranger maintained that he heard a few clicks on the park radio system around 4:00 p.m., about when Christensen's accident may have taken place. But the clicks could have just as easily been something else. In fact, the seriousness of his injuries might have left him unable even to speak, much less operate his radio. He did have the wherewithal to wrap his head in the T-shirt he carried in his pack, and to put on a parka against the chilling mountain air; evidence also indicates that he walked a ways from the original site of the accident. Whether he did so in any organized way, or whether he was simply stumbling about, disoriented and hazed with pain, is yet another unknown. Eventually, though, he came to rest about five miles from where he initially hit the trail, and he died sometime in the near-freezing night.

Around 6:00 p.m., the shift ranger realized that Christensen hadn't yet called for someone to pick him up and attempted to reach him via radio. (Another sad irony: the ranger who attempted this contact used the wrong radio call sign—234 instead of Christensen's 233.) Five hours later, with the lost ranger's car still parked at headquarters, the alarm went up. Searchers looked for him at the Lawn Lake trailhead and at his home, with no success. Calls to his cell phone went unanswered all night, and at 6:30 the next morning the official park-wide search kicked off. Over the next few days, one hundred volunteers would scour twenty-six square miles of the Mummy range looking for Christensen, coming within mere feet of him on a few occasions.

Three hikers discovered his body on Saturday, August 6. By the time he was found, searchers had begun to assume the worst; that many days and nights out there, even for a backcountry expert like Christensen, would have proved a tall survival order. Particularly given the small amount of gear the ranger carried—official reports showed that he toted no food, no first aid kit, and no compass, let alone matches to fight off the cold in a pinch. He also carried no alternative means of communication, like a whistle or mirror, to signal for help.

Why such a seasoned outdoorsman, let alone a professional park ranger, would not carry elemental, necessary survival items on a thirteen-mile hike through the backcountry defies all explanations save one: Christensen suffered from a textbook case of hubris. He'd fallen prey to his comfort level out there, a contentment that, to his expert mind, rendered basic safety procedures unnecessary. (This foolhardy confidence and lack of respect counts among the most common factors in outdoor sport-related deaths.) According to the official investigation of Christensen's death, his boots were also worn to the nubs, far beyond usefulness in rough terrain; the pictures included in that same report bear this out, showing a pair of chewed soles that had clearly seen more gripping days. Even worse, Christensen didn't leave any written record of the route he planned to take. He discussed it with the ranger who dropped him off that day but decided once on the trail to take a detour. Not having extra radio batteries or any alternate way to draw attention, his ability to communicate with anyone went dead as soon as his radio did, or as soon as he was unable to work the gadget. A whistle, far less technical in nature, may have saved his life. Instead, he died alone and incommunicado, without proper equipment or a proper plan, and no one will ever know exactly how.

Which leads to yet another question: Why was Christensen hiking alone in the first place? Hikers regardless of skill level are admonished constantly never to travel the backcountry alone and to always keep in touch with fellow hikers on the trail lest they be left behind. And generally, the ones doing the admonishing are park rangers, such as Jeff Christensen. Why would one charged with keeping the backcountry safe, with enforcing trail discipline, break this cardinal rule, particularly in country he'd only covered one other time?

The unfortunate answer: everybody's doing it. National park rangers often patrol the backcountry alone, which is only surprising if you don't take into account plummeting funding levels for the Park Service across the board. Even now, rangers in Rocky Mountain National Park—and just about every other park in the system—travel solo into nearly untouched wilderness, a backwoods high-wire act with no net if the ranger happens to fall, or to run across the wrong grizzly at the wrong time.

Christensen's death did not happen in a vacuum, however. Though solo patrols continue, the first ranger fatality in Rocky Mountain National Park's history brought about a number of rule changes in that park's backcountry patrol procedure. Rangers now must leave a written account of the route they choose to take, and have to radio in with more regularity to give headquarters a better idea of their locations. They must also carry a number of items that Christensen didn't have, including the "Ten Essentials" of backcountry travel. If you have ever hiked in wilderness areas, you're probably familiar with this ten-item list, which varies a bit depending on who's ticking off the list.

Every hiker should ostensibly carry these things on every trip into the wild. None of them are exotic in any way; in fact, a common-sense packing job would probably get most of them into your backpack anyway. A map, a compass, matches and kindling, extra water, extra food, extra clothing, a first aid kit, a good pocketknife, makeshift shelter materials (i.e., a blanket and some rope), and a signaling device. That's it, more or less, though some lists also include sunscreen and shades as protection from exposure. These are all common-sense items that, prior to Christensen's death, no ranger at Rocky Mountain National Park had to carry.

The essentials, more frequent radio calls, written itineraries—perhaps none of these would have saved Jeff's life. And no one would deny that what happened to Jeff Christensen was a tragic accident; he was a good ranger by all accounts, and whatever happened probably involved bad luck rather than incompetence in nature's house. But denying the man's mistakes out there only makes it OK for the next victim to fall into the same comfort trap. Nothing demonstrates the capricious possibilities of the western backcountry better than the fact that even the most experienced, strongest hiker can, and did, find himself in deep trouble. Christensen may still have fallen with proper footwear, on his original trail, leaving earlier in the day, even if he'd set out with another ranger.

But he may not have.

Jeff Christensen clearly made certain mistakes, but the ranger had experience and erred not out of ignorance, but confidence. He didn't treat the backcountry as the dangerous place it can be because he *lived* there, at least part-time, and he thought he had a pretty good handle on it, much as someone living in central Manhattan who leaves his wallet inside his newspaper on the train, simply getting too comfortable and consequently not being careful enough. Christensen had acclimated himself to the backcountry the way city dwellers acclimate to the hustle around them, and he quite possibly would be alive today had he paid more respect to Rocky Mountain's vagaries.

More mystifying than Christensen's case, though, is that of folks who set off to places unknown to them with no clear idea of what they are doing out there, possessed with romantic and often dangerous notions of communing with nature on its own terms. Christopher McCandless, the tragic subject of Jon Krakauer's classic *Into the Wild*, starved to death in an abandoned bus in the Alaskan wilderness after such rosy thoughts infected his mind, blinding him to the hard realities of the backcountry. This impulse usually ends after the first cold night sleeping in a soaked tent, but occasionally—as in McCandless's case—it simply ignites a stubborn willingness to tough it out in the face of nature. And occasionally, nature takes the would-be trailblazer to task for his lack of respect.

The western U.S. has played host to hundreds, if not thousands, of these deluded souls. Most escape with only their egos injured, perhaps after a bit more exposure to the elements than they might have wanted. A few, however, suffer extreme privation and even death. When they do, their ordeals redefine agony; the wild takes its time with them, seeming to revel in some way as the wayward realize their fate, then succumb to it after days of anguish. The most punishing areas of the West—the deserts, the massive snowcapped crags, the trackless woods—offer little in the way of quick exit. Unless, that is, the victim in question decides to end his plight himself.

Raffi Kodikian and David Coughlin planned to spend only one night in Carlsbad Caverns National Park. By the time help reached them, they'd spent four hellish nights there, marooned in a tiny canyon only a mile or so from their car, and Coughlin was dead. According to Kodikian, Coughlin had asked to die, rather than suffer any more at the merciless hands of the New Mexico desert. The story is a classic of backcountry naiveté, with a dollop of murder mystery—maybe—thrown in for good measure.*

Kodikian and Coughlin first met in 1994, when Kodikian was attending Northeastern and Coughlin was attending the University of Massachusetts a few miles away. The two met through mutual acquaintances and became fast friends over the next two years. By 1999, however, both were feeling the pull of the West: Coughlin had dreams of attending graduate school on the beaches of California, while Kodikian felt compelled to wander as he had during a previous cross-country jaunt. Meant to mimic the American odyssey

---

* *David and Raffi's story receives an excellent telling in Jason Kersten's book* Journal of the Dead *(Perennial, 2004).*

of his hero, Jack Kerouac, Kodikian's 1997 trip was, in his own words, "one of the greatest experiences I could have imagined." He managed to have his adventures printed in the *Boston Globe*'s travel section, obviously large potatoes for a journalism student only a year past graduation.

Ironically (very ironically, given subsequent events), Kodikian spent some time camping in the desert during this earlier trip, too—namely at the White Sands National Monument about two hundred fifty miles west of Carlsbad and within spitting distance of the Trinity nuclear test site. That detour took a nasty turn when a sandstorm blinded him and nearly sent him off in the wrong direction. He eventually found his way back to his Jeep, but the experience clearly didn't convince him to improve his sense of direction or carry a compass on later adventures.

The boys set off for the wide open West in July 1999 and spent the next six days winding their way from Boston down through Pennsylvania, where Kodikian was from, then on at a breakneck pace through Virginia, Nashville, Graceland, New Orleans, and Austin. While in Austin, they decided to take a slight detour on their way to the Grand Canyon, and see Carlsbad Caverns.

Carlsbad spotlights two worlds in geological opposition. Yet they lie in unquestionable alignment, too; both are environments largely hostile to human life, though for completely different reasons. In 1898, a cowboy named Jim White rode out to investigate a suspicious column of smoke in the desert. As he got closer, he discovered that the black ribbon was made of bats—seemingly endless, emerging from the ground to feed. White proceeded to explore the caverns he found, and became the foremost advocate of the wonders he saw there. Despite his enthusiasm, it took more than thirty years for the U.S. government to agree and declare Carlsbad Caverns a national park. While most people came to see the majestic caverns in subsequent years, others of more rugged stock took on the miles of desert backcountry that stretched out aboveground, a region perhaps even more challenging than the cold, damp world below it.

Underground, caverns born of twelve million years' worth of seeping, dripping rainfall open into magnificent rooms, decorated with majestic formations of onyx large and small. The caves lie within an ancient fossil reef, and there are more than one hundred, including Lechuguilla, the nation's deepest limestone cavern. Like the Grand Canyon, Yosemite, Yellowstone, or Mount Rainier, Carlsbad demonstrates just how geologically unique the West is. Only rarely will you find chambers as completely, stereotypically like your mind's conception of "cave." The bats are still there, too; every night, visitors congregate to watch them blot out the sky as they exit their subterranean lair and search for food. (Though the sky blotting used to be a lot more impressive—the caves only hold two hundred thousand to three hundred fifty thousand bats now, depending on the season, food availability, etc. Back in 1936, that population was around 8.7 million. Thanks, DDT.) Like any cave system, Carlsbad Caverns hold immense potential for danger, though you'll see little of that potential on trips along the well-traveled routes of the park.

On the surface, a more traditional, yet somehow still alien, nature reigns. In 1978, Congress declared much of the park's 13,406 surface acres a wilderness area, protected from any further development forever. Not that developers were clamoring at the gates anyway; the area's solitude, punishing climate, and isolation have turned it into a poster child for backcountry preservation—a place where people can hike primitive, dusty paths into a world that has lived essentially unchanged for eons, as the caverns themselves have. But while the caverns exist in a climate-controlled, nearly static state of splendor, the desert above experiences wild mood swings, with temperatures capable of dropping—or spiking—up to fifty degrees Fahrenheit at a shot. Temperatures in the summer can peak at one hundred ten degrees, then fall close to zero in the winter. Though little rain falls in the bone-dry Chihuahuan desert that constitutes the Carlsbad backcountry, when it does come down the resulting flash floods have been known to sweep away the unwary.

But the main difference between the surface and what lies beneath remains water. The simple difference: underground, you find it. Above, you don't. Kodikian and Coughlin somehow remained unaware of this fact, even though the day they arrived was scorching hot, even though they were coming specifically to stay in the desert, and even though Kodikian had once before become lost in such a place without being properly prepared. Despite the fact that the ranger on duty that day, Kenton Eash, read the boys the list of dos and don'ts for camping the backcountry. One of those recommendations: "There is no water in the backcountry. So you must carry what you need. A minimum of one gallon per person per day is recommended." The two young travelers proceeded to buy three liters of water total, and headed to the site Eash recommended: Rattlesnake Canyon.

They got to the trailhead, parked, and set out. Although they didn't carry the entire complement of the Ten Essentials, they did carry a fair number of them—knives, hats, sunglasses, food, matches, a topographical map, and a lighter. They didn't have a compass or any means of signaling if they happened to get lost. But what were the chances of that? They were only hiking in a mile or so, after all, to the bottom of the canyon where they would set up camp and spend the night before setting out again for Phoenix and the Grand Canyon beyond it.

They hiked into the canyon and made their first terrible decision: they took a primitive, less-traveled route rather than the main one, and ended up pitching camp in an unmarked side canyon. After that, they opened up their third container of water—they'd already begun drinking from the other two during the hike down—and boiled hot dogs with it before turning in.

The next morning they headed back to where they thought the car was, and ended up wandering in unfamiliar territory. The topographical map they carried might have helped under the circumstances, had either one known how to read a topographical map. Worry began to set in as they roamed, searching for familiar territory, though it dissipated somewhat when the skies opened around noon and quenching rain began to fall. The rain bought them another three-quarter pint of water each, but the next few hours of searching didn't get them any closer to salvation. They pitched camp again, and during the night they thought a distant light at the top edge of the canyon might have been a headlight. They set out in that direction the next morning, hoping to reach a highway.

They didn't. Instead, they hiked to the top of the canyon, using as much water in three hours as they had the whole previous day, and saw nothing but desert stretching out before them in all directions. They saw no shade, no road, and no civilization, even though, according to Jason Kersten:

> They were standing on the same plateau as the visitor center, which lay on the opposite side of the canyon, about six miles away and a good five hundred feet lower in altitude. They should have even been able to see the square bulge of the cavern's elevator tower to their left, a small yet distinct speck of human geometry in the distance. Even closer were the twenty-foot-high water tanks that they had passed on the road in. Any of these would have told them the general direction of their car.

They saw none of them.

How they managed not to see any of these landmarks remains a testament to panic. Faced with their predicament, they failed to rise to the occasion, and instead began succumbing to it. Another chance for escape passed when Coughlin sighted Rattlesnake Springs, an oasis the park annexed in 1931 for its water supply, about five miles off in the distance. Kodikian, however, lay under a bush suffering from exhaustion, so Coughlin simply sat down and joined him, rather than setting out alone. They hung their shirts from the only largish bush around—a small mesquite—and tried to hold off the midday sun.

Their lack of outdoor experience made things worse. When vultures began to circle above—a common behavior for the birds, brought on more by curiosity and social nature than anticipation of a meal—the boys seemed to panic, thinking they were in some B-level western and that the next scene would be dramatic views of their bleached, white bones.

They trudged back down into the canyon, convinced there was nothing else to do topside, even after expending all that effort to get up there (and with Rattlesnake Springs right there, visible, in the distance). At this point, their dehydration seemed to enter dangerous territory; according to Kersten, they began hallucinating, seeing bottles of water off in the distance, and jumping to the conclusion that the rangers were playing tricks on them by dangling cold water just out of reach. The boys found their way back to camp (another surprise, given their lack of directional sense) and cursed the rangers who couldn't get it together to find them.

The next day, they searched again, found nothing, and as the day's temperature reached up toward one hundred ten degrees, they began to seriously consider the possibility of dying. "Dave has asked that his remains be cremated & thrown over the edge of the Grand Canyon. I leave the handling of my remains to my family," wrote Kodikian in the diary he'd been keeping throughout the trip. (Kodikian, a writer and Kerouac disciple, took his journaling seriously even as things degenerated for him and Coughlin.) Pretty hard to argue about where the boys were headed at that point.

But I should pause here to mention that, in terms of desert survival, the boys were far from goose-cooked even as they went to bed that fourth night, at least according to many of the experts who testified at Kodikian's trial. They had been eating prickly pear cactus fruit over the previous days, a fair source of water. They had no shortage of these plants nearby. They were, however, close to or already into what Edward F. Adolph, a pioneering researcher in the field of water deprivation, would call severe, or third-stage, dehydration, in which the body has lost more than 10 percent of its water supply. Experts at the trial estimated that they had lost anywhere from 10 all the way up to 18 percent of their water. Their blood thickening, limbs tingling and uncoordinated, pounding headaches morphing into dementia—there's no way to know if Coughlin was already too far gone or not when Kodikian decided to honor his final wish.

That night, Coughlin vomited uncontrollably, probably in reaction to the prickly pears he'd eaten. (Though they can mean life in the middle of death for people lost in the desert, unripe prickly pears can cause severe reactions in some people—including, apparently, Coughlin.) As the dawn of August 8 approached, according to Kodikian's court testimony, they decided to end their lives rather than suffer any more. The boys tried to cut their wrists, but didn't succeed; when Kodikian was found, he had some cursory cuts on his arms, though nothing that serious. According to Kodikian's journal, Coughlin then asked Kodikian to kill him. "Dave had been in pain all night," the journal read. "At around 5 or 6 he turned to me & begged that I put my knife through his chest. I did, & a second time when he wouldn't die. He still breathed & spoke so I told him that I was going to cover his face. He said OK." The unnerving frankness of the passage betrays just how close death was to them; after four days of wandering the desert with no water and no food, lost and getting weaker by the minute, they had little use for euphemism. The entry is, nonetheless, eerily calm for someone who has just killed his best friend, in the same way Kodikian himself seemed too calm when he was picked up only a few hours later.

When the authorities rescued Kodikian and began probing into the circumstances of Coughlin's murder, few believed the survivor's story. The pieces simply didn't add up, from the relatively obvious location of their camp to the fact that neither man showed serious physical symptoms of acute dehydration. There is also the small matter of Kirsten Swan, Kodikian's ex-girlfriend and a good friend of Coughlin's. After the murder, someone familiar with the situation revealed that Coughlin had been "intimate" with Kristen, a fact that might have come out as the two friends, believing they were facing eternity, talked the desperate hours away. Coughlin's friends also had trouble believing he would beg for death, given his generally upbeat and positive demeanor. And given all the writing the boys were doing, reasoned Sheriff Mark Anthony "Chunky" Click of Carlsbad's Eddy County, why didn't Coughlin write anything about his request, perhaps asking people to absolve Raffi Kodikian of responsibility? (Though the boys had made a suicide pact, and Coughlin might have thought Kodikian was going to die, too.)

The real circumstances will never be known. But Kodikian did stand accused of Coughlin's murder and went to trial over it. He was eventually found guilty, thanks mostly to the fact that any killing in New Mexico—even a supposed "mercy killing"—qualifies as an illegal act. Though the judge didn't see Kodikian as "a threat or danger to society," he did perceive a crime, and thus sentenced him to fifteen years with the majority of it to be suspended. (Kodikian pleaded no contest to the charges, rather than proceeding with an "insanity by dehydration" defense.) Kodikian would serve sixteen months in a New Mexico prison as a model inmate, then go home to Pennsylvania. Dave Coughlin's remains did eventually make their way to the Grand Canyon, when his parents scattered his ashes there in 2001.

Raffi Kodikian and David Coughlin should not have been hiking in the New Mexico desert. Period. They had no idea what they were doing out there, to the point that one is forced to wonder why they decided to camp at all, anywhere, much less in the potentially punishing environs of Carlsbad in August. These were two guys who got lost *a mile away from their car.* Their final camp sat only 275 feet from the path they were searching for over the previous four days. The road was visible from the hills above their camp, and not one but two trail markers sat within spitting distance. Kodikian had already proven himself unable to rely on his sense of direction; the fact that he didn't compensate for this deficiency with a compass at the very least seems odd. At the most, it's mighty suspicious.

In fact, of the Ten Essentials, the boys carried only a few. Sure, they were going only for a night, and the car was parked nearby, but the fact that these things didn't matter in their case pretty much proves that you carry emergency items with you for a reason—namely in case of an emergency. And the quantity of certain items, particularly the presence of an unusual number of knives, in lieu of other useful things, makes as little sense as the rest of the situation. The question "What were you thinking?" seems relevant, though again, as in most backcountry accidents, we are certain to receive no satisfactory answer.

We do know, however, that dying of thirst might just be the most horrible break you can catch. It takes a long time, causes profound pain, and destroys the mind as it hammers the body. Human beings, like all animals, require near-constant hydration to survive; go too long without water, and truly dreadful things happen to you. The following is a fine, if nerve-wracking, description of thirst's ravages, courtesy of William Langewieshe from the *Atlantic Monthly* Web site:

> Thirst is first felt when the body has lost about 0.5 percent of its weight to dehydration. For a 180-pound man, that amounts to about a pint of water. With a 2 percent loss (say, two quarts), the stomach is no longer big enough to supply the body's needs, and people stop drinking before they have replenished their loss, even if they are given ample water. This is called voluntary dehydration, though it is hardly a conscious choice. Up to a 5 percent loss (about one gallon) the symptoms include fatigue, loss of appetite, flushed skin, irritability, increased pulse rate, and mild fever. Beyond that lie dizziness, headache, labored breathing, absence of salivation, circulatory problems, blued skin, and slurred speech. At 10 percent, a person can no longer walk. The point of no return is 12 percent (a three-gallon deficit), when the tongue swells, and the mouth loses all sensation. Because swallowing becomes impossible, a person this dehydrated cannot recover without medical assistance. ... Now the skin shrinks against the bones and cracks, the eyes sink into the skull, and vision and hearing become dim. Urination is painful, and urine is dark. Delirium sets in.

As the body dehydrates in a hot desert climate, a disproportionate amount of water is drawn from the circulating blood. The blood thickens and can no longer fulfill its functions, one of which is to transport heat generated within the body to the surface. It is this heat that ultimately kills. The end comes with a rise in body temperature, convulsions, and finally blissful death.

So dying of thirst rates pretty high on the "Most Excruciating Things Ever to Happen to a Human Being" scale. Being thrown into a blender might even be better—at least quicker by a long shot. But people still journey into the desert without proper preparation, still take a chance on the desert's awful power to kill without hedging their bets. They still head to places like Death Valley thinking that the moniker must be a cute nickname, rather than a literal description of what's lurking down there.

Death Valley National Park is the hottest, driest, least hospitable environment in the United States. It's not "in the running," or "one of the worst"; during the summer, it's literally the place where you will survive the shortest time if you happen to get lost in an unprepared state. In July, for example, the average high temperature is around 115 degrees. In August, it's 113. Those are *averages*, mind you—roughly the temperature it's going to be on any given day. Average rainfall during those months: a combined 0.21 inches. In other words, the only water you are going to find is whatever you bring with you.

Technically, heat illness covers a whole list of ailments that occur when the human body is subjected to extreme heat. Its worst manifestation—heatstroke—happens when body temperature gets above 106 degrees or so, and the body starts malfunctioning as a result. The human body relies on two main methods to cool itself: pumping more blood to release more heat at the surface of the skin, and sweating out moisture in order to take advantage of naturally cooling evaporation. When temperatures reach Death Valley levels, even slight dehydration will stop the sweat glands from functioning, leaving the body only one option. Thus the victim's temperature starts to rise, and the one method left to deal with the heat—pumping blood—can't get the job done as that blood thickens in the veins like concrete. Body temperature rises, and things go downhill quickly from there.

Once heatstroke does set in, the person afflicted needs quick medical attention—an estimated 80 percent of people who aren't treated immediately for heatstroke end up dying from it. Cardiac arrest can happen because the heart is forced to work so much harder, pumping more blood in its attempts to cool the body just as that blood is getting heavier and heavier. The body gets overwhelmed very soon at this rate, and chances of recovery shrink every minute the vicious cycle carries on.

The typical Death Valley fatality goes something like Kinhluan Nguyennogoc's final experience. The fifty-year-old amateur photographer set out on July 23, 2005, from Stovepipe Wells sand dunes, where he parked his car. He'd come to the park to photograph the landscape that would eventually claim him, apparently with no knowledge of how to handle it. He hiked into the dunes carrying his camera and one bottle of water, and wore no hat to protect himself from the one hundred twenty-degree heat of the day. At some point, Nguyennogoc became disoriented and couldn't find his way back; it must not have taken long, since a helicopter patrol found his remains only three-quarters of a mile away in the midst of the dunes.

Later that same week, rangers found Robert Darmer Jr.'s body deep in the desert wilderness, a victim of grandiose belief in his own abilities and chronic disregard for signs that said "you probably shouldn't try this backcountry thing anymore." Darmer was headed to one of Death Valley's best-known and most controversial sites—the Saline Valley Warm Springs, a system of hot springs popular among nudists, who began frequenting the area before Death Valley's boundaries extended to include it in 1994. Infamously, it once served as a home base for Charles Manson and his followers. (He thought one of the springs might lead to an underground paradise, which might explain why he was Charles Manson.) The freewheeling history and culture of the spot attracted Darmer's attention, and he set out in his van on July 23 to have a little fun out there.

The road to Saline Valley didn't amount to much—a rutted track that became impassable with snowmelt or rain at different times throughout the year. He got his VW van stuck in a salt marsh on the way in and proceeded to spend the next six days sitting with the van waiting for someone to come along. Unfortunately for him, no one did, and in a state of panic he set out in search of help. In an incredible stroke of good luck, a pair of fourteen-year-old English boys found Darmer just as he'd drained his last water bottle, eliciting tears of relief from the would-be dead man. The boys were members of the League of Venturers, a British organization of youths "dedicated to Helping People and Animals in Danger or Distress on Land and Sea," according to their official credo. He caught a ride back to the closest ranger station with the troupe, where he kissed the ground in gratitude.

His prostration in the face of nature's ability to whack him did not last. Another expedition to the marooned vehicle succeeded in pulling it from the mud, but with two flat tires and a ton of mechanical problems, he wasn't going to be driving it anytime soon. So he went back to his home in Bishop one more time, collected the supplies he figured he would need, and told his aunt to report him missing if she did not hear from him in three days. (One would imagine this directive made the poor woman feel great about his chances.) On July 25, another Good Samaritan dropped him off at a wash in the road fifteen miles from the Palm Springs campground. His idea, apparently, was to reach the campground and recruit some people to help him fix his van.

Unfortunately, things got off to a bad start and deteriorated from there. Darmer's ride had arrived via a route he was not familiar with, a piece of information Darmer did not make enough of a big deal about, apparently. He stashed his supplies at the drop-off point, and started walking along the road. He made it about ten miles on the chopped-up track before heading into the desert in search of some water. The death march probably took him about two days; most likely, he was already dead when his aunt followed the three-day directive he had given her and called the authorities. Searchers found his body about two miles from the hot springs and assumed that Darmer, most likely crazy with heatstroke by that point, had set out for the only water source he knew about. (This last part is unfortunate given that there were other water sources closer by—Darmer just was not familiar enough with the area to know about them.)

The ridiculous circumstances of Darmer's unnecessary death earned him a Darwin Award, passed out to those people who, in classic evolutionary fashion, "improve our gene pool by removing themselves from it." A little callous, maybe, but to call Darmer's ill-fated expedition anything but foolish doesn't make much sense.

Both of these incidents happened within the space of one week, a rare coincidence of frequency. And in fairness, the three fatalities in 2005 marked a bad year for Death Valley, despite the punishing conditions and the park's massive size (at 3.4 million acres, it's the largest national park outside of Alaska). In actuality, most people follow the life-or-death rules out there; when it comes down to it, doing so will almost always see you through. If, that is, you are able to equip yourself for the situation.

If you can't do so, the consequences are predictable, dire, and almost inescapable. One ongoing saga has proven this fact with gruesome frequency and pushed the western desert into the national consciousness, though its more horrific points are usually lost in oceans of political rhetoric on both sides. Few western news stories receive as much public scrutiny as that of illegal immigrants from Central and South America moving north to the United States; and few groups suffer at nature's hands more than they do. Whatever your opinion on this issue politically, it is impossible to ignore the fact that every year, hundreds of people are struggling and dying along that desert border, their last moments spent in a haze of pain and thirst. Obviously, this is nothing to wish on anybody at all, whether you approve of what they are doing or not.

Nonetheless, it happens throughout the summer months from southern California to Texas, anywhere Mexican or other Latin American immigrants decide to chance crossing massive expanses of desert to see what's on the other side. And it happens more now than it used to—in fact, back in 1994, before the U.S. government implemented its current "control through deterrence" model for illegal immigrants, fewer than thirty people died trying to cross into the country. By 2005, that number hit 451, according to Border Patrol and Mexican consulate guesses. That's about two cataclysmic plane crashes' worth, if you're keeping track.

The real estate the immigrants cross is nothing less than hellish in the high summer months of June, July, and August. Though the Sonoran desert classifies as one of the world's soggiest—rainfall averages three to sixteen inches per year—summertime temperatures are still punishing, spiking up to more than one hundred thirty degrees in the shade. The human body requires about a gallon of water each day, more when sweat and exertion come into play. With water weighing as much as it does and taking up as much space, we can assume that illegal immigrants, moving with as much speed as they can manage, are usually not carrying the proper complement. When thirst catches up with them, with the pounding sun and ground temperatures reaching up to one hundred sixty degrees, the air practically boiling around them—well, what the outcome will be isn't hard to figure out.

"Heartbreaking" properly describes it. As men, women, and children trudge along, the coyotes—criminal smugglers who specialize in getting people across the border with absolutely no regard for their safety—herd them forward, keeping them from highways and other things that might be of help in an emergency. Of course, straying too close to such arteries might get their groups caught and cost them tens of thousands of dollars; the flip side, of course, is that when something goes wrong, there is nowhere in sight to get help. As such, the coyotes, according to nearly all accounts, simply shrug and carry on, abandoning those incapable of following.

This is exactly what happened to Edith Rodriquez Reyes and David, her three-year-old son. They had attempted to cross the border in order to join the boy's father, a construction worker in Tennessee, and had set out under the "care" of a coyote across the Tohono O'odham Indian reservation, a stretch of blazing desert the size of Connecticut. After two days of walking in unholy heat with not nearly enough water, David became sick and couldn't go on. The group abandoned Edith and David rather than take them to civilization, which was only a few hours' walk away in the form of a major highway. To take them to safety might have gotten the entire group captured, so the coyotes and their other ten charges pressed on, while Edith stayed back to care for her little boy.

She kept close so she wouldn't lose him, and searched for water in the baked, powder-dry desert. The next day David died, and Edith set out on her own, wandering for another whole day before the Border Patrol found her on the roadside. She suffered from massive dehydration and shock, and it wasn't until an hour later that she was coherent enough to tell her rescuers about the little boy still out in the desert. "My baby is out there," she said.

The agents stormed into the desert, desperate to find the boy, who they thought might still be alive. They sent scans of Edith's shoe soles to search and rescue teams, who then followed the woman's staggering tracks into the bush. Six hours later, they found the boy under a small mesquite tree, his shoes removed and neatly arranged by his side, arms carefully folded on his chest. Border authorities considered prosecuting Edith Reyes for child endangerment, but eventually decided not to, sending her back to Mexico instead.

David's story is particularly tragic given his age, but with hundreds dying every year, he is hardly the only casualty. Sometimes, whole parties end up dropping to the desert floor, desiccated, their fates sealed, like the fourteen men who lost their lives in Arizona's desert in May of 2001.

They set out from Veracruz and Guerro, numbering about twenty-four strong in the beginning. All men and boys age sixteen through thirty-five, they began with a two-day truck ride to Los Vidrios, right on the border. They each paid about a thousand dollars to the coyote who smuggled them into the United States, and they entered on foot with a few cartons of water and some bags of clothes on Saturday, May 19. They had seventy miles to make before hitting Interstate 8, and set out in temperatures already pushing one hundred degrees.

The group passed near the Cabeza Prieta National Wildlife Refuge the next day, seeing nothing but desert landscape and the occasional creature in the brush. Cabeza Prieta plays host to some of America's loneliest, least hospitable country; temperatures clear one hundred degrees for ninety or one hundred days in a row, and shade—outside of the slim shadows cast by giant saguaros—barely cools the ground. For thirty miles in every direction, nothing beckoned but more desolation. Still, the men pushed on. By Monday, they had run out of food and water, and the temperature continued climbing toward 115 degrees. That day their guides set out alone, saying they would return to the group with water. Before they left, they instructed the men to walk "a couple of hours" to the highway—neglecting to tell them that it was still about sixty miles away.

The coyotes never came back, and in fact one of them died in the desert just as so many of his charges would. The other man—Jesus Lopez Ramos—was arrested in June 2001, and eventually received a sixteen-year prison sentence for his part in the tragedy. But the men he left behind suffered far worse fates; they continued to walk, watching their hellish situation deteriorate. They dealt with the ordeal in different ways—some busted open cacti and drank the juice inside; others resorted to drinking their own urine. Others dug into the soil, hoping to find moisture in the roots of the desert flora. When none of these methods proved sufficient, they began shedding their clothes, exposing more of their flesh to the sun's merciless heat, and calling out for their families and God as their minds cooked and dementia took over. Then they began falling one by one, their equilibrium baked away by the sun, while the remaining group pushed on and left the dead and weakened behind.

Border patrol found the party in various states of desperation. One man lay facedown in a ditch he'd dug to get away from the sun; another had been digging at the sand in a vain search for water. In all, seven of the dead men and boys came from Atzalan, a tiny village forty miles west of Veracruz steeped in poverty. The men returned to the village in their coffins, reminders of the treacherous path they had chosen. The town's mayor, Ramiro Barradas, told reporters that the tragedy might "cause the rest of our people who are thinking about crossing the border to think twice."

The warning hasn't seemed to take. Politicians, along with the rest of us, debate immigration policy as hundreds of people continue to stream across the border every day, even in the blazing height of summer. The stark, simple fact is that about two thousand people have died crossing the Mexico–U.S. border since 1998. More have died in attempting this crossing than in any disaster or catastrophe this book talks about. More have died crossing the border than have lost their lives in all outdoor sporting activities combined. Politics melt away in the face of barren, awful facts like these: in 2004, Arizona and New Mexico saw 583 murders, according to the U.S. Bureau of Justice Statistics. In that same year, about 325 people died crossing the border—that we know about. No one actually knows just how many bones lie in the desert, buried or waiting for discovery.

The Sonoran desert is the West's bloodiest killing field, hands down. And it will keep killing, though when you get down to it, it's not the desert itself that is pulling the metaphorical trigger. People who die in the backcountry, whatever the circumstances, have to get there first. In doing so, particularly when they come unprepared, the elements can only do what they always do— blaze with heat, blow with bonebreaking force, and otherwise remind us that nature does not suffer the unwise or unprepared.

≋ 艸 ≋

Dave Coughlin's death, whatever its actual circumstances, rates as a tragedy that could have been prevented had some things gone differently—had the boys accidentally taken the right turn instead of the wrong one, or brought more and better gear, or if a regular backcountry patrol had happened by earlier. We know, in hindsight, the general gist of the story, if not the devil in the details. But what about those families who lose loved ones to the wild and never know any details at all? The ones who never know how their family members met their fates, if they suffered, or even if they're actually dead or not? Wilderness disappearances, even more so than fatalities, leave so many open questions that closure—the certainty of a known outcome, rather than some fuzzy psychological idea—becomes impossible. Passing time will, of course, make death more and more probable; but only by attrition, as more hopeful scenarios hit their statutes of limitations. What's left is a tortuously slow-dwindling hope, and the mystery.

Backcountry disappearances happen every year in the West's national parks, largely because the parks represent both the biggest expanses of wilderness and the most popular backcountry destinations. It's tough to get lost forever when, for example, a five-mile walk in any direction will get you to a 7-Eleven. But when you're trekking into Yellowstone National Park's 3,472 square miles, you just might find yourself in some places that few people ever see, and may not see again for an awfully long time after you.

Some disappearances leave less doubt than others. If the victim falls into a hasty river or off a cliff, never to be seen again, the outcome is a safe, if crushing, bet. Twelve-year-old Luke Sanburg's body, for example, has never been recovered from the Yellowstone River; he is still missing, technically speaking. But the circumstances of his 2005 disappearance have led even his parents to conclude that he is gone. Unfortunately, there's no doubt that they are right.

On June 24, Luke and his fellow Boy Scouts were pushing logs into the Yellowstone near Knowles Falls when a chunk of wood caught him on the leg, knocking him into the water. Unfortunately, the Yellowstone River is not one you would want to get dropped into without lifeguard-like swimming skills; its 671-mile length makes it the longest undammed river in the lower forty-eight states. Throughout that flow, rapids with names like Sleeping Giant and Man Eater smash water and debris against the jutting rocks. Sanburg fell into this maelstrom and was last seen floating downriver with his head above water. Only his tennis shoes were ever found, about five miles downriver.

A host of volunteers spent days trying to find him, stationing themselves up and down the river at bridges and hillocks along the Yellowstone's rough banks. By that Sunday, two days after Luke fell into the river, two hundred fifty volunteers were combing the area, to no avail. Though his parents had admitted as early as June 27 that their boy probably would not come home alive, efforts continued for the next two weeks in the event of a miracle.

And miracles do happen, as a story out of Utah the previous week reminded the searchers. Eleven-year-old Brennan Hawkins had disappeared from his Boy Scout campsite on Friday, June 17 in Utah's Uinta Mountains, inciting a massive search effort that came up empty for three days. On the fourth day, however, a man named Forrest Nunley surprised the wandering boy and brought him back to his parents. (Brennan was following his parents' advice not to talk to strangers so well that he didn't seek out the searchers who had been in the area.) Having made a wrong turn on the way back to camp, the boy spent four days wandering area paths and drinking stream water to stay hydrated. By all accounts, from rescue professionals to his parents, the boy's survival under those conditions rated as a miracle—the kind of revelation Luke Sanburg's parents surely hoped they would experience, too.

By July 8, though, the National Park Service had scaled back efforts to find Luke, and his fate, while not definitively known, had been assumed. Luke's body—indeed, no other trace of him at all—has ever been found. The Yellowstone River simply swallowed him up. His family will probably get no more news of him, unless his bones surface someday, somewhere along the river's merciless length.

Right around the same time Luke's body was swept away, two other disappearances in Yellowstone attracted media attention: nineteen-year-old park employee Candace May Kellie lost control of her Ford Explorer and plunged one hundred feet down into the Yellowstone River, also never to be found; and fifty-nine-year-old Joseph Miller of Seattle disappeared after launching his canoe in high, choppy water near the Lewis Lake campground. Miller's body eventually turned up days after his backpack, lifejacket, and canoe washed onto the lake's northern shore. Why he decided to take the lifejacket without using it—witnesses say he set off without wearing it—remains one of those frustrating, inexplicable truths that raise the unhappy possibility that Miller's fate could have been averted.

In all, these tragedies made for a bad summer at Yellowstone—three deaths inside of two weeks never bodes well for your basic tourist spot. But considering that upwards of three million people visited the park in 2005, the shock of those few weeks looks less like real danger and more like bad timing. Which, honestly speaking, it was. That doesn't change the pain the three families felt, or the awful fates the victims suffered; getting swallowed up by wilderness, never to be seen again, is a terrible way to go, even if it does happen infrequently.

Wilderness accidents in general happen only occasionally, though certain environments hold more dangers than others for the unwary. It may be that no park has the ability to ruin your day like Grand Canyon National Park, home of the biggest, craftiest maw in the West. The plentitude of different disasters that can befall you there makes every hike in the vicinity a potential problem, particularly when conditions converge on the wrong side of good.

Death swings by Grand Canyon a few times every year. According to Michael P. Ghiglieri and Thomas M. Myers, authors of *Over the Edge: Death in Grand Canyon*, ninety people have fallen into the canyon to their deaths, doing everything from posing for photographs to free-climbing canyon walls. (Doing the latter in Grand Canyon is an extremely bad idea, given the crumbly nature of the sandstone that makes up those sheer cliffs.) Another seventy-three died of heat exposure or other environmental causes, while over eighty more have drowned in the Colorado for various reasons (as of 2004). Plane crashes have darkened its skies, and helicopters carrying terrified tourists have plunged into its depths. For people trying to commit suicide, Grand Canyon has the same allure as a fifty-story building, with none of the troubling stair climbing to the top, since that's where you're starting out; around fifty people have checked themselves out using gravity and Grand Canyon's rocks.

While all Ghiglieri and Myers' stories spell tragedy for the people involved, some speak to the kind of mistakes Jeff Christensen made, and others bear the hallmarks of truly rotten luck, a lot of which seems to hang over Grand Canyon. If, for example, a piano-sized piece of rock breaks from the canyon wall and smashes into your chest, as Rosalee Heaney experienced in 1992, death is pretty much what you get—wrong place, wrong time.

Then there are the ignorant types—jumping hundreds of feet into four yards of water, drinking mass quantities of alcohol before wobbling off on narrow canyon paths, eating poisonous plants found along the trail just to see what happens. One plant found in the canyon, *Datura,* holds a sacred place in local American Indian circles, as it induces intense visions when properly prepared. But when simply eaten or incorrectly whipped up, it kills hallucination seekers deader than disco. Anthony Krueger, a twenty-year-old in search of Enlightenment, or a high, or something in between, died way back in 1971 after drinking some tea made with *Datura* and jumping into the Colorado River. He didn't do that, however, until after he'd eaten some dirt, talked to (and heard from, apparently) invisible people, and attempted to lift a few giant boulders. He stripped down to nothing before he jumped in, and his body didn't turn up until five weeks later, seven miles downstream.

Yet despite high profile, nearly public fatalities like Mr. Krueger's, most deaths in Grand Canyon take place out of sight, vanishings rather than straightforward accidents. And, as the case of Iryna Shylo demonstrates, that big hole in the ground can hide one little human being as easily as one might stash a couple pennies overboard in the middle of Lake Superior. Iryna's story is simply one of the latest about people who lose their way in the canyon badly enough to vanish completely. In her case, as with Luke Sanburg, a big river is the prime suspect. Iryna and her hiking partner had set up camp near Hermit Rapid in July 2006, planning to stay the night before hiking back up the next day. Sometime during the night, Iryna got up to go to the bathroom and never came back. Her shoes turned up downriver, one of them nine miles away and the other a mile beyond that, but nothing else gave any indication of her fate. The Colorado has notoriously quick undercurrents, which could have sucked her out into the river; if this happened, the fifty-degree water would certainly have played a factor, disorienting her as it carried her farther from safety.

Shylo's body actually did turn up in August 2006, in the same area as her shoes, demonstrating that the Grand Canyon does have a way of coughing up the missing weeks or months after they disappear. (Not always, of course; sixteen-year-old Richard Tarr set off alone during a hike with his family and a tour group, and was never heard from again. His body was never found, though it's suspected that he also fell into the Colorado River at some point.) After all, as big as the canyon is, it's still a semi-arid environment, with sparse ground cover and lots of sunny visibility throughout the year. Even if there is nobody around to see the fall, or the slip, or the leap, victims of the place seem mostly to turn up sooner or later. The previously mentioned day-tripper Anthony Krueger showed up weeks after his ill-fated swim; Andrew Gradzik turned up four hundred feet down in the canyon three years and five months after he sent a postcard back home saying he'd found a guide to give him "private hikes." (This cryptic statement has never been deciphered.) In fact, people who plummet into the canyon are seldom *not* found, thanks both to the landscape and the fact that so many people are constantly looking around down there.

Sometimes, when easy explanations aren't available, wilderness disappearances take on a more sinister air. Gilbert Gilman's vanishing, which happened in Olympic National Park in June 2006, is one such bit of potentially fishy business. Gilman certainly had creden tials for the backcountry: a former Army paratrooper, he'd served in both Kuwait and Somalia, and had even worked for a year in Iraq as a civilian contractor. Before his disappearance, he'd taken a job with the state, as a deputy director for the Department of Retirement Systems.

Olympic National Park, unlike Grand Canyon, stands perfectly willing to swallow up the lost and never release them. The dense forest, almost all of it protected old growth, remains as primeval a spot as can be found in the lower forty-eight, with eight plants and fifteen different animals that are found nowhere else in the world except in those woods. Ninety-five percent of the park's forests are classified as "wilderness" by the Federal government; in other words, they must be preserved in their natural condition, hold no permanent human presence, and be allowed to develop as nature sees fit to develop them. Into this hinterland Gilman went, and there something happened to him.

The search for Gilman produced nothing, despite the operation's incredible size and intricacy. Searchers logged more than five thousand hours on the ground and used everything from dogs and helicopters to high-tech underwater sensing devices and cameras. The searchers followed every conceivable angle and traveled every path they could imagine Gilman taking from the park's Staircase parking lot. But in the end, it all came up empty; on July 4, park officials reduced the scale of the search, assuming the worst. By the end, the hope his family brought into the effort had dwindled to tears and that unfulfilled worry that afflicts every person who loses a loved one without the benefit of knowing where they went. In fact, the search turned up absolutely no clues—no hint or indication of what happened. That empty feeling won't be going anywhere for a while, as far as Gilbert Gilman's family is concerned.

The fact is, he might have gotten lost. He may have fallen, or run into any number of troubles out there. But the weather was beautiful with temperatures staying in the fifties after dark and pushing ninety during the day, and Gilman was experienced in survival techniques and quite healthy. His disappearance shocked everyone who knew him, and though foul play was never suspected, the completeness of his vanishing leaves far more questions than it answers. In terms of enemies or people who might *want* him disappeared, there were none, at least according to press accounts. In fact, chances are that the same thing happened to Gilman that has happened to so many others out there: he met up with more trouble than he was prepared to deal with, or had a split-second accident of circumstance, and it got the better of him. Maybe, like Jeff Christensen, his experience worked against him, and a lack of preparation was obscured by confidence. But the fact remains that this well-trained man was day hiking in a relatively well-traveled area, and managed to disappear with absolutely no trace. It is the stuff mysteries are made of, particularly when they end with indictments years later.

These disappearances, all different in their details, nonetheless demonstrate a unifying raw deal: even in a relatively "tame," well-traveled backcountry, nothing is certain. Parks like Yellowstone and Grand Canyon attract millions of visitors every year; during the summer, both places are practically crawling with people. These are parks with *traffic jams*, for Pete's sake. Yet despite the encroachment of tourists by the millions, despite being some of the most heavily trod wilderness in the world, they still swallow up a few people every year, some never to be seen again. They are that expansive—in every sense of the world, wild. Keep in mind, too, that most of the disappearances recounted here have taken place since 2000; in other words, awful things happen in the wild, and continue to happen even as the world at large looks ever tamer and smaller.

It is enough to humble you next time you are waiting in line, grumbling about the crowds, to see Old Faithful or Yosemite's waterfalls.

≋ ☖ ≋

Climbing mountains doesn't present the same easy diversion that simple hiking does. Technical expertise, specialized equipment, clear-headed decision making—good climbers must put all these elements together on every single climb, lest they find themselves at the bottom of a very deep crevasse or hip-deep in drifting snow as a blizzard rages around them.

People die every year in climbing accidents, in all sorts of different ways. Each story provides a lesson to those mountaineers lucky enough to make it through the season. In fact, the American Alpine Club and the Alpine Club of Canada publish a book called *Accidents in North American Mountaineering* every year, chronicling the depth and breadth of mountaineering mishaps for that period alone. What other sport do you know of that *has* enough fatal and near-fatal accidents to fill a single book, let alone one every year? Suffice to say that not respecting the backcountry when it happens to include a very tall, snow-covered mountain peak stands a good chance of being the last mistake you will ever make.

Among western mountains, few match the unfortunate record that Mount Hood has amassed. It may not be the tallest, or the coldest, or even the most difficult; it does, however, seem to be the major western peak that rates the least respect, and thus draws people prone to make terrible mistakes. More than two million people live within two hours of the mountain; as a result, Mount Hood gets a lot of use. And with that use comes the inevitable crossing of unprepared, unfocused, or simply ignorant people with natural forces that have the ability to kill them. What's more, you don't need any special permits or permissions to climb—or attempt to climb—Mount Hood. You simply make the drive, gear up, and go to it as best as you know how. Maybe that's why upwards of one hundred thirty people have lost their lives on this mountain, making it one of the country's bloodiest. (By contrast, at the end of 2004, 186 people had died while climbing Mount Everest; of course, only 2,249 people reached the Everest summit in that time, while Mount Hood is thought to be the second-most climbed mountain in the world after Mount Fuji.)

The peak lies in northern Oregon, about fifty miles from Portland, and stretches 11,235 feet into the sky over the Cascade Range. It has earned a bit of fame due to its status as an active volcano, though it hasn't erupted with any authority for two hundred years or so. But most people these days know it as a good introduction to high-altitude climbing, thanks to its relative ease and comparatively shallow summit. Of course, saying any mountain is a good introduction to high-altitude climbing is akin to describing the Red Triangle as a great place to introduce yourself to swimming with great white sharks—in no way is Mount Hood free of the dangers typical to this type of climb, nor is it to be climbed without all due diligence, care, and respect. Get into a bad way up there, and things will go just as wrong, just as fast as they will on a humungous mountain like Everest or K2. Hood's weather turns on a dime all year long, and blinding curtains of whipping snow never lie that far off. The result: hundreds of visitors within inches of being buried, thrown into a crevasse, or otherwise mangled as the mountain continues marching capriciously on.

In May 1986, nineteen people from the Oregon Episcopal School—most of them high school sophomores—set out on their annual Mount Hood outing, determined to reach the summit in the shortest time they could manage. In their haste, they failed to account for the number-one factor in any alpine climb: the state of the mountain in question. Their rush to the summit, coupled with lack of preparation and bad decision-making, eventually resulted in what came to be known as the Episcopal School Tragedy, the worst climbing accident in Oregon's history.

The group set out from the Timberline Lodge on Monday, May 12, at around 2:30 a.m. The lodge lies at around six thousand feet elevation, putting another five thousand feet or so between the young climbers and the summit. May marks the beginning to middle of the Mount Hood climbing season; for the most part, winter's storms have wrapped up, and the temperatures hop up to the low thirties or high forties. On their face, conditions favored the group, but the devil in the weather details somehow escaped them; forecasts showed a strong possibility of stormy weather, a rare occurrence in May, but certainly not unprecedented. In fact, a number of the area's guide companies cancelled climbs that day, thanks to the nasty forecast and overcast, chilly conditions.

But the Episcopal group wouldn't alter their plan, due in part perhaps to the reason they were up there in the first place. Every student at Oregon Episcopal had to make the climb, part of a required outdoor program called Basecamp, and 1986 marked the thirty-sixth year the students faced these outdoorsy graduation requirements. Those who didn't want to do Hood could finish the program with forty hours of community service, but high school students being high school students, most elected the daylong climb instead. (Expediency coupled with a dash of adventure, versus a full-time week picking up trash—it's not hard to see why most did.) The climb's leader, Father Tom Goman, had extensive climbing experience, too, specifically in leading expeditions of novice student climbers eager for the summit. On the face, it seemed that the group had little to worry about, other than a strenuous climb and lots of spectacular summit views to look forward to.

But things looked rough enough from the start to raise concerns. Right out of the lodge, the group seemed to move too slowly; temperatures dropped into the low thirties and the winds kicked up over thirty miles per hour, alarming some observers who noted that this early leg of the journey was by far the easiest. As the party forged on, students began dropping out and returning to the lodge, complaining of soreness and exposure. Courtney Boatsman, just sixteen at the time, had little physical trouble, but experienced that strange compulsion one could only call premonition: "It was something that was bugging me all the way up. Kind of like a voice saying 'Go down.'" Not arguing with that voice probably saved Courtney's life; she, along with four other students and one chaperoning parent, turned back before the snow started and things really got ugly.

Once that snow began to fall, it blew down with the force of reprisal. After a few hours, total whiteout conditions prevailed, and the group still inching its way up the mountain found itself in deep trouble. Four boys, six girls, Gorman, professional guide Ralph Summers, and dean of students Marion Horwell were unable to see more than two feet in front of them, while sixty-mile-per-hour winds ripped through their clothing. Nonetheless, they reached a point below the summit, then decided not to go any farther. (Some accounts put the group one thousand feet below the summit while others—including that of Molly Schula, one of the survivors—assert that the group had come within mere feet of the peak when the storm hit in earnest.) One member of their group, student Patrick McGinnis, had succumbed to hypothermia on the way up and needed help walking. Six o'clock p.m., the group's scheduled arrival time back at the lodge, came and went.

Whenever it happened, the party eventually realized they were walking off course and decided to dig in for the night. They spent Monday afternoon constructing a shallow snow cave by hand, digging for approximately two hours in the blistering conditions, before settling in for the night with no heat and little additional food or clothing. What's more, the group left some of their supplies under a tarp outside the cave, where they were unable to retrieve them later. And even after all the effort, the cave measured only five feet by six, adding claustrophobia to the list of terrors the increasingly desperate group faced.

The litany of things the Episcopal party could have done differently can, and has, filled pages. Goman and Summers—one or both of them, depending on who was really in charge up there—obviously drove their charges too far. In subsequent reports, Summers maintained that Goman ultimately made the calls, employing Summers as a "technical assistant"; neither man, however, seemed to take it seriously when some of the students said they wanted to turn back, or when Marion Horwell complained of breathing trouble. Estimates after the fact asserted that they should have turned back about eight hours before they actually did, at around 8,500 feet. Not paying attention to the forecast also seems tragically ignorant, especially when other professionals in the area clearly knew what might happen up there. Equipment, or the lack of it, played a part, too, as the climbers didn't carry enough shovels, not to mention an altimeter or even a proper topographical map of the mountain.

Their ultimate fate played out in tortured increments over the next three days. Sometime Tuesday morning, Summers and Molly Schula left to find help, Summers making a macabre promise to "keep walking until we found help or until we died." Leaving the cave, they found the blizzard still blowing strong and the wind chill at fifty below, but decided to have a go at it anyway.

They descended the mountain, picking their way through the blinding snow until, by luck and grace, they found their way to Mount Hood Meadows, one of the peak's six ski areas, three and a half hours later. Later that afternoon a search began, though conditions on the mountain made the ground search difficult and air reconnaissance impossible.

The weather did not improve markedly until Wednesday morning, and as it did the aerial search got underway. Around six that morning, spotters in the air found three more climbers at around 8,300 feet, comatose and with core temperatures around forty-three degrees Fahrenheit. They had left the cave, perhaps as their minds succumbed to the cold. (When body temperature drops below eighty-six degrees, pleasant warmth replaces the edge of cold, and victims are known to do strange things—lie down in the snow, take off their clothes, etc.) Doctors tried all day to revive the students, and actually got a heartbeat in one of them, but ultimately all three died in the hospital that same Wednesday.

The most grisly discovery, however, was not uncovered until 5:20 p.m. the next day, when searcher Charlie Ek struck something under the snow with his twelve-foot prodding pole. Four to five feet below the surface, the rest of the party lay stacked like cordwood, half-frozen. Of the remaining eight climbers, only two showed signs of life: Giles Thompson, sixteen, and fifteen-year-old Brinton Clark. Father Tom Goman, the leader of the expedition and ostensibly the man responsible for the decisions leading to the disaster, paid for those decisions with his life.

Giles and Brinton both ended up surviving their ordeal. Thompson, an athletic teen who played on the school soccer, ski, and track teams, ultimately lost both his lower legs to frostbite, after suffering through no less than twenty operations. For her part, Brinton Clark suffered no permanent physical damage and returned to school the next year, though she chose to grant no interviews about the incident.

Most of the students' families found it within themselves to chalk the incident up to bad luck, rather than incompetence. Father Goman had a great reputation among the parents and teachers of Oregon Episcopal, and few saw a reason to blame him in death. "For whatever reasons, whether he was suffering from hypothermia or whatever, he simply, to put it mildly, had a bad day," said Donald McClave, whose seventeen-year-old daughter Susan died on the mountain. "We'll never really know the answer to it."

This might, in hindsight, be the best reason not to blame Goman, despite his obvious mistakes and a possible dose of that old hubris brought on by outdoor experience. The man did, after all, know what he was doing up there, having led many previous expeditions. In fact, he had even climbed Hood two weeks before the journey that killed him to make sure conditions would be favorable. But blaming him, or Summers, or the mountain itself is simply an exercise in hindsight and futility. No one becomes less dead, regardless of what or who is to blame.

The Episcopal School disaster will go down as one of the worst outdoor sport accidents ever, both for the number of people killed and their youth. The worst accident in the history of Mount Everest, the 1996 storm Jon Krakauer wrote about in *Into Thin Air*, claimed eight lives—a tragedy for sure, but most of the Mount Hood victims had yet to go to prom, either. The seven students and two adults who lost their lives on Mount Hood certainly deserved better than they got all the way around. From leadership to simple luck, everything seemed to fail them that day, with predictable, and horrific, results.

≋ 年 ≋

Nothing happens to anyone alone during a mountaineering expedition. The sport requires teamwork, in terms of assisting climbers lower on the rope than yourself, as well as extravagant dependence on your climbing partners if you happen to be one of those further down the line. In fact, few other activities require such extreme trust in one's teammates; you are, after all, literally tied together, and the fate of one climber is often the same as that of the people tied to him. If one member of the group cannot ascend a peak, for example, chances are good that—if the climbing team is smart and stays together the way climbers should—no one else will either.

This dependence forces good climbers to work a certain way as they climb. First off, lead climbers simply shouldn't fall; when they do, they risk dragging the whole group down with them as they fall past the folks trailing and build up unmanageable momentum. For this reason, the most experienced climber in any given group will usually take the lead spot. In addition, smart climbers rarely climb in a vertical line, preferring instead to take individual routes in close proximity to avoid collisions in case someone does fall. This latter strategy doesn't do much good on a crowded mountain, however; a falling climber from one group is likely to tangle into other groups farther down the slope, resulting in a human avalanche with potentially disastrous consequences.

By 2002, nearly ten thousand climbers were attacking Mount Hood's summit every year, nearly twice the number that made the trek back when the Episcopal School expedition met its end. Such numbers of people, most of whom made their ascent during the high season in April, May, and June, create crowded conditions on mountaintop lanes. With so many groups on the mountain at once, the whole bunch essentially becomes one team—what happens to one group is, for better or worse, likely to happen to everybody else in the vicinity.

Four teams were sharing Mount Hood's popular southern route the morning of May 30, 2002—two on their way up and two, having already reached the summit, making their way back to the base. The group highest on the mountain consisted of four men: Harry Slutter and Chris Kern, both experienced climbers; Bill Ward, a less experienced though nonetheless competent mountaineer; and Rick Read, on his first climb after extensive training in mountaineering technique. Typically on an ascent, the best climber will take the lead position, with the weakest bringing up the rear; on the way down everyone reverses, so the weakest climber once again stands little chance of falling into more experienced climbers and taking them down the mountain. Slutter, however, was leading his group on the way down, with Read coming last in line.

The men descending also failed to respect another fundamental mountaineering rule: descending climbers are expected to hold their positions until ascending climbers below them can complete what they are doing. This courtesy keeps the mountain clearer should someone fall, and prevents the kind of event that eventually enveloped all four parties on the southern route that day.

At some point, Rick Read and Bill Ward, the climbers farthest up the mountain, began falling, crashing down to the snow. That day the snow was hard, and their rapid acceleration began immediately. (An eyewitness would say later that Ward fell first, as he tried to reposition himself on the mountain and gain better purchase on the slippery slope.) Falling down a steep, icy surface like the upper reaches of Mount Hood feels like falling down a cliff in that there is little or no friction to hold you back. Little, that is, unless you have the presence of mind to stab your ice axe into the snow properly in what is called a "self arrest." Ideally, doing so will stop a slide such as Read and Ward experienced, but in hard snow conditions, when ice axes don't penetrate more than an inch or two, their use as anchors disappears. Hard-snow conditions reigned that morning, putting Read and Ward in an untenable position extremely quickly. And, as their plight exploded into major danger, everyone on the mountain below them became subject to it.

As one might imagine, things happened quickly from there. Chris Kern, the second climber in line, didn't hear any verbal warning as his friends blew by and pulled him off the mountain. Slutter also heard nothing before momentum yanked him out of his arrest position. By the time they reached Slutter, Read and Ward had traveled more than one hundred feet each, ample distance to build up real speed.

John Biggs and Thomas Hillman were descending the mountain below this team, satisfied with having reached the summit but deliberate given the treacherous snow conditions. Hillman later said that he heard someone yell,

"Falling!" and looked up in time to see Biggs go down in a tumble of ropes, crampons, and bodies. Hillman, a seasoned climber himself, instinctually assumed the arrest position; as the falling group's rope tangled itself with his, Hillman knew he was going for an awful ride. As the weight of five men hit his ice axe, snow and ice plowed out in front of him, and he joined the group as it careened inexorably toward a thirty-foot-deep crevasse known as the Bergschrund (German for "mountain crack").

The whole mess of climbers and gear continued down the mountain, building up more speed. The two ascending groups, made up mostly of firefighters from the Tualatin Valley Fire Department, saw them coming and struggled to get clear. One group, comprised of Jeff Pierce, Cole Joiner, and Jeremiah Moffitt, didn't succeed and found themselves joining the procession downward as their gear melded into everyone else's. They were twenty to forty feet above the crevasse when they got hit; Joiner said he tried to get out of the way, but the other climbers in his threesome had assumed the self-arrest position already, anticipating the impact. In any case, no one succeeded in avoiding the avalanche, and all three were swept along and into the Bergschrund. The second Tualatin Valley team, safe on the downhill side of the crevasse, could only watch in horror as all nine climbers disappeared into the cold dark.

The whole event happened in fewer than ten seconds. In just that time, nine climbers had crashed into the wall of the crevasse and plummeted to its bottom, though each one had done exactly what they had been trained to do. Every climber, in fact, from the inexperienced Read on down, assumed the arrest position quickly and properly. Unfortunately, the first one hundred feet of momentum gained in that first second or two proved enough to pull everyone down. Even proper training, it seems, can't compete with simple gravity.

The men suffered in varying degrees after careening into the crevasse. Evidence indicates that the three who died—Rick Read, Bill Ward, and John Biggs—did so fairly quickly, with the sixty-two-year-old Biggs possibly suffering a concussion, or worse, in the initial collision.

Five hours after the accident, the HH-60G Pave Hawk helicopter sent to rescue the survivors began wobbling just as it was preparing to lift the injured Jeremiah Moffitt off the mountain. The chopper's refueling probe stuck into the snow, pitching it sideways and slamming its rotors into the snow. The massive blades sliced the ground and eventually tore off as the Blackhawk began a one thousand foot roll down the mountain. The whole thing took place in front of national news cameras there to cover the climbing accident, and all initial indications pointed to more tragedy.

Fortunately, no one died in the helicopter mishap, sparing Mount Hood more bad ink on a day already rife with it. Quick thinking and action by the pilot and crew saved the day; they quickly released the cable holding Moffitt, probably saving the man from a punishing, fatal ride down the face of the mountain. The pilot realized that a wind change was causing him to lose power, so he steered away from the accident scene to avoid dropping on top of the people there. Though the crash spread debris all over the mountain, no one was hit. The six crewmembers all survived, albeit not without some serious injuries, and three of them were even able to walk away from the crash. In all, it was a far less awful ending than it could have been.

While Mount Hood represents the West's most-climbed peak, it is far from the only one that has claimed victims in pursuit of its reaches. In 1997, two climbers scaling the ice on Mount Rainier suffered a fifty- to eighty-foot vertical drop after one of them tried to knock some snow out of his crampons as they walked along a crevasse lip. Don McIntyre, the man who had tried to clear the snow from his feet, died before rescuers could get to him. The climbers had already reached the mountain's summit and were working their way down when disaster struck. In 2005, four more people lost their lives on Rainier. Two of the deaths happened in May, when a pair of climbers had apparently set out in fairly bad weather improperly dressed, and died about 8,500 feet up the mountain after hypothermia overtook them. Another unfortunate climber fell to his doom when he lost his footing on a steep chute of ice and plummeted more than nine hundred feet over protruding rocks.

In fact, almost every high peak in the West has seen its share of death. Even Mount Shasta, a relatively tame climb—the main route isn't even classified technical—saw fatalities in 2000 and again in 2004. The 2004 incident involved a twenty-one-year-old Indonesian man named Lukman Latif Tardia, who fell down to the snow and wasn't able to arrest his fall. He slid about one thousand vertical feet, knocking into rock outcroppings along the way. He came to rest at the bottom with multiple and profound injuries, including a vicious bang to the head. His brother hiked out for help, which didn't arrive until about seven hours after the fall. By then, of course, it was too late, though it was most likely too late immediately after the whole thing happened.

The previous Shasta incident happened in April 2000, and involved two climbers caught out in one of the mountain's infamous spring blizzards. This one dumped about two feet of powder on the upper mountain, which sealed the climbers' fates and hampered the search effort. Actually, another four feet fell in the next ten days, as rescue personnel desperately tried to find the lost hikers. In the end, they discovered that one of them, Craig Hiemstra of England, had fallen and broken his neck. His companion, John Miksits, froze to death as the subsequent snows fell. During the search, yet another helicopter—a National Guard chopper—crashed into the snow, brought down by hard winds. Once again, thankfully, none of the seven people aboard suffered any injuries.

More amazing than accidents like these, however, may be the fact that so many people who do not know what they are doing manage to get off the mountains in one piece. In most cases, only one factor keeps these lucky souls away from death's door: the heroic efforts of rescue personnel. In June 2005, for example, Mount Rainier rangers caught wind of a three-person team that had become stuck at about 13,500 feet. They had left for their climb without a tent or stove, and—in a head-scratching piece of decisionmaking—brought only one sleeping bag. Stories like these, albeit involving a slightly higher level of preparedness, if not skill, happen dozens of times every year at Mount Rainier and across the entire national park system. If not for those search and rescue personnel, this book would be significantly longer, and outdoor recreation far less popular.

Though climbing a mountain to reach its frozen reaches only occasionally results in trouble, the reverse—mountain snows taking a run downslope—never ends all that well. At the very least, an avalanche will scare the bejezus out of you; at worst, a serious slide will bury everything in its merciless path under dozens of feet of snow and ice, paralyzing and suffocating anyone unlucky enough to get caught.

Avalanches are to snow what tidal waves are to seawater—massive, driving accumulations, moving at unholy speeds and slamming into whatever happens to be in their paths with crushing force. And according to the Forest Service's National Avalanche Center, about 95 percent of avalanches get triggered by the people they afflict and sometimes kill. As with so many other backcountry calamities, avalanches result from people acting improperly, whether they know it or not, and suffering the consequences. Steep slopes, combined with unstable snowpack and changing weather, usually add up to dangerous conditions waiting to be set in downhill motion by a fourth factor: human beings who don't recognize the dangerous mix of circumstances in front of them. Backcountry skiers in particular are prone to cause avalanches—not a surprising fact, given skiing's downhill slope requirement. Snowmobile riders run a close second in avalanche-related incidents, since the vehicles are more powerful, and thus more capable of climbing sheer mountain slopes, than ever before. As they make their way up these steep expanses, heavy snowmobiles can easily break the tenuous connection between surface snow and the forces that bind it in place.

Once a hapless skier or snowmobiler triggers an avalanche, the destruction comes on quickly and angrily. The typical snow slide travels about three to five hundred feet, and runs about five feet deep. They can get a lot bigger and deeper, though, and really major avalanches with a lot of ground in front of them can reach blinding speed—over one hundred miles per hour in the worst cases. Typically they don't fly down the hill quite that fast, but consider the deadly results even at slower speeds: about one in three people who get caught in avalanches die in them, making the avalanche, event for event, perhaps the most deadly natural occurrence to afflict the backcountry.

There are a number of different types of avalanches, all of which present a problem under the wrong circumstances. (Even a so-called roof avalanche, which involves a slab of snow sliding down to the ground from the rooftop above, has the potential to kill—think wet, heavy snow and two or three stories' worth of gravity.) The worst variety, however, is known as a slab—that is, a slab of snow on the surface detaches from its moorings, and gravity takes over to chuck it down the mountain. Avalanches of this variety often happen when the unwary travel directly onto the slab about to break off, thus ensuring a fast, suffocating trip downhill.

Only five people died in Colorado during winter 2004–2005 from avalanches. Previous years, however, were far more deadly. The worst in modern memory remains 2000, which saw eight people in Colorado and thirty-five across the nation die in snow slides. (The year1910—when the Wellington avalanche swept two trains off their tracks up in Washington, killing ninety-six people— probably ranks as the worst ever.) Seasons with less snowfall, such as 2000 and 2001, result in an awful catch-22: less snowfall isn't likely to generate the large avalanches that destroy property. But with less pack, sliding snow is more likely to reveal the rocks and other debris hiding underneath, resulting in more fatal accidents. In fact, during the two deadly years mentioned above, sixteen people total died in Colorado; in the same period, no property damage was reported, according to the Colorado Avalanche Information Center.

Not so many people used to die in avalanches. In fact, between 1950 and 1980, avalanches killed more than ten people annually only seven times. After that year, however, there were only four years in which ten or more people *didn't* die, with most years since 1992 passing twenty fatalities each. The five-year moving average of avalanche-related deaths, according to the Northwest Weather and Avalanche Center (NWAS), has increased from less than five in the early 1950s to just below thirty today. Without a doubt, the increase in fatalities relates to increased ski and snowmobile presence in the backcountry, where massive sheets of snow receive little or no traffic until some unsuspecting ski bum decides to shred into them.

Backcountry skiers have learned to deal with the slides by taking care and carrying some basic avalanche gear: a transceiver that sends out a signal, in case they're buried under a few feet of snow; a shovel, to get that snow out of the way; and a probe, to pick out where buried comrades might be if things go badly. Without this equipment, getting yourself found after an avalanche is next to impossible unless you're lucky enough to have a glove, ski, or other bit of you sticking up above the snow.

Still, people die every year under very similar circumstances—by being buried, mostly, though some perish after being swept into lakes and other bodies of water. In early 2002, one man skiing alone at Aspen Highlands slid past the ski area boundary and triggered a small avalanche, "no wider than his skis" according to the CAIC. Unfortunately, the small slide was enough to immobilize him, and having no one around to dig him out, he asphyxiated. The irony in such backcountry accidents lies in the fact that most people do not even go out there unless they are pretty good on their skis or snowboard; unlike hikers in over their heads, these people have some skill going for them, and manage to die anyway.

Mountain climbers see their share of avalanches too, as might be expected. In 1998, first-time climber Patrick Nestler and his mountaineering school class were climbing in Rainier's wet, early summer conditions. The warm temperatures came after two chilly days that saw new snow fall on the dormant volcano, followed by about an inch of rain and sunlight that loosened up the whole mountainside. Conditions could barely be riper for avalanche.

The slide happened at about 2:00 p.m., just when the effects of the temperature and precipitation would most likely cause snow to break off. The group had actually reached the summit already, and was headed back down. They were all climbing with Rainier Mountaineering Inc. (RMI), the biggest guide outfit on Mount Rainier, and were four days into a five-day climbing school. The summit run had energized the whole lot of them, thanks in part to the gloriousness of the weather. "This was one of the most spectacular days I've ever seen," lead guide Curt Hewitt said afterward. "It was like that right up to the accident. It was euphoria, and then chaos."

That chaos began just as two climbing teams were reaching the downslope edge of Disappointment Cleaver, a rough dorsal of black rock. One of the climbers, an ophthalmologist named Scott Pressman, sighted a largish snowball tumbling down the mountain at them, and watched as it blossomed into an avalanche before his eyes. "It was just a snowball," he said afterward. He also said he'd never climb Rainier again, given the events that snowball portended.

The full-fledged avalanche slammed into the two groups. The first group, three climbers and guide Curt Hewitt, was making its way across the downslope clipped to an eight hundred foot safety line, held in place by three aluminum spikes. As the snow smashed into them, two of the three aluminum anchors yanked out of the ground, though miraculously that last anchor held fast. The safety line pulled down the other five-person group as they tried to run clear of the avalanche's path, bringing them down the mountain until they came to rest on various ledges, or simply dangling out in midair.

Nestler and his party got caught in the slide, which swept twelve of them down toward Disappointment Cleaver, a rough dorsal of black rock. Many tried to bury their ice axes in the snow and arrest their descent, but the mushy conditions confounded their efforts, and they continued to slide toward oblivion. As they slid, the various teams ran into each other and tangled up, their ropes somehow holding despite the jagged rocks they slid over.

Chaos had blasted down the mountain quicker than either group could react to it, though they were all lucky enough to remain clamped to their ropes. Though things were still far from certain, at least no one had gone plummeting into space on broken ropes. Patrick Nestler dangled about one hundred feet down from the cliff he'd fallen from; Wreatha Carrier, another climber who had witnessed the avalanche and was the first to call in the emergency, tried to get to him but couldn't.

Despite the fact that he stayed attached to the group, Nestler still settled into the worst position possible: he simply hung out in the air with nothing supporting his body save the rope attached to his middle. Other RMI guides and rangers had begun rescuing the climbers stuck in various states of rope-wrapped discomfort on the mountain, but they could not see Nestler dangling below. They did, however, hear him moaning and screaming.

Nestler suffered some blunt-trauma injuries on his way down, but hypothermia ultimately killed him. He'd come to rest in the path of a snowmelt "drip," a drenching mini-waterfall that magnified the cold as it penetrated his clothing. His jacket and pants, wet and getting wetter by the second, were soon soaked through, and thanks to his position at the end of the line, he never had a chance. Rescuers didn't reach him until three hours after the fall, when it was far too late.

The rest of the rescue effort, however, proved phenomenal in its success. Things could have been far worse; the line connecting the second group to the safety line, for example, nearly snapped as the rocks cut into it during the slide. It held by mere strands as the rescuers arrived on the scene. Another climber, Deborah Lynn, dangled thirty feet off the cliff in a snowmelt stream like Patrick Nestler; luckily, the rescuers were able to pull her out in time. Ultimately, all eight of the other climbers came off the mountain alive; some of them even walked off themselves. The fact that so many were rescued without a hitch, given the mushy, dangerous conditions up there that day, speaks to the quick and dedicated work of RMI guides and Mount Rainier's rangers.

Patrick Nestler's first major climb killed him. His death, however, was no accident of amateurishness; he was climbing with experienced people, utilizing proper safety procedures. Unfortunately, natural conditions rose against him and the rest of his party, resulting in his fate. Not so with some other avalanche victims whose fates, tragic as they are, don't really surprise anyone.

Snowmobiles, ATVs, and the like have given those who might previously have no business in the backcountry a two-way ticket there and back, though sometimes the mountains have something to say about it. The weight, noise, and vibrations of these machines—and six hundred horses bring along a whole lot of all three—trigger avalanches. If you happen to be acting the fool on top of all this, you might find yourself trying to breathe through six feet of freshly churned powder.

Craig Rogers was one such snowmobiler who did not quite understand the rules of the backcountry road. In 1998, he and a bunch of other snowmobilers were gathered in Washington's Wenatchee National Forest, engaging in a "sport" called high marking. The point: to drive as far as possible up a forty-degree slope, the winner being the one who could make it the farthest. Rogers, to his credit, won the day with the highest mark. Unfortunately, his winning run started an avalanche that eventually buried him under three feet of snow, fifty feet from his snowmobile.

Not a nice fate, to be sure, but certainly a predictable one.

CHAPTER TWO

American Chaos
Natural Disasters of the West

*When we saw the tsunami, we cried, because we felt so bad for
those people. We hugged each other and asked, 'What would we
ever do if one of us lost the other?' Man. I never imagined. . . .
I still don't know, baby.*

— JIMMY WALLET,

*Relating a conversation he had with
his wife Mechelle in late 2004.*

On January 10, 2005, four hundred thousand tons of mud and debris slid from the hills over La Conchita, California, killing Mechelle and three of their children along with six others.

Natural disasters have earned a Hollywood-esque, unreal status in the United States, mostly because they seem always to happen somewhere else. Hundreds of thousands died during the tsunamis of 2004; more than eighty thousand died in the cataclysmic 2005 Kashmir earthquake. These events took place in only the last few years; such disasters strike around the world with depressing regularity. Of course, these horrible events took so many lives partly because they slammed into buildings of grass and mud, or no buildings at all. It does reveal something about our modern ability to protect ourselves from the elements that the United States has never seen a catastrophe of that magnitude. Still, the fact is that natural factors brought these catastrophes to pass, and had they happened on American soil, the results would have been bad by any measure.

Historically, we have been extremely, blessedly lucky on the natural disaster front. It took a catastrophe of Hurricane Katrina's proportions to remind us that even our cities, even our sturdy, concrete and steel cities, are subject to the same destructive forces as the rest of the world's. Yet even in the face of this spectacular destruction, only about fifteen hundred people died—an awful tragedy, to be sure, especially for those who saw their neighbors and loved ones drown, but one would be hard-pressed to equate America's losses in New Orleans and its surroundings to the death of hundreds of thousands in Indonesia under crushing walls of seawater.

But Katrina *was* something special. The fourth most-powerful hurricane ever to strike the U.S., she reached category five—as bad as hurricanes get— and happened to hit land exactly where her ten- to fifteen-foot storm surges would do maximum damage. Her winds maxed out at around one hundred seventy miles per hour, hard enough to propel shards of debris through trees like arrows. Hurricane-force winds whipped out even two hundred thirty miles from the storm center, and the storm itself released as much energy as a ten-megaton nuclear weapon every twenty minutes. (Perhaps more—that figure comes from the National Oceanic and Atmospheric Administration (NOAA), and simply describes "a fully developed hurricane." Katrina, as a category five, may have belted out even more energy.) New Orleans and the Gulf Coast never had much of a chance once this abomination rolled into town.

The western U.S., luckily for the folks who live there, doesn't suffer from hurricanes, cyclones, or any other storms bad enough to receive names. It also doesn't see many tornadoes, the bane of the Midwest. What the West does see, however, are drenching, inundating rains that raise rivers and lakes until, sometimes, they start sweeping away houses and people. In fact, flooding represents the most deadly natural event in the West; even without hurricanes, the West has suffered immobilizing accumulations of water, and seen dozens die in their soaking wake.

Lots of different things cause floods—rain is the most obvious culprit, though the whole concept of "flood" is a human thing when you get down to it. Consider: when people don't live near the body of water in question, changes in water level don't attract much attention. If, however, you happen to live near the Mississippi, the Missouri, or the Nile, hard rains produce floods.

Floods come in two main varieties: the awesome, biblical floods that result when rivers burst their banks and water spills out into the surrounding area (known as the flood plain); and flash floods, usually far smaller than their giant cousins but more dangerous if you happen to be in the wrong place at the wrong time. They generally happen when massive storms hit and dump several inches of rain within a short time, faster than the ground can absorb it. That water, with nowhere to go, simply accumulates, bringing up river levels and running downhill regardless of what stands in its way. Big ones like the Great Flood of 1993, which drowned some towns off the Mississippi for upwards of two hundred days, destroy lots of property and cause no small amount of suffering. Big flash floods, however—cataclysms like the famous Johnstown flood of 1889—can kill thousands as they scrub the landscape clean of human presence.

Colorado's Big Thompson flood falls into this latter category, both in terms of its classification and the amount of death it dropped on this popular alpine retreat. The Big Thompson Canyon meanders between Loveland and Estes Park, cradling the Big Thompson River and U.S. Highway 34. The sheer walls, pretty meadows, and gentle hiking trails attract thousands of outdoor enthusiasts every year who populate rustic cabins and tents in campgrounds up and down the valley. On July 31, 1976, fresh off the huge bicentennial celebrations of July 4th, Colorado's campers were still in a festive mood. After all, the state celebrated its own centennial the day before, a Friday, and lots of vacationers had decided to skip town and hit the Big Thompson for a bit of summer fun. Twenty-five hundred to thirty-five hundred people made their way into the valley for the weekend.

The valley itself pushes in tight at some points, pinching the highway and river together like fingers threading a needle, and spreads out into gorgeous vistas at others, revealing stands of ponderosa pine and Douglas-fir at the top fringe of the canyon. These slopes, consisting of hard rock like the rest of the canyon, don't absorb very much water; the soil is thin and spotty, just enough to give the trees something to hold on to. Normally this inability doesn't mean much, as storms tend to blow from the head of the canyon and move quickly on through, carried by powerful mountain winds. July 31, 1976, was an uncommonly calm day however, with weak breezes rather than the winds that ordinarily propel a developing thunderstorm once the skies open. The thunderheads that developed that day, born of moist mountain air condensing in the daytime heat, grew and exploded forth with no way to go anyplace else.

The storm, instead of running through the valley as storms normally do, took a leisurely crawl. Clouds towered sixty thousand feet into the air, a black and roiling mass stalled in its tracks. Tons of water began falling into the rock canyon, funneled ever downward into the river. Within the first minutes, the water level started to rise.

Rain fell by the dumpster full. Witnesses said the air even became hard to breathe from all the water in it. According to NOAA, eight inches of water fell during a one-hour stretch. The storm inched its way east, gaining force as it traveled the twenty-five miles between Estes Park and Loveland, dumping rain into the Big Thompson proper as well as its tributaries—Fox Creek, Cedar Creek, the Thompson's North Fork—until the water acquired crushing intensity. According to Larimer County's account of the accident, by 9:00 p.m. the river was flowing close to 31,200 cubic feet per second; its normal flow at that point—near Drake, midway up the canyon—is about 137 cubic feet per second. The gentle two-foot-deep stream built into a nineteen-foot-tall deluge, sweeping boulders and entire houses in front of it as it rocketed toward Loveland.

Two inches had fallen by 6:30 p.m., when the river began to rise; by 10:30, more than ten inches had fallen, a deluge that meteorologists called a three-hundred-year storm for its intensity and rarity. (Storms are often classified in this way, according to the historical weather and water flow data of the water body in question. A ten-year flood has a ten percent chance of happening in any given year, and constitutes a pretty bad time; a five-hundred-year flood has a 0.2 percent chance, and causes a whole lot more trouble, as river flows reach their five-century high-water mark.) After all was said and done, ten to fourteen inches—an entire year's worth of rain—fell in about four hours, causing a deluge of black, chunky water that blasted through the valley and carried off everything it touched.

The water bludgeoned Highway 34 into rubble, washing out the main avenue of escape. Even if it hadn't, however, the rush of water would have made getting out via that route impossible. People who tried found themselves stuck in their vehicles and washed into the maelstrom, with many of them failing to escape. Those who had the best luck in surviving scrambled for the high ground, climbing slicked canyon paths and walls that, only hours before, they'd been tooling around on at a leisurely summertime pace. Lightning struck continuously, and the ground shuddered with the various forces of the storm.

People sought shelter wherever they could—under rock ledges, up in the trees at the top of the canyon. Eventually the water washed all indications of Route 34 away, leaving the canyon in a primeval state of pre-humanity. The pockets of people huddled all around didn't fail to notice. "It was kind of cool, pristine," said survivor Mike Fink on the thirty-year anniversary of the disaster in 2006. He spent that night crammed between vertical rock slabs twenty feet above the former roadway. "All signs of man had been erased." By the storm's end, nothing remained of the road save some bits at the river's curves. The riverbed deepened by ten feet, carved down through schist and granite, boulder-size pieces strewn miles downriver. Fink and his group—twenty-five of them in all—survived the night and flagged a rescue helicopter the next morning as hypothermia was just setting in. They made it out alive.

Knowing the highway's fate, it's not hard to imagine what befell the canyon's homes and vehicles. The water destroyed 418 homes and 52 businesses in a place that didn't have a lot of houses to begin with. It cost more than $1 million just to remove the accumulated debris in the valley—in excess of 320,000 cubic yards of broken, battered trash that had washed into every crevasse. Two hotels located at the junction of the north and south forks of the Big

Thompson simply disappeared without a trace, swept off the map and leaving not a single scrap of evidence that they'd ever existed at all. Cars and other vehicles turned into coffins as people, trapped and caught up in the flow, were simply dashed into the general mess of debris flowing downriver.

One hundred forty-five people died in the flood, though six of them were never found in the cleanup effort, and victims kept turning up even two months after the initial deluge. That there weren't more fatalities attests to luck and most people's ability to reach the high ground; large groups like Fink's huddled in high-ground cabins and under whatever they could find through the night, and were evacuated the next day. For the amount of traffic in the canyon that day, things could have been far worse. Perhaps the fact that most of the people there were outdoors to begin with had something to do with their collective ability to scramble up the canyon and out of harm's way.

The Big Thompson flood remains Colorado's deadliest disaster. But by the next day, things were returning to normal, at least as far as the river was concerned—water levels had fallen, and people could get back into the canyon with little trouble. This aspect of the Big Thompson disaster defines the flash flood—namely its capricious, temporary nature. Flash floods will sneak up, drag you down and along until your lungs stop, and then melt away into the ground once the rain stops falling. Perhaps no geological feature compliments the *blitzkrieg* nature of a flash flood like the slot canyons of the Southwest.

Slot canyons are narrow corridors through rock—usually sandstone, since it erodes quickly and with even a trickle of water—that are lots of fun to explore when they're dry. In any western you've ever seen, the nooks and crannies where the outlaws hide are slot canyons, mysterious passages in which the long arm of the law might be avoided.

Ribbons of orange and red run through sandstone slot canyons, which usually spread only a few feet wide but can reach a couple hundred feet in height. Their walls undulate smoothly, beckoning exploration and making for very cool desert hiking. One thing you never want to do, however: hike a slot canyon during a rainstorm. Because the very factors that made the Big Thompson such a death trap are also present in the slot canyon to a far higher degree, with the additional drawback of not providing a way to climb up and out of harm's way. At least in the Big Thompson Flood, you could head to the high ground.

Most slot canyons are tucked pretty deep into the backcountry, where few people even see them, much less worry about hard rains whipping up a flood and sweeping them away. But as I've explained before, more people are heading into the backcountry these days, which makes such tragedies more likely. In the Southwest, it's the monsoon season that brings the heavy noise, running water down the slot canyon and perpetuating that force—erosion—

that put the sandy passage there in the first place. The fact that the passage is so narrow makes the amount of rainfall less relevant, too; it doesn't take much water (rainstorm-wise) to fill a three-foot-wide passage beyond your ability to breathe or move in it. Even the Southwest's slight rainfall, less than ten inches a year in many places, can get dangerous waters moving. In fact, it only takes about a half-inch of rain to create troublesome conditions, especially in the narrow, hard-packed soil common to slot canyons and the desert in general.

On August 12, 1997, at the height of monsoon season, twelve men and women, mostly tourists from Europe, descended a rickety wooden ladder into the most famous slot canyon in the West: lower Antelope Canyon. Antelope, located near Lake Powell and Page, Arizona, is instantly recognizable from the thousands of pictures it has inspired over the last several decades; grooved, sand-colored walls, shooting up into a near-canopy, pools of light on the ground the only indication that the photographer isn't standing in a cave. At some points, the canyon walls press in only three feet away from each other, making for one of the most interesting, breathtaking hikes in the whole American West. Truly, Antelope Canyon holds an iconic place—if not exactly known by name, it certainly represents the image foremost in many a mind's eye when it comes to Arizona and the Southwest in general.

There's ample evidence that European tourists might appreciate this heritage even more than we ourselves do; during the summer, for example, most of the people you'll find in scorching Death Valley are Europeans. "It's something you don't have in Europe—this hot wind," Nicole Becker of Germany said during a 2003 Death Valley visit. (As far as is known, no one responded, "You can keep it, sister.") The stereotype of the fascinated German/French/English tourist wearing cowboy boots and listening to Merle Haggard is well established among those who live in Arizona or Nevada, and quite commonly encountered if you visit Tombstone, Grand Canyon, or any other western landmark.

These particular tourists entered Antelope Canyon at exactly the wrong time: just as a thunderstorm was breaking about fifteen miles to the south and—most importantly—uphill. Conditions for flash floods get ripe based on a number of factors, one of the most important being the lack of absorption in the ground. The desert that day, as it does practically every day, resisted the rainwater, providing no ingress as it traveled two thousand feet downhill toward Lake Powell. All that water just built up speed, momentum, and debris as it traveled; by the time it hit Antelope Canyon, it accelerated even more, thanks to the canyon's narrow profile. Like water shooting through a hose, it built up even more speed.

Arizona's monsoons gave birth to the region's slot canyons over the course of millennia. Officially, *monsoon* describes a weather phenomenon in which the wind reverses course during a certain season of the year, bringing moisture into generally dry areas and creating massive storms. The monsoon season in India, for example, happens from April through October when southwesterly winds bring titanic storms, versus the rest of the year when a dry northeasterly breeze brings little moisture at all. Arizona and New Mexico catch the tail end of just such a phenomena happening annually in Mexico, where summertime winds pull moisture from the Pacific and the Gulf of Mexico and dump it over that country and the American Southwest.

Even tropical storms from the eastern Pacific Ocean can result in drenching rains; over Labor Day weekend of 1970, for example, tropical storm Norma's remnants dumped over seven inches of rain in some places and killed twenty-three people in Arizona, fourteen of them when Tonto Creek flooded faster than they could escape it. Because the creek was running so deep, people swept into its flow had little chance for escape, and even less so considering that many were swept away while inside their vehicles. The death toll makes this event the deadliest natural disaster in the history of an otherwise weather-placid state.

Generally, sunshine is the order of the day all over the Grand Canyon State; between 10:00 p.m. on September 4 and 10:00 p.m. the next night, however, the rain gauge at Workman Creek measured 11.4 inches of rainfall. In Arizona, with its sunbaked ground and lack of regular rainfall, such a deluge has few places to go, so the places it accumulates fill up and burst their bounds very quickly. For its part, the air brought forth a tornado that touched down into Scottsdale and Tempe, tearing into roofs and patio covers (though it left only twenty-five thousand dollars' worth of damage—not a lot, even considering the value of those 1970 dollars). The vast majority of people who died in the flood met their end as they tried to escape the deluge in their cars. As news slowly made its way into the papers, the death toll continued to rise. At one point, estimates ran as high as thirty-six dead.

The Tonto Creek disaster may have claimed more lives than any other natural event in the state's history, but biblical rain isn't foreign to Arizona despite its being one of the nation's driest states. The normal monsoon season starts in mid-summer around the beginning of July, and continues through the middle of September. The storms cause serious damage, often when decaying thunderstorms give rise to microbursts, concentrated cells of wind and furious rain that can produce gusts topping fifty miles per hour. In 1996, one such burst created wind gusts of one 115 miles per hour, and did $160 million in damage. From 1996 through 1999, in fact, severe thunderstorms did more than $225 million in damage around the Phoenix area, most of it happening when winds carried whatever they were able to carry into the closest building, car, or person.

At Antelope Canyon itself, only a little rain fell on August 12. But the rainfall nearby, three-quarters of an inch within fifteen short minutes, grew into a ten-foot-high wall of brown, muddy water as it rushed along. (Some observers reported heights of fifty feet in certain sections, a nightmarish thing to contemplate if true.) In fact, as the twelve-person tour group descended into the canyon, some other parts of the canyon had already been closed due to the rain.

The warnings, in hindsight, should have stopped the expedition. In addition to these closings, the National Weather Service up in Flagstaff had already issued a severe thunderstorm warning. According to the Associated Press, a ticket taker working for the Navajo Nation (the Nation charges people for access to the canyon) warned the group before they set out, and to proceed at their own risks. Yet tour guide Francisco Quintana, working for a company called TrekAmerica that specializes in showing young Europeans the American sights, took his group of five down into the canyon. They descended despite everything, and suspected nothing until they heard the roar of the water.

Quintana knew what was coming. The welder-turned-wilderness guide had only been at it for a year, but even with the lack of experience he realized that the exit ladders, about one hundred feet away, were already out of reach. He wedged himself against a wall with two of his charges, and the water began to sweep past their ankles. It was up to their knees in seconds, and inside of a minute they were all swept away, their clothes stripped from their bodies by the raging water.

The people above, looking down into the canyon, saw everything—the sweeping water, the hikers disappearing under it, some never to be seen again. Seven from France, one from England, one from Sweden, and two Americans succumbed to the water; two of the French citizens were parents who had left their little girls back at their hotel. The girls, ages eight and thirteen, got nervous when their parents never came back from their hike; their lack of English caused them to delay telling the hotel staff until they were fairly panicking. They were remanded to state custody in the aftermath of their parents' death, and though they wanted to ask Quintana exactly what had happened down there, they never got the chance—he returned to California immediately after the accident without talking to the press or much of anyone else.

Quintana, amazingly, had managed to grab a rock as the water and mud bashed into him. He reported seeing a few of the other hikers flying by, their expressions rictuses of panic, before they disappeared into the deluge. Then he lost his grip and struggled to keep his head above the water as he grasped at the canyon walls, trying to find some purchase as the water smashed him along. Rescuers eventually found him about a quarter-mile further down, where he finally succeeded in grabbing a rock and clinging to it. He was naked, as his clothes had been flayed from his body.

Rescuers pulled all the stops in their search for the missing hikers, bringing dogs, divers, and even miniature submarines to bear. Most of the victims turned up farther down the canyon, though some didn't surface at all—three of the hikers were never found, their bodies probably washed four miles downstream and into Lake Powell's depths. Powell, the massive result of the Glen Canyon Dam and the flooding of its namesake, may be the prettiest lake in America, situated in the middle of Utah and Arizona's red rock country. It is certainly one of the biggest, with over 1,900 miles of shoreline (more than the Pacific coast of the U.S.) and around a hundred side canyons to explore. But at a mean depth of 132 feet, a sink to the reservoir's bottom is, for all intents and purposes, a complete erasure.

Two years later, Francisco Quintana sued Young's Tours, the company that charges to lead tourists to Antelope Canyon. He alleged that they hadn't told his group about the potential for danger down in the canyon; he also revealed that during the flood, he'd held his breath so long that he ruptured the lining of his stomach, and had since had it replaced with a metal mesh. His lawsuit came after his tour charges' families decided to sue *him*, blaming the guide for the deaths of their loved ones.

Who actually deserves blame? Perhaps everyone—no one ended up saying "no" and heading back to the parking lot after the ticket taker warned them. Quintana let his people climb down into the canyon, and the Navajo themselves continued to let people in. It seems a compilation of tragic miscalculations, culminating in one of the worst wilderness disasters in Arizona's history, and certainly the worst due to flood in recent memory.

Other flash floods deaths have punctuated monsoon season since then, though few of those match the ironic twist of George Mancuso's demise near the Little Colorado River around August 7, 2001. Mancuso might have been better acquainted with the Grand Canyon than anyone else ever has been. Ken Phillips, a ranger at the canyon for eighteen years, said that Mancuso probably knew it better than anyone on the park's staff. The photographer described himself as "obsessed" with his "big ditch," and it overrode everything else in his life. Ironic, then, that his first love—the geographical icon he forsook even his family for—would end up killing him in the end.

Mancuso was, by many accounts, not an easy guy to get along with. He admitted that the canyon managed to wedge itself between he and most people in his life; according to Mancuso, "My relationship with the canyon comes first, and because of that, my personal life has not always been so good. During the seventies and eighties I didn't do so well with women." In spending so much time there, however, Mancuso developed a rare eye for the canyon's many scenic treasures, and brought back some of the best photography of

Grand Canyon around. He made about twenty pictures into postcards to sell around the canyon, and by all accounts his work was top-notch.

Around the time he died, George Mancuso was working on a new project: *La Femme de Grand Canyon*, which he described as an effort to "capture on film a unique portfolio of prints displaying the sensual, artistic, natural, and spiritual expressions of the female form within a beautiful outdoor setting." He may or may not have been working on this project with Linda Brehmer, the friend Mancuso was camping with that early August and—according to her journal—with whom he shared a romantic relationship. Mancuso was quite experienced in the outdoors, but one detail escaped him as he and Linda set out for the Little Colorado: they did not seek permits from the park itself, a decision that served to delay search efforts since no one knew there was anyone to search for.

In fact, no one thought to look for them until they were ten days overdue, after authorities received a missing persons call regarding both of them. Not that this was anything new; Mancuso had a reputation for coming home late from canyon excursions, and once even turned up a few days after being reported missing, tagging along with a river rafting expedition. He was, after all, extremely good in the backcountry and knew the canyon better even than people who'd dedicated decades on the ranger staff.

Rescue teams took the call seriously, though, and soon found remnants of the couple's camp, where water, food, and sleeping bags were still neatly laid out. The camp was at the bottom of a tortuous backcountry trail, one that, according to the Coconino County sheriff's office, required ropes to get down. It turned out that Mancuso and Brehmer had set out for a fairly long side hike, according to Brehmer's journal. She wrote that they decided to visit Emerald Pool, a remote backcountry landmark located about twelve miles from the original campsite. The route there, however, had seen a few flash floods recently, as Arizona's monsoon rains continued to fall nearby. The result: roiling masses of water shooting through slot canyons like the one the couple walked through, a terrible demise waiting but not identified until too late.

Of course, no one knows exactly what happened next. They may have struggled; then again, they might have been too beat up by the blasting water and its masses of logs, mud, and stone to stay conscious for very long. What we do know is that Mancuso's body ended up near the confluence of the Little Colorado and Colorado Rivers, a place that he had visited no less than fifty times. He was found six miles downriver from Linda Brehmer, partially buried in deposited sediment.

Once again, George Mancuso was a consummate outdoorsman, as well as an expert on the Grand Canyon's vagaries. And he *still* got killed there, during one of the canyon's best displays of raw power. Unfortunately, he never filed for his permit to hike the backcountry; even without it, however, chances are rescue teams would have been too late to pull him and Linda Brehmer out of harm's way. In his search for the perfect picture, looking through his lens, he may have missed the big picture. And though he did take his eye off the ball (so to speak), the canyon country he loved so much ultimately dealt the killing blow, once again proving that nature does occasionally hurt the ones who love it.

≋ ䷸ ≋

Massive sheets of drowning water aren't the only threat big-time storms can bring to bear. Even the average thunder boomer releases as much energy as a twenty-kiloton nuke, the force of which gets dispersed as the rain falls and takes the thunder, so to speak, out of the clouds above. But that energy gets expended in a more spectacular way, too—as lightning. Lightning happens high in cumulonimbus storm clouds, which can reach forty thousand feet into the atmosphere. As water droplets in the cloud's lower reaches collide with ice and snow crystals above at speeds up to fifty knots, a massive electric field builds. The roiling snow and ice create positive and negative regions in the cloud itself, and lightning starts jumping around between the two. Then, as the clouds move, induced positive charges on the ground attract negatively charged energy from above; a column of air known as a step leader flows down to the ground, and positive charges from the ground reach upward. Once the two connect, electricity fires from the cloud into the ground (or the tree, or the person) and then back up in what is called a return stroke.

That little technical description translates into one of nature's scariest, deadliest, and most breathtaking phenomena. The return stroke heats the air around it to fifty thousand degrees—five times hotter than the sun—in a few millionths of a second, creating a crushing shock wave that blows off for about ten yards, then continues outward as sound, namely thunder. Lightning happens literally all the time; twenty million cloud-to-ground strikes happen every year, according to NOAA, and cloud-to-cloud flashes happen five or ten times more than that. The whole event takes less than a second, but if you happen to be the subject of the electrical attraction, that bit of time probably ranks as the worst half-second you'll ever spend.

It's a wonder that we all haven't been cooked a few times over, given this frequency. Again, it's our brains that keep us unzapped, for the most part— lightning safety must get taught to schoolkids fairly effectively these days, as the number of people hurt or killed by lightning is relatively small compared to the good ol' days. From 1940 through 1949, for example, lighting killed 337 people—more than tornadoes, floods, and hurricanes combined in that decade. And those were just the cases people reported; lots of lightning strikes go unreported even now, especially those that result in simple injury.

Today, lightning ranks behind flash floods in terms of fatalities. Between 1990 and 2003, 756 people died from lightning strikes, with 126 of those deaths taking place in Florida. While that state saw the most fatalities, the main Rocky Mountain states—Colorado, Utah, and Wyoming—held the top three spots for strikes by population. In Wyoming, two people per million died by lighting during the 1990s, while Utah and Colorado came in at 0.7 per million and 0.65, respectively. In terms of property damage, lightning causes many of the forest fires that regularly devastate the West; in Arizona and New Mexico, for example, experts at Northern Arizona University estimate that 60 to 70 percent of forest fires start as a result of lightning strikes. And in Florida, according to the federal government, lightning ignited 2,282 fires in the summer of 1999, causing $390 million in damage. House fires, lumber fires, brush fires—capricious lightning strikes cause thousands of these conflagrations every year, resulting in over $1 billion worth of property damage annually.

Obviously, the Rocky Mountains have a lot to do with why people get struck out West; lightning seeks the highest point to hit, and the Rockies are about the highest point we have in this country. More people climb those peaks than ever before, creating a whole new group of potential lightning victims. As long as people decide to scale the Rockies and their surrounding features at the wrong times, turbulent storms will have juicy targets to fire on.

That being said, lightning is liable to strike anywhere conditions are favorable to it. The National Lightning Safety Institute has collected stories of lighting traveling through ductwork to metal closet rods and burning up the clothing that hangs on them, injuring people holding onto various household appliances that catch voltage from a nearby strike, and even describes a man suffering slight injuries and temporary blindness when a bolt struck outside the window he was watching the storm from. It would seem that a force of nature as powerful as lightning will, ultimately, hit you if it feels like it, regardless of where you sequester yourself when the dark clouds roll in.

These incidents demonstrate that lightning doesn't necessarily have to hit you directly to ruin your day. Standing next to a tree or large, wet rock formation will cause the lightning to arc around it, and possibly into you. Hanging out in a cave isn't much better, as the electricity will travel through the rock and shock across the enclosed space as it jumps from one surface to another. People conduct better than rock does, so anyone who happens to get in the way of such an event is a prime candidate for well-donehood.

Not that all lightning strikes are fatal. In fact, there's a pretty good chance you won't even have burns on your skin, much less be reduced to a pile of smoking ashes. Lightning only kills about 10 to 30 percent of the time, depending on who you ask, though survivors are seldom left unscathed. Such a massive jolt can scramble the brain and nervous system for the rest of a person's life, resulting in chronic headaches, personality changes, seizures, and a host of other problems. Physically, victims can experience impotence, chronic pain, and even complete disability from muscle and cellular damage. Really serious strikes cause strange injuries associated with the electricity exiting the body—soles of the feet blown off, massive craters at the point of exit, and smoking burns wherever electricity spent too much time in contact with the skin. Death by lightning, however, comes almost exclusively by cardiac arrest, as the electricity courses through the blood vessels and shocks the heart into stalling out. No two lightning-related injuries seem exactly the same. It all depends on where you get hit, how bad it gets you, and where you are when the strike happens.

And contrary to popular opinion, lightning will strike the same place twice, or a dozen times; witness the Empire State Building, which receives dozens of strikes every year. Or the great Roy Cleveland Sullivan, a park ranger at Shenandoah National Park who suffered a world-record seven lightning strikes between 1942 and 1977. (The fourth strike set poor Roy's hair on fire, so he began carrying around a pitcher of water after that. Smart move—the fifth strike set his hair on fire, too.) Roy eventually came to believe some cosmic force was out to get him, and he would cower in his truck whenever a storm rolled in while he was on duty.

He might have been right, too. Take that fifth strike in 1973, for instance; according to Sullivan's account, he saw clouds forming and headed in the opposite direction. Once he thought he was far enough away, he got out of his truck—and promptly saw a bolt come arcing out of the clouds and straight for him. (Of course, the chances that he saw the lighting coming are probably a bit exaggerated, since it moves pretty much instantaneously.) That bolt, in addition to setting his head ablaze, also blasted off one shoe without untying it. The pain of the strikes themselves weren't the only negative, either; people avoided being near him when storms rolled in, lest they inherit his rotten luck. It all ended for Roy in 1983, when he apparently shot himself over a lost love at the age of seventy-one. In all, as we can see, the title "Human Lightning Rod" isn't such a great thing to have.

Roy's susceptibility to lightning probably had something to do with him, and something to do with his job—he was in harm's way a lot out there in the sticks. A wet roadway also classifies as someplace not to be if you can help it, as motorcyclist Gary Missi discovered to his misfortune on June 21, 2006. Riding a motorcycle in a lightning storm qualifies as fairly high-risk behavior, as you don't have anywhere near the same kind of protection from the elements that you do in a car; in addition, the smaller, upright profile of a person on a motorcycle, riding on a large, flat surface, makes for a pretty inviting lightning rod. Missi was heading west on U.S. Route 36 near Westminster, Colorado, when a lightning bolt struck either him or his bike and shot down into the ground, blowing a twelve-inch crater into the highway and spraying asphalt on the surrounding vehicles. Missi's bike kept traveling at highway speed for another one hundred fifty yards, until it slammed into the center wall and flipped Missi over into oncoming traffic. The strike probably killed him almost immediately; witnesses tried to find a pulse as he lay propped up on the median, but could find none.

As crazy as this story sounds, it was the second such incident in Colorado within only three years. In 2003, another biker, this one from Florida, was riding his Harley-Davidson when lightning struck him right in the helmet, causing him to lose control and pitch into a culvert. He was alive when paramedics arrived, but didn't stay around for long—the injuries he'd sustained in the strike eventually killed him. In both cases, the bikes sustained little damage—telltale evidence that the lightning most likely killed both riders, rather than the ensuing crash.

Herd animals often feel the effects of lightning strikes, too. As they graze, they are generally the highest point in massive stretches of grassland. This fact leads to some truly terrible, if not downright bizarre, incidents. Take, for example, the sixteen horses of El Paso County, Colorado, who died from a lightning strike in 2005; some of their eyeballs burst with the energy of the strike. They were standing near some barbed wire fencing when the lightning descended, a terrible idea whether you're man or beast. Or consider the twenty-four cattle that died as the tree they stood under sustained a massive bolt.

In fact, cows seem to stand under trees during thunderstorms a lot; newspapers around the world carry periodic accounts of massive die-offs due to bad positioning during a storm. Sixty-eight died in a 2005 storm in Australia, half of farmer Warwick Marks' herd. Another thirty-one died the year before in Denmark while they stood—you guessed it—under a massive tree. Apparently, cows the world over don't get much lightning safety education.

Following the bovine/equine example and putting yourself in an exposed position will exponentially raise your chances of being blown into oblivion. Say, for example, you're hanging onto a metal cable on a two-thousand-foot rock face during an electrical storm. This course is, as you might expect, an extremely bad move. Nevertheless, one of the best-known lightning accidents in U.S. history happened under just these circumstances, thanks to some very bad judgment at a place where such a thing can get you killed quickly.

If there's a more famous hunk of granite than Yosemite National Park's Half Dome, I'm not sure what it is. Visitors once believed Half Dome, rising 4,737 feet above Yosemite Valley, couldn't be climbed. The first successful ascent happened in 1875, and from then on the parade to the top has gotten more and more crowded. Accessibility isn't so much of a problem anymore, so long as you're in reasonably good shape; two cables run up to the top along the most vertical section of the trail. Climbers hold on to the cables and pull their way up the face, using wooden footrests every ten feet or so for stops. Even little kids and grandparents climb Half Dome these days, though very few of them would do so under the conditions that Adrian Esteban, Tom Rice, Bruce Weiner, Brian Jordan, and Bob Frith faced.

July of 1985 was a particularly bad weather month for central California's massive belt of national parks, running from Yosemite south through King's Canyon and Sequoia National Parks. In fact, on the very same day that the men listed above decided to climb Half Dome—July 27—twenty-seven-year-old James Wunrow was hiking alone in King's Canyon when thunderheads rolled in above him, and electricity began charging the air. Wunrow's life had already been touched by the crack and charge of electricity; back in 1984, while working for the Forest Service in Superior National Forest, he'd touched a live power line and received a terrible shock. By all accounts, he wasn't the same afterward, as he suffered from terrible headaches and occasional disorientation.

As the storm opened up the skies above him, dropping rain and hail by the ton, Wunrow ran toward a rock formation off the trail and took shelter between two boulders with a broad slab sitting on top of them. He rested in this makeshift cave when the lightning struck, entering his head and stopping his heart. The next day, passing hikers simply assumed he was a fellow traveler taking a nap, until two curious passersby noticed that his feet were sitting at an unnatural angle. They found him laying inside, a small puncture wound behind his ear (probably caused by his glasses), some singed hairs on his arms and head, and tiny, cauterized pinholes in his back the only external evidence of what had befallen him. It didn't look like he'd suffered a direct jolt, but as he sat in the cave, a nearby strike must have coursed into the space he occupied and entered his body. The wet ground and rocks would certainly have conducted, making the whole area a potential deathtrap that poor James Wunrow never anticipated as he covered his head and searched for a comfortable spot to wait out the storm.

In Yosemite, fewer than a hundred miles away, the same storm system would eventually find another group huddling in another cave, with results just as deadly.

The day's promise had mostly evaporated when Adrian Esteban and Tom Rice set out for Half Dome. By 5:00 p.m. or so, the two friends were just coming to Sub Dome, the bottom of the steep, 442-step granite staircase that brings hikers up to the steel cables leading to the top. On their way up, they passed two frantic teenagers, Ken Bokelund and Rob Foster, who were hightailing their way back down after attaining the summit only a short time before. The two boys had already seen the worst of Half Dome's weather; the previous night, they'd endured a drenching storm complete with multiple lighting strikes on the rocks around them, which repeatedly sent electric charges through the wet rocks and into their hands and feet. The scared hikers managed to stick it out that night once the storm abated, and spent all day Saturday, July 27, reaching the summit with a frenzied sense of impending doom. They summited the dome around 5:00, just as more black clouds were blowing in, then pointed themselves down the mountain and started running. They blew down so fast their hands burned on the metal cables, and as they bounded down the granite stairs they passed Esteban and Rice.

Bokelund and Foster warned the older climbers, but they would not be turned away. Nor would the other groups on the rock that day, two in addition to Esteban and Rice's, all focused on reaching the summit of Half Dome, an accomplishment worthy of braggadocio once things wrapped up back at the bar. Esteban and Rice had been conquering the great outdoors together since high school, Rice assuming the role of prophet and risk-taker and pulling Esteban along for the ride. By the time they came to Half Dome in July 1985, they'd already climbed the rock many times together, so much that it had become an iconic constant in their young, turbulent lives. Esteban in particular, already divorced in his early twenties and often dissatisfied with his job and life in general, came to see Half Dome as "the one solid entity in his drifting life," according to Bob Madgic, who chronicled their fateful climb in the excellent book *Shattered Air*.

On July 27, Esteban and Rice came to Half Dome with seven other hikers: Bob Frith, Esteban's boss, who in turn brought his friend Bruce Weiner; Bill Pippey, a longtime friend and fellow adventurer; Karl Buchner, another of Esteban's co-workers; twins Brian and Bruce Jordan, whom Pippey brought along; and Steve Ellner, a friend of Buchner's. The motley group straggled out that morning, first to the Happy Isles trailhead and then up to Nevada Fall, where they stopped for some lunch and skinny-dipping. One other group out to conquer the rock that day showed up at the falls around the same time. Disgusted by the raucous goings-on, they left for the long hike up at around 1:30 in the afternoon—right about the time dark clouds were beginning to mass overhead and the first growls of thunder were echoing through the valley.

By this time, the weather already looked forbidding, certainly bad enough to turn around and head back down for the safety of lower climes. Still, Esteban, Rice, and the other members of their party pushed on at varying rates and in different locations on the trail. Pippey and Bruce Jordan, far out in front, eventually met with a lucky obstacle: Pippey's clairvoyant gastrointestinal tract. "One minute, I'm fine. The next, I can barely keep my bowels from exploding," he said later, a condition Pippey thought might be a signal to keep him from going any farther. Esteban, Rice, and Brian Jordan kept moving up the trail behind the first pair, despite the warning they got from frightened climbers Ken Bokelund and Rob Foster. Further back, Buchner and Ellner wound their way up, Ellner expressing nothing but doubt as the black clouds roiled. Even farther behind, Weiner and Frith struggled, exchanging their forty-five pound pack of gear every fifteen minutes or so.

The arduous hike brought Rice and Esteban to the cables first, about six hundred feet from the summit. They hesitated, knowing they could reach the relative safety of a cave at the summit within about twenty minutes with a strong climb up the cables. Then again, lighting had begun arcing across the sky, thunder booming out with each stroke. They would be exposed, out in the open as the storm, fully raging, moved in. They decided to keep going, believing nothing could go wrong on "their" mountain.

The two leaders banged their way up the slope, driven by adrenaline and the pressing need to get out of the weather. Brian Jordan, Bob Frith, and Bruce Weiner followed them up and joined them in the cave at the top; Bill Pippey and Bruce Jordan would have been right behind them, but about twenty feet up the cables, they witnessed a terrifying lightning strike smash into North Dome, across the Yosemite Valley from them. Bruce confessed his fear and didn't want to climb anymore, a decision Pippey seconded as they turned around and headed back for the base to pitch camp. Buchner and Ellner also managed to stay below the danger zone and were down there when lightning struck Half Dome's summit right around the cave their group had taken refuge in.

Bob Frith and Adrian Esteban were outside when the strike happened. Esteban took a hard jolt that pinned him to the ground; Frith fared less well. He had been sitting outside the cave on a formation Esteban and Rice had dubbed the King's Chair. The lightning either entered or exited through a one-inch slice on his forehead—either way, one can only hope that the charge turned off his brain during his last few living moments. His body convulsed, vomit and spit spurted from his mouth, and he flopped much too close to the edge of the King's Chair and its 2,200-foot drop to the ground below. Esteban and Weiner, smoking and blistered themselves, attempted to pull Frith back from the brink, but to no avail—with their legs nearly useless for leverage, they had no choice but to save themselves from plunging over with him. Bob Frith's fall off Half Dome ultimately killed him, but judging from the descriptions of his condition before he fell, the lightning strike very well might have killed him without it.

Wiener, Tom Rice, and Brian Jordan were sitting inside the cave when the lightning hit, firing current across every wet surface. The inside of the cave, the refuge they'd sought during their desperate scramble up the cables, afforded no shelter under these circumstances, and they felt the brunt of the charge as if they'd been standing outside. Brian Jordan, sitting between two metal-framed packs at that moment, died almost immediately, electricity passing between the packs and into his body. The arcing charge blew huge holes in each of the bags, indicating how powerful the charge must have been. Rice suffered a horribly mangled leg as well as burns across his body. Wiener didn't take much damage from that initial strike, though a subsequent bolt threw him to the ground and left him seriously injured. Rice and Wiener, in fact, suffered a similar slate of injuries: their legs, shot through with electricity, had sustained massive tissue damage to the point that amputation might become necessary. The burns also released poisonous fluid into their systems, which overloaded their kidneys and brought on catastrophic fluid weight gains. Had they not been rescued the same night they'd been struck, they almost certainly would have died, too.

Rice and Esteban, the unequivocal leaders of the expedition, bore much of the blame for how things turned out, though ultimately each member of the group came to terms with his own role, and the fact that none of them turned back despite the massive evidence practically begging them to do so. Bruce Wiener, who endured a long, excruciating road to recovery via physical therapy and several operations, suffered ten years of mental trauma in the form of nightmares, social withdrawl, and irrational fear. He, beyond his injuries, also suffered the sight of seeing his best friend, contorted and insensate, slipping from the uppermost reaches of Half Dome to crash down on the rocks below. Of the incident, he says:

> We passed signs that gave specific warnings about not going to the summit when there are signs of a thunderstorm and not taking cover in a rock enclosure. Frith and I were adults capable of thinking for ourselves, so we had little excuse for our own actions. We were the only ones with college degrees, for God's sake!

Despite the fact that it can hit anywhere and anything, when you get down to it not even lightning, the very symbol of nature's randomness, strikes with complete capriciousness.

≋ ⚡ ≋

Long before Prometheus gave us the spark, fire was a natural phenomenon. Few people know of the controversial debate among forestry types between those who believe fire is a positive, benevolent force in nature, responsible for consuming dead things and clearing the way for new life, and those who maintain that any burn is a bad burn, and that we'd be better off just putting out fires when they pop up.

In fact, many in the wildfire-fighting game believe both in the regenerative power of fire *and* its potential to wreak havoc. "Wildland fire, always a natural and necessary part of the North American landscape, is now seen as the way forests and grasslands renew themselves and create healthy habitat for wildlife," writes John N. Maclean, author of two excellent books on wildfires and the people who combat them. And yet, he continues, "try telling that to someone whose Colorado dream house and majestic view have just been turned into a moonscape. Living in fire country today is like having a grizzly bear hibernate in your backyard: it's a thrill, but at some point the bear wakes up." The question: how to preserve fire's wild function while saving those million-dollar woodland mansions, along with thousands of more modest homes.

The grizzly analogy couldn't be more apt. Wildfires are simply awesome to behold, even from a dozen miles away. Massive towers of inky smoke climb from the ground like a hellish fog in reverse, bleeding into the white clouds of the sky; flickering matchheads on the horizon become, with closer inspection, immense conflagrations stretching for miles, cutting down everything as they march forward with uncanny, malevolent speed. These modern fires, fueled by overgrown ground cover and unnaturally dry conditions resulting from years of drought, have scorched staggering expanses of land—in July 2002, for example, the Biscuit Fire of Oregon burned a half-million acres before firefighters finally tamed it. Fires this huge inevitably reach out from their wild birthplaces—regions where the burn actually does a lot of good, removing dead brush and clearing the way for new growth—into so-called "red zones," where human settlement bumps up against woodland and necessitates a line of defense.

Wildfires, and the conditions that start them, all share a few characteristics. Natural fires tend to start when uncommon dryness intersects with abnormally high temperatures and blustering wind. The Mann Gulch Fire of Montana, for example, sparked up when temperatures in nearby Helena reached ninety-seven degrees, with temperatures in the gulch certainly a few degrees higher than that. The so-called Big Blowup of 1910 began in late August, when punishing winds smashed into the Idaho panhandle and stoked small lightning fires into blazes that literally, according to writer John Maclean, destroyed men's minds.

Towering flames and smoke could be seen for hours before they arrived. The sight drove men insane. One firefighter shot himself to death; two others on a crew in the Selway National Forest became unhinged. One of them was held down in a creek by comrades; a ranger later recounted that the other "danced around singing a lullaby." Both men survived, but the "lullaby boy" spent the rest of his days in a lunatic asylum.

The fire strode across the countryside like Death's angry brother, covering dozens of miles at a stretch, consuming three million acres in a matter of two days, and producing smoke visible in Boston. Eighty-five people eventually died in the fire, most of them burned to bones and blackened meat. The Big Blowup birthed the Forest Service's longstanding policy of fighting every wildfire that springs up, a strategy that may have set the kindling in place for the early years of the twenty-first century, when the most horrendous fires in decades burned their way across the western U.S.

The year 2002 marked a particularly bad fire season, though in a few cases the very people who were supposed to be protecting us from such disasters were helping them along. Leonard Gregg, an unemployed fireman with the Bureau of Indian Affairs, started Arizona's Rodeo Fire. (He set the fire to give himself work, mirroring a common Depression-era practice of setting forest fires to create labor for jobless masses.) The Chediski started when a motorist who'd run out of gas two days earlier lit a single fire hoping to attract attention to her plight, after which she promptly lost control of the thing. Eventually, the two fires merged and mutated into the Rodeo-Chediski, the biggest fire in Arizona's history. It destroyed nearly 500 homes, torching 467,584 acres in the process.

The worst of the recent fires, however, remains the 2003 blazes that reduced large swaths of the California coast to smoking ash. Wildfires in California are a somewhat different beast than those that take place in, say, rural Nevada or Arizona; in those places, the fires sprout and burn in largely backcountry areas, and endanger firefighters more so than civilians whose houses may be lying in the path of destruction. Though people live in those out-of-the-way places, there just aren't that many of them; in the Rodeo-Chediski, for example, for all that burning, only 467 homes were lost, or one for every thousand acres burned. In California, however, the red zone is long and broad, running almost the entire way up the coast from San Diego to San Francisco. As a result, wildfires spring up quickly and become mortally dangerous just as fast, reaching tentacles into suburbs, rural enclaves, and even the large cities themselves.

In late October 2003, the skies above Orange County and the surrounding area burned bright red as the sun tried—and largely failed—to penetrate the smoky haze layering the landscape. Smaller fires born throughout the region had fused into a single wall of flame that seemed to march toward the coast with unceasing, martial dedication. The Siege of 2003, as that fire season eventually came to be known, hit its pinnacle during those dark, ash-flecked days. Only the brave work of California's fire personnel, coupled with hard-earned lessons of previous fires, prevented 2003 from being far worse.

That year, fire season began with an air of competent preparedness. Previous seasons had raised awareness among residents and fire personnel to the point that multiple plans for combating the blazes to come were already underway: projects to create "defensible space" around homes in the fire zone, dead tree removal to deny potential fires easy fuel, and an allocation of fourteen million dollars in federal funding to fight fires and institute preventive measures across the region.

Unfortunately, nature has a way of rendering such preparations a moot point. Chronic drought conditions continued to kill trees throughout the region, creating more dead wood even as state and federal authorities worked to remove it. Hot Santa Ana winds blew upwards of seventy miles per hour, providing rapid means of locomotion for any blaze that started, more than enough momentum to jump fire defense lines. And random circumstances—a stranded hunter setting a signal fire, lightning strikes, the vagaries of nature in general—provided the sparks that would eventually burn over three-quarters of a million acres among some of the most densely populated regions of the country.

On October 21, three fires sprung up within four hours, from Fontana in the north down to the De Luz Canyon between Los Angeles and San Diego. That first day, 1,750 acres burned, and 1,166 firefighting personnel dedicated themselves to putting out the fires. Things simply spiraled out of control from there; as firefighters contained one blaze, another would spring up in its place, continuing to chew up acres of forest and grass and turning them to ash. By Saturday, October 25, the fires were racing across California from Santa Barbara to San Diego, some covering distances of ten miles in just seven hours. Speeds like these changed the firefighters' missions, according to Larry Hood, a Fire and Fuels Specialist with the U.S. Forest Service: "When a fire does that, your efforts are turned from the firefight to firefighter and public safety. You just hope you can get all the people out of the way in time." One fire, the Old Fire burning east of Los Angeles, grew from just twenty acres to ten thousand in eight hours.

October 25 also saw hunter Sergio Martinez get himself lost in a remote part of the Cleveland National Forest. Sergio, remembering the training he'd received in a 2002 West Covina hunting safety class, lit a small fire meant to attract attention to his position. Unfortunately, Martinez's ability to control the fire was about as good as his sense of direction, and he soon lost control of it. Friendly fire, an accident, incompetence—call it what you will, Martinez's mayday became known as the Cedar Fire, and eventually grew into the second-worst in California's history, burning over 280,000 acres and costing more than $27 million to fight. (Martinez was up for criminal charges over his fire, but the judge eventually threw out the case because he didn't show any malevolent intent when he started it. Rather, he simply followed the instructions given to him by a safety professional without considering the consequences of doing so in such a fire-prone environment.)

Each day the news got worse. Then-governor Gray Davis declared a state of emergency from San Diego to L.A. on October 26; that same day, the Cedar Fire killed thirteen unsuspecting people north of Lakeside who had no idea the fire was bearing down on them until it was too late for evacuation.

Gary Edwards Downs was probably among the first to die in the area. He jumped into his car with his two cats and tried to outrun the fire, but the winding area roads didn't provide much opportunity to build up speed. He was found outside his car with the cats. Residents of Lake View Hills Estates, a higher-end community, realized the fire was coming only fifteen minutes before it blocked the only entrance to the property. Just that quickly, escape had become impossible.

Some residents successfully weathered the firestorm; a retired firefighter named Larry Redden staved off disaster with his garden hose and a few buckets. Another couple, Barbara and Robert Daly, leapt into their pool and watched their home be immolated before them in relative safety. Before deciding on this course, however, Robert had tried to walk out via an access road to the San Vicente Reservoir, a plan he abandoned after walking fifty yards and feeling heat too intense to deal with. On his way back home, he passed his neighbors, James and Solange Shohara, along with their son Randy, and pleaded with them not to go that way. Unfortunately for them, they continued on; two of their bodies were found in the burned-out car, while another was fifty feet away.

Around the same time the unfortunate residents of Lake View Hills were making the decisions that would either kill or save them, the Paradise Fire killed two more people. The federal government soon declared Los Angeles, San Bernardino, San Diego, and Ventura counties disaster areas. By Monday, October 27, twelve major fires were burning, fifty thousand people had lost their power, fires had entered San Diego's city limits, and the coastal air carried stench and powdery ash throughout the whole bottom half of the state. Even the NFL fled the scene, as the San Diego Chargers played the Miami Dolphins in Phoenix rather than in the Chargers' Qualcomm Stadium. The stadium's parking lot had been pressed into service as an emergency relief station.

Nothing seemed to go right for those fighting the encroaching flames. New blazes, numbering 183, had sprung up across the state and been contained, but the flames kept grinding on, thanks to unseasonably hot and windy weather, pounding the fire crews into dust and creating an atmosphere more akin to a war zone than a natural disaster area. Firefighters on the Cedar and Paradise Fires worked two days continuously, as they didn't have any backup of any kind. Besides stoking the flames, the strong winds kept fire-suppressing planes on the ground, further hampering the efforts of people on the front lines. A few firefighters lost their lives over the course of those darkest days, adding to the casualty count; by Wednesday, October 29, the fires had claimed eighteen people, including three firefighters.

Hellish walls of fire reached two hundred feet in height. They marched over acres in less than a minute. They belched enough smoke into the sky to close nearly every airport in southern California for some period of time, including LAX. More and more buildings burned, and four more people died, raising the casualty count to twenty-two. Slowly but surely, however, the weather turned in the firefighters' favor, slowing the major fires and reducing the number of new ones. Although not by much—143 new fires started on the tenth day of the siege, as conditions were getting *better*. A nuclear winter of sorts descended on the region, as the smoke held out the sun and cast the state in an otherworldly shade of orange.

In its aftermath, Californians took inventory of the damage and death the fires left in their collective wake. All told 3,710 houses burned, along with 56 commercial buildings and 1,484 other structures. The Cedar Fire alone destroyed 2,232 homes, and killed 14 people while injuring 107 others. The fires left 750,043 acres destroyed, and 22 people dead across the state (though two bodies discovered after the fires would bring that total to 24). The cost of fighting the fires: over $123 million, not to mention the monetary damage of the fires themselves in property damage and repair costs. At the peak of firefighting efforts, 16,000 people were involved in fighting the fires, 14,000 of them on the front lines, along with 1,600 engine companies and 160 fire-suppressing aircraft.

Among the many disasters to afflict the West over the last century, the Siege of 2003 certainly ranks among the worst in terms of damage: $2.5 billion, by the time all was said and done. Only the Herculean efforts of firefighters prevented more human casualties and property damage; in fact, given the number of buildings and acres burned, given the fact that these fires didn't burn out in the middle of nowhere, but right in the middle of densely populated suburban areas, that only 24 people succumbed to the flames rates as a downright miracle. It remains the most expensive conflagration in California's history, at least in terms of money.

If there's a deadliest single wildfire in California's long and terrible history of fires, however, the distinction would have to go to the 1991 firestorm that descended on the hills outside of Oakland, a fire that very well could have spread into the city itself, creating a modern-day fire to rival the legendary Chicago blaze of 1871. It came quickly, burned for a comparatively short time, and resulted in more destruction than any other blaze until the conflagrations of 2003. It exploded from the tiniest ember within a shockingly short period of time, and the problems it highlighted brought reform to city firefighting systems across the country.

Tinder makes the difference between a little wildfire scare and conflagration. In October 1991, the hills overlooking Oakland blossomed with fuel in the form of dry native vegetation and transplanted eucalyptus trees, which burn as if soaked in gasoline. A small brush fire under these conditions becomes a lot bigger really quickly, and can, under the worst confluence of circumstances, grow into a major horror show rapidly. In this case a brush fire became the horror of the Oakland–Berkeley Hills Fire, which was one of the worst urban disasters in American history both in terms of property damage and loss of life.

The fire started small on October 19, a grass fire that was promptly extinguished. Unfortunately, that first fire didn't die completely despite firefighters' best efforts, and it re-ignited the following day. Eyewitnesses say that a sole ember floated up and into a dry tree just outside the area of the previous day's fire, and that the tree subsequently exploded into flame. The firefighters on the scene quickly found themselves overwhelmed.

The fire grew with the help of San Francisco's signature foehn winds— hard, hot breezes that occur when air travels up a mountain ridge, losing moisture as it cools, then descends the other side and heats up. The result: a gusting and dry wind that can raise the air temperature thirty degrees in just a short few hours. In addition, the lack of moisture in the air makes it a perfect tool for fanning fires. Couple such a wind with tinder-dry brush and a fledgling blaze, and the outcome is easy to predict. (Ironically, these winds are known as "Diablo" winds in the Bay Area, most likely because they tend to blow in from the Diablo Valley.) The day's record-high temperatures didn't help things, either; at a time when average temperatures generally peak around seventy degrees, the mercury that day shot up into the mid-nineties.

In the Oakland Hills, the result came with terrible speed and force. By 11:00 a.m., the brush fire began spreading southwest, and jumped Highways 24 and 13 within an hour. Local firefighters found themselves overwhelmed with alarming speed, and unable to contain the fire. It spread out in every direction, consuming the tinder-like plants in its path until it reached the middle- and upper-class neighborhoods that coated the Oakland Hills. As it began moving through those homes, the roads were clogged with people struggling to escape and fire personnel trying to get in. Perhaps worst of all, a choking black smoke covered the area and caused people to collapse in pain.

A number of factors made this fire difficult to fight. First off, it spread in many different directions, rather than along a single front. What's more, the local water supplies were largely dry, thanks to previous firefighting efforts and citizens' attempts to make their houses less amenable to fire by wetting their roofs and yards. Then, as the fire burned, the situation got worse as the power failed, and outside engine companies that came to help out were unable to hook up to Oakland's fire hydrants, which use three-inch hose couplings as opposed to the more standard two and a half-inch coupling. The hydrant problems rendered much of this outside support useless, and convinced Oakland's city officials to replace their hydrants in the firestorm's aftermath. If that incompatibility wasn't enough, the radios Oakland's fire personnel were using often didn't jive with the communications equipment the other agencies brought, eliminating the ability of the various units to talk to each other. The radios also overloaded with all the vocal traffic, a problem the various agencies would solve afterward by moving to bigger bandwidths.

The solutions didn't come in time to help on that terrible day, although fire-suppressing aircraft for hundreds of miles around made the trip and ultimately helped out. But the fire got the best of its combatants within the first few moments, and simply overwhelmed them from there. The first building was burning within fifteen minutes of the fire's beginning, and the strong winds whipped the flames into a firestorm—a tornado-like spiral of heat and destruction—within that same span of time. The fire started pushing out, completely uncontained, on four sides: west toward Highway 24; north toward the Claremont Hotel, a local landmark first established in 1908; south toward Broadway Terrace; and east in Contra Costa County's direction.

People began dying soon after the blaze escaped control. It came quickly, but residents nearby saw what was happening and clogged the roadways trying to get themselves away from the conflagration. Not that clogging this roadway was too difficult; Charing Cross Road, the main street in the picturesque area, was only twelve to fourteen feet wide, barely enough for two-way traffic. As the escaping residents sat in their cars, trapped on the roadway, a two-thousand-degree tongue of fire lashed over them; eleven people ultimately died in the traffic, unable to move through such a cattle chute. Eight more died outside vehicles but in the same stretch of roadway. Some were disabled, and couldn't evacuate quickly enough; others were senior citizens unable to outrace the fire's dreadful march. No firefighters were in that particular area to stand up to the advancing fire, adding to the charnel-house scene.

Elsewhere, however, first responders gave up their lives attempting to evacuate the East Bay Hills. Oakland police officer John Grubensky died trying to lead a group of five citizens to safety. He'd placed them in his car, intending to get them out, but the fire simply came too fast. (Grubensky also performed with distinction during the Loma Prieta earthquake, when he crawled and scrambled through the Cypress overpass wreckage looking for stranded motorists.) Battalion Chief James Riley also perished in the fire, attempting to save Kimberly Robson, whose body turned up next to his.

The fire came under control relatively quickly, though it didn't seem that way to the firefighters involved. Many of them fought the blaze for twelve hours and more without a break. They suffered exhaustion, burns, smoke inhalation—yet they continued to fight, once again proving that the number-one factor in saving lives during a fire is the dedicated group standing between it and the rest of us. But despite their valiant efforts, the damage had already been done by the time they could assume a strong stance. In fact, most of the carnage took place in the blaze's first two hours, when people unable to evacuate quickly enough succumbed to the flames. A downpour rolled in by October 26, soaking the ground and bringing scant comfort to those who lost loved ones in the fire and surely wished the rains had come a week earlier.

Ultimately, the Oakland blaze killed 25 people, more than all the conflagrations of 2003 put together. It destroyed 2,843 residences, and damaged or destroyed another 3,469 more. (Interesting side note: the venerable Claremont Hotel sustained almost no damage, despite the fact that homes all around it went up like kindling.) These numbers become even more terrible given the total area the fire burned: only 1,520 acres, or 5.25 square miles. For one second, imagine what huge blazes like the 2003 specimens would do in such densely populated areas, and then try to stifle your shudder. The dollar cost: $1.55 billion, up in smoke within three days, making the Oakland-Berkeley Firestorm the third-worst urban fire in U.S. history, after the San Francisco Earthquake of 1906 and 1871's Chicago fire.

≈ ⚏ ≈

In 1995, residents of La Conchita, California, were assaulted by a terrible, yet strangely majestic sight: part of the massive hill behind the beachfront town detached from its rocky moorings and slid down the slope, crushing everything in its path. Nine homes eventually succumbed to the rolling mud and rock, more than forty-six million cubic feet of detritus, though thankfully no one lost their life in the tragedy. Soon after, Ventura County declared La Conchita a Geological Hazard Area, meaning the state was acknowledging the community's century of landslides and mudflows, and warning the residents there to acknowledge it, too, lest they suffer a more catastrophic event in the future. In subsequent months, the county built a wall on the hillside, ostensibly to prevent additional debris from falling on the tiny town of two hundred sixty people, but did little else. The residents themselves did little too, gradually returning to their daily lives and forgetting about the tons of potentially deadly debris poised in the hills above them.

As beachfront property values will tell you, California's unstable coast's tendencies to such slippage have encouraged pretty much no one to leave it behind. The fact that most of southern California's population lives on such geologically unsound terrain doesn't bode well for the future, particularly since larger geological events—like earthquakes, which strike California literally several thousand times every year—come and go in the Golden State like nowhere else. The doomsday scenarios given such conditions are scary, and completely within the realm of possibility.

Rock and mudslides don't just happen on the coast, either; in July 1996, for example, a one hundred sixty thousand-ton slab of granite tore off the southeastern face of Glacier Point, falling from as high as twenty-two hundred feet and blasting one hundred sixty mile-per-hour winds out into the surrounding forest on impact. The cataclysm buried everything in the Yosemite Valley under two inches of dust, and witnesses described one horrific scene— trees fell flat as if a bomb had gone off, and the initial dust cloud rose some three thousand feet into the air as it marched over the landscape and blotted out the summertime sun.

Yosemite's slides aren't the same species as those that occur on the coast. Those waterlogged floods of mud and debris come from too much rain, falling too long, and washing away ground that is already quite loose. A rockslide like the one at Glacier Point took a million years to get started; as the big rocks formed and pushed upward from the molten interior of the earth, the older layers of the rock begin sloughing off. Temperature changes, water, even plant roots growing into the rock can expedite the process. The whole thing's known as exfoliation, and also results in all the little handholds that make Yosemite such a climbing destination.

Unfortunately, the rocks occasionally decide to exfoliate with more authority than it takes to make a little ledge. This particular event started generating its choking cloud when a deafening "crack" signaled the break. Then the massive "flake," two hundred feet across in some places, plummeted to the ground, literally exploding into powder and dust on impact as it struck the ground at around two hundred thirty miles per hour. The falling rock hit so hard that seismometers one hundred fifty miles away registered it as a magnitude 2.15 earthquake. Thick, gray fog radiated outward, but only after the initial shockwave flattened everything in its path.

The slide injured up to fourteen people but killed only one: Emiliano Morales, who was standing at a nearby ice cream stand when a tree felled by the rockslide crashed down on him. The stand itself was also destroyed. This incident certainly takes the cake for the biggest, scariest rockslide in Yosemite's recent history, though in the annals of natural disaster, the rain-induced mudslides that plague the coast are both more deadly and more frequent (at least in terms of real damage-causing, potentially fatal events).

You would think the residents of Malibu, Santa Barbara, and the rest of those beach communities would have learned by now. (Though, to be sure I, too, would be loath to evacuate my three-million-dollar pad overlooking the beach.) Southern California has seen fourteen serious rain and mudslide seasons since 1905, and lost more than one hundred people to their fury. Bad rainfall during the winter season starts things going most of the time—typically days of continuous downpour that anyone who's spent time on an ocean coast has experienced at one time or another. La Conchita is among the communities that bear the brunt of these wet seasons, as it did in 1995, and would again, with far more terrible consequences, in 2005.

The flow that year was far smaller—less than seven million cubic feet, all of it from coming from the deposits of the 1995 event. (Together, according to California's State Mining and Geology Board, these two landslides represent only ten percent of the potential landslide material in the hills over La Conchita, making the fact that people still live there something of a mystery.) But it started much closer to populated areas, and thus blew into town far quicker.

In addition, slides and heavy rain earlier that week had closed down nearby roads, keeping kids at home from school and adults from work. Some people had already left town, while others were considering it, even though mud had closed Highway 101 just north of town, at a cost of ten million dollars a day to California's coffers. Still, the way south still lay open, and some people were taking the hint provided by these earlier collapses up the road.

But when the big slide came on January 11, it didn't give the people left in La Conchita much chance to act. The land simply detached and began moving, burying or flinging everything in front of it, popping through entire rooms with firecracker bangs, shooting glass shards as it smashed windows. According to eyewitnesses the whole thing took about fifteen seconds, but in just that amount of time La Conchita saw a massive gash open down its middle and fill with mud, live power lines, crushed houses, cars, even a bus.

In the mudslide's immediate aftermath, only six people were known dead. Another thirteen remained missing. Efforts to save them began as six hundred rescue workers rolled into town and began digging, finding nine more people alive under the rubble. The survivors had been lucky enough to find pockets to hide in as the mud flowed down; Greg Ray, for example, dove between two parked cars before the flow reached him, flattening the cars to scrap but providing just enough space for him to survive until rescuers dug down and pulled him out.

Others like Jimmy Wallet and his family weren't so fortunate. Jimmy himself survived, but suffered as his wife Mechelle and his three youngest daughters lost their lives in the disaster, buried under three stories of rock, mud, and debris. All the more heartbreaking, the family had decided that very day to leave town and wait out the rains elsewhere; the oldest of the Wallet children, sixteen-year-old Jasmine, had already left, as she lived in Ventura part-time.

Before the rest of the family evacuated, Jimmy went out to get ice cream for his kids. Minutes later, the river of destruction, routed by other houses and cars and moving "like chocolate milk with swirls of green," according to Jimmy, crashed into the house the Wallets shared with his friend Charlie Womack and family. (Womack also died in the mudslide that day.) As it moved through the house, Wallet described the smashing sound as sequential booms, "Just explosions like there was dynamite in there." He ran back to the house and began clawing at the new swell of debris, convinced he could hear his six-year-old daughter Raven's voice under there. Other rescuers joined him, but it was simply too much to move. No one within the Wallets' former household when the slide hit survived it.

Ultimately, ten people died in the La Conchita landslide, half of which were in the Womack–Wallet house. Thirteen homes were leveled, out of the community's total one hundred sixty-six, with another nineteen seeing significant damage. The disaster scarred the town's residents in terrible ways, causing some to turn to drugs, while others simply left, never to return. The hills above still loom, poised to come down again, a constant source of paranoia in those left behind. A year after the disaster, La Conchita's residents sued Ventura county for not doing enough to protect the community during the disaster. In fact, they maintained, that wall built after the 1995 landslide actually helped to channel mud into the community. The state, for its part, maintained that the residents should have known that two weeks' worth of torrential rain would weaken the hills above, and that anyone still in the town at that point only had themselves to blame. Things haven't looked good for La Conchita so far; the town lost a similar suit after 1995, and the judge has already dismissed a number of claims in the latest suit.

Given these outcomes—the destruction, the lack of recourse—it's easy to say that people shouldn't live beneath unstable, muddy hills. You might even say that they shouldn't live in the Golden State at all, given its seismic instability. But take a look around Big Sur's cliffs and beaches, the ocean off Santa Barbara, or any number of other breathtaking coastal spots. Go for a drive on the Pacific Coast Highway at dusk, with San Francisco pulsing up over the next rise. Or take your board out into the surf just as the sun's coming up and the swells are particularly tasty. This place, for all its shifting and shuddering, might just be worth the risk.

And "risk" is not too strong a word. It's a bit of a cliché now, but one rooted in truth: California sees a *lot* of earthmoving activity, particularly earthquakes. A *whole lot*. More than you can imagine. In fact, they're probably having one right now. In fact, I will bet you one thousand dollars that somewhere on the

West Coast there's some shaking going on. Please, feel free to go check.

Now that you're back, and you owe me one thousand big ones, consider this: southern California sees about ten thousand earthquakes every year. Most of them, admittedly, you can't feel. Fifteen or twenty, however, reach up over 4.0 on the Richter scale, which means they shake the surface of the Earth and at the very least knock over the knick-knacks in the china cabinet. At worst, they do a whole lot more. And California isn't even the most earthquake-plagued state; that honor goes to Alaska, which sees at least one magnitude seven earthquake every year, and an eight every fourteen years or so. If Alaska was as densely populated as California, this would be very, very bad news, as a magnitude seven quake will make short work of any buildings that happen to be located above its origin point within the earth. (Alaska has even seen magnitude nine quakes, which can kill people thousands of miles away via tsunamis. But more on that—namely the 9.2 quake that caused flooding on the northern California coast in 1964—later.)

Magnitude seven quakes strike California with some regularity, too. In the twentieth century, according to the California Geological Survey, about sixteen quakes of that power or above hit the Golden State, while another thirty-seven passed the 6.5 mark. Quakes like these cause major damage and generally kill people unless they happen in unpopulated mountain or desert areas. Take the 7.4 quake that struck west of Eureka in 1980, for example; that shaker injured six people and caused two million dollars in damage. The Loma Prieta quake of 1989, by contrast, only weighed in at 6.9 on the scale; as it happened to strike just outside the San Francisco and Oakland areas, however, it caused far more destruction, and killed many more people, than the far stronger shake farther north nine years earlier.

The Loma Prieta quake happened at 5:04 p.m. on October 17, just before the third game of a World Series that, ironically enough, pitted the Oakland Athletics against their cross-Bay rivals, the San Francisco Giants. TV coverage of the game showed little—the screen simply went to static, with someone yelling, "We're having an earth…" just before the whole thing cut out and *Roseanne* filled screens across the country. At the stadium itself, people screamed as the right field upper deck cracked apart, huge sections separating by six inches, and cracks began running down what had been, only seconds before, immutable concrete. Pieces of the light towers rained down as they shook, though thankfully no one was killed at the stadium.

The quake rated as the worst to hit San Francisco since the infamous 1906 quake that ultimately caused huge portions of the city to burn down. Like that quake, Loma Prieta knocked out the city's electrical system, leaving it at least partially dark until October 20, when power was finally restored. Emergency help didn't come as fast as it could have in the quake's aftermath, either, thanks to a fire that broke out in San Francisco's 9-1-1 telephone equipment room. That fire was one of twenty-seven that broke out across the city, burning up large swaths of the city but blissfully less than the 1906 blazes, which struck a city of wood rather than one of metal and man-made stone.

The worst of the quake's damage happened in Oakland, specifically when the Cypress Street Freeway collapsed, its top layer smashing down onto its bottom and crushing everything in between. Opened in 1957, the freeway didn't have very much in the way of earthquake preparedness; certain sections of the elevated highway, in fact, had only one base support, a dangerously inadequate circumstance in earthquake country. What's worse, the highway's foundation sat on an ancient streambed rather than solid rock, so pitches in the earth underneath impacted the structure more than it might had the freeway been built on more solid footing.

When the quake hit, it took only about fifteen seconds for the whole thing to come down. The upper level's braces snapped like dry twigs, blowing outward as if pushed down by giant hands. As they collapsed away from the structure, it fell, about two million tons of concrete, asphalt, and steel, destroying vehicles underneath by the dozen. After the initial collapse, the rest of the elevated expanse followed suit; starting from the northern end, sections of the freeway began dropping as the previous falling sections yanked the next downward.

People began dying immediately; they also began saving each other, a testament to grace under pressure and, really, a pretty good argument for people being all right underneath it all. The Oakland fire department, victim of budget reductions in previous years, only had limited personnel to send, especially given the fires breaking out across the city. Luckily, first dozens, then hundreds of people from the surrounding neighborhood pitched in to help under extraordinarily dangerous circumstances, while the freeway continued to literally fall apart around them. And in an amazing stroke of luck, about sixty Department of Public Works employees were attending driving school at a nearby public works yard, and rushed into the fray immediately, removing massive pieces of debris with earthmoving equipment.

The heroism of the next few hours, in which hundreds were evacuated from the wreckage, almost defies belief. Take navy corpsman Bill Wicker, who was driving his ambulance toward the structure when the quake struck. He climbed to the top deck and began giving first aid to everyone he found, despite the fact that, according to a navy report of the incident, "he was drenched in gasoline from ruptured fuel tanks, and risked certain death should a fire break out." In the hospital, doctors had to physically restrain him from returning to the freeway. And Tim Petersen, who became a firefighter after the quake but on that day was rescued by some. He survived after his truck, moving on the lower section of the freeway, smashed down to about eighteen inches high under a hundred thousand tons of concrete. Somehow, Petersen survived long enough for rescuers to find him, despite suffering a broken back and other profound injuries.

Then there are the people who lived in the West Oakland neighborhood that the freeway ran through—people who, when the freeway was built, protested its presence as a blight on their community. For decades the Cypress Freeway stood for oppression in the largely African-American area, a stark reminder of Victorian houses that once stood in the neighborhood by the thousands, but were bulldozed to make way for an eyesore of a highway. Neighbors came running as word of the collapse spread, and started pulling injured people out of their ruined cars. The locals who pitched in so valiantly made up the backbone of the heroic volunteer effort; it's hard to know exactly how many people their efforts saved that day, though without a doubt many of the one hundred fifty people injured on that highway would have ended up on the fatality list without West Oakland's selfless charge to the rescue.

Things would certainly have been far worse without all those helpful people. Unfortunately, no amount of Good Samaritanship could have spared everyone caught in the massive collapse; after all, two million tons of concrete fell in only fifteen seconds' time, on top of a San Francisco highway at five in the afternoon. *With the World Series going on*, no less. In the end, forty-two people perished in the Cypress Freeway collapse, making it the most fatal incident associated with the Loma Prieta quake.

But the quake killed elsewhere, too. In Santa Cruz, the historic downtown section's quaintness in stable times made it deadly as the ground shook; buildings fifty to one hundred years old proved unequal to the quake's power, and bricks began tumbling off the buildings almost immediately. Six people ultimately died there, while the businesses destroyed moved into tents as the neighborhood began its slow recovery. The San Francisco Bay Bridge saw a partial collapse, in which one person died; had the quake gone on a few more seconds, the bridge very well might have dropped into the bay, a cataclysm too horrible to imagine. The bridge, one of America's busiest, carries about two hundred seventy thousand vehicles every day over ten lanes on two levels. We'll never know the number of cars and people on the bridge at that moment, though its collapse would have certainly made Loma Prieta California's most catastrophic seismic disaster, if not one of the worst in U.S. history.

The Loma Prieta quake ultimately killed 62 people, injured another 3,757, and left more than 12,000 people without homes for some period of time. The San Francisco Marina District was practically destroyed, thanks to major fires and buildings that simply sunk into the muddy ground as it pitched, sinking deeper with each aftershock. The Embarcadero Freeway, a double-decked twin to the Cypress across the bay, almost collapsed as well. The entire Bay

Area looked as if bombs had fallen, but the repair effort to follow ground along slowly but surely. In the end, the ultimate price tag came in at around six billion dollars to repair the entire earthquake zone.

Ironically, however, the aftermath of Loma Prieta worked out pretty well for the cities injured. In San Francisco, the Embarcadero Freeway—long an eyesore on that city's pretty waterfront—simply went away after its near collapse. The Cypress didn't come back either; traffic patterns were re-routed, and even the name of the street changed. The formerly divided neighborhoods of West Oakland came together, and urban renewal projects have moved the area forward in ways they never could have if the freeway still stood. The San Francisco Marina today shows practically no sign of the quake; both San Francisco and Oakland have new city halls as a result of quake damage. Santa Cruz, its old buildings shaken to rubble, has rebuilt its downtown to dazzling effect.

And so people all over the Bay Area, like most people in California who have suffered at the Earth's hands, have moved on. They joke about the instability of the ground they build their houses, their roads, and their businesses on. And when disaster strikes, they rebuild. Disasters like La Conchita, Loma Prieta, and any number of lesser tragedies force us to wonder, though, just how long Californians can flirt with disaster before they get something truly monumental to worry about. The Earth works in small steps most of the time—and yes, for the planet Loma Prieta is but a hiccup, if that—but occasionally it also works very, very big. Recently, with the drowning of New Orleans, we've seen just how big. Here's hoping that people living the good life off those Cali beaches get to do so for a very, very long time.

Back to that "big" part for a minute. The natural disasters we're talking about here are truly awful, particularly for those who lose their lives in them and the people they leave behind. However, let us take just a minute to discuss a *potential* disaster, only because if it happened, the western U.S. would not just change—it would, most likely, cease to be, anything much more than a wasteland for a long, long time.

The source of such a cataclysm, ironically enough, draws more visitors every year, from all over the world, than just about anything else in the entire nation. I'm talking about Yellowstone National Park—or more specifically, what's going on underneath Yellowstone. Most people don't know that Yellowstone gets its scenic geysers and mud pots from the massive caldera that the park rests on. (A caldera is what happens when a giant volcano erupts—so much magma leaves the space under the eruption that the ground on top collapses down, creating a depression.) Few regions on earth roil with as much volcanic activity under its ground, nor are there many bigger potential disasters on this little blue rock.

Yellowstone has erupted three times before, most recently about six hundred thirty thousand years ago. That last one tossed ash from Ventura to Des Moines, about six hundred cubic miles' worth of soot, rock, and magma. By contrast, Mount St. Helens generated 1.4 cubic miles during its eruption (though the subsequent rock slides, as we saw, created more terrestrial junk). Yellowstone's eruption area was so big, in fact, that it wasn't discovered until the 1970s, when an intrepid U.S. Geological Survey scientist named Bob Christiansen found the three sites of eruption and mapped them. The massive size of the Yellowstone caldera has led to the urban legend that it was discovered from the air, since the best way to see it in its completeness is from aloft. In fact, it was Christiansen's research that led to Yellowstone's being recognized as a volcano—a potentially active one at that.

Actually, not just a volcano. Yellowstone classifies as a "supervolcano," one of a few in the world. Supervolcanoes, when they erupt, must expel more than two hundred forty cubic miles of debris to earn the moniker—more than enough to give anyone within a thousand miles or so a serious problem. The last supervolcano eruption took place seventy-four thousand years ago, when the Toba Caldera in Sumatra exploded and nearly doomed the human race to extinction, thanks largely to the murderously cold volcanic winter it produced.

An eruption in Yellowstone would pretty much duplicate these effects, with the added "benefit" of taking place on American soil. It would also mean a whole lot less of that soil: Montana, Idaho, and Wyoming would be blasted clean of all life, as a few meters to a few miles of volcanic ash buried the whole area; volcanic gas would smash into the atmosphere, dropping temperatures worldwide; and the explosion would create a massive hole in the ground akin to the three already in Yellowstone, the largest of which (created during the first eruption, 2.1 million years ago) measures sixty miles across.

Luckily, we don't have too much to worry about in our lifetimes. Though Yellowstone is overdue for eruptions in terms of its historic cycle, Yellowstone's own geologists put the chances of an eruption at a miniscule one in seven hundred thirty thousand, the same chances of a one-kilometer asteroid striking our planet. Far more likely are small-scale lava flows, which would cause some pretty tough driving conditions if you happened to be in the park at the time but little trouble at all if you weren't.

I include this Yellowstone aside to reiterate that we Americans haven't seen the worst of it. We haven't even seen the hind end of the worst of it. For that, ask the surviving residents of Indonesia, who saw 111,000 of their countrymen die in the tsunamis of 2004. Or the people of Armenia, where a 1988 earthquake killed fifty-five thousand. Two hundred thousand died in 1927 when a killer quake struck Nanshan, China, just seven years after another earthquake in China killed another two hundred thousand people. By contrast, 1,417 people died during Katrina and its sordid aftermath. Twenty-two hundred lost their lives in the Johnstown flood, widely considered one of the worst natural disasters in U.S. history. The actual worst natural disaster, in terms of lives lost, was the infamous Galveston hurricane, which took eight thousand lives in one day on September 8, 1900.

Mother Nature has visited the West—and the whole United States, for that matter—in all her worst moods, in all kinds of ways. We have not, however, seen the kind of punishing natural events that much of the rest of the world has experienced. As in so many other things, we have led a charmed life. One hopes that we will continue to do so for decades to come.

CHAPTER THREE

The Terrible Aristocracy
Animal Attacks

*I heard a noise, like 'whoosh,' like a submarine, like a boat going
by fast. ... I knew it was a shark. It almost brushed me. I saw its
dorsal fin. I don't know what kind it was; all I know is, it was big.
Big. It was big enough to kill.*

— CLIFF ZIMMERMAN, witness to a fatal
*shark attack just north of Fort Bragg, California;
quoted in the* San Francisco Chronicle

When it comes to the terrible aristocracy of nature, Man sits
pretty low on the totem pole. Despite our apparent control
of the natural world, despite our efforts to shut it out, domesticate it, and
otherwise bend it to our will, the earth continues to do what it has always
done—shake from time to time; explode in furies of magma and rock; whip
the oceans into a fury of storm and wave.

When we get down to brass tacks, the simple fact is that we are utterly
at this planet's mercy. Now this is generally all right, given the fact that you
are reading this without drowning in biblical rain, and I was able to write it
without being sucked into a lava-filled crevasse. But when nature goes bad—as
the previous chapter demonstrated—it tends to go very bad indeed.

Though large-scale disasters such as the Loma Prieta earthquake and the
Big Thompson flood remain the most terrifying examples of nature's fury,
smaller disasters are no less deadly. Whether from the jaws of a large predator

or the needled, poison-filled teeth of a slithering one, the West's natural world does not necessarily *need* grand gestures to kill the unwary and unlucky.

We view animals in a certain way when we are hunting them, or when we see them in a zoo—as prey, or sport, or entertainment. But in the wild and without the trappings of civilization, their presence—more specifically, what animals we find ourselves facing during our time there—defines the natural world in store for us. Come within a few dozen yards of graceful, bounding antelope removed from the hustle and bustle of humanity, and you have a pastoral paradise. Call in Thoreau and start the moon-eyed odes to beauty. Get into a staring contest with a mountain lion that you are catching on the tail end of a long hunting drought? You are liable to be lunch. Look for a big rock to throw, very quickly. Either way, you have absolutely nothing to do with the outcome.

Which explains why animal attacks are so nerve-wracking to think about: you have little say in whether an attack happens or not. Lots of tragedies mentioned in *Death in the West* involve people short on smarts and common sense; on the other hand, a lot more people with deficiencies in both areas survive similar situations with nary a scratch. But in terms of bad luck, nothing quite measures up to a random animal attack. They are so rare, and so unavoidable once they begin, that to experience one must certainly feel like a curse.

Of course things happen to cause animal attacks; the problem is, the vast majority of them occur in the attacking animal's brain. That animal holds all the cards when you are on its turf, and if it wants to go at you, you stand little chance of influencing its mind, which is utterly alien to you despite any ideas you might have otherwise. Sure, you can follow the conventional wisdom and wave your arms, shout and throw things—after all, the animal is generally more afraid of you than you are of it—but ultimately there is a brain at the other end of the equation, animal though it might be, and ultimately that brain decides whether to attack or not. You simply have to wait and see, which is no easy thing when you are passing the time within striking distance of a fifteen-foot great white or a grizzly bear with four paws' worth of knife-like claws backed up by six hundred pounds of muscle.

Much of the time, people who are attacked do not see it coming. Great white attacks, for example, often happen so fast that the victims do not even realize they have been bitten until they look down and discover parts of them missing. And however rare animal attacks might be, all indications are that they are on an uptick; the 1990s hold the record for the most shark, bear, alligator, and cougar attacks on North American soil, and so far the twenty-first century hasn't been a whole lot tamer. The primary reason for the increase: habitat encroachment—people moving deeper and farther into animal territory, and animals understandably surprised at finding so many human beings running (or swimming) around. Another factor that most would consider a positive—everyone except for the people killed or maimed in animal encounters—is the recovery of many species to pre-endangerment numbers. The grizzly bears of Yellowstone National Park, for example, made their way off the U.S. threatened species list after numbers in the park escalated to six hundred, from a low of around two hundred bears thirty years ago (though the bear is still listed as threatened in other areas). With so many more bears around, increased interaction between them and visitors to the park is nearly inevitable. Purportedly, mountain lion populations have also increased, in some areas to the point that populations support active hunting. And still, even with efforts to thin them out, the lions sometimes come in a little too close, resulting in a tragic choice of menu items.

The apex predators off the California coast—namely great white sharks—are not numerous so much as concentrated. (Though, like so many things about the great white, no one really knows how concentrated they are.) And when that area of concentration offers the kind of recreational choices that the Red Triangle near San Francisco does, you can imagine that people are going to be in the water, whether or not there are Suburban-size sharks with massive, serrated teeth swimming around underneath them or not.

Great white sharks live all over the world, but the so-called Red Triangle, a patch of ocean from Año Nuevo Island to the tiny, barren Farallon Islands off Sonoma County, contains a whole convention's worth of these massive predators. In early summer and late autumn, the sharks congregate to hunt elephant seals and sea lions in the waters between San Francisco and Monterey. So much has been written about great whites that it's hardly worth the rundown here; suffice to say that these sharks, like all others, have their share of truly fascinating behaviors. Unfortunately, massive helpings of myth, conjecture, and flat-out lies have resulted in little sympathy for sharks when conservation groups try to draw attention to the extermination they face in the wild. Estimates are that more than one hundred million sharks are killed every year, the majority of them for their fins, with many of those simply caught, de-finned, and dumped back into the water to bleed to death.

Still, the fact remains that great whites attack people and have done so in California more than anywhere else in the world. From 1916 through 2005, sixty-eight great white attacks were recorded off the California coast, with seven of those attacks resulting in fatality. In other regions of the world, great whites kill more efficiently; in Australia, for example, if you fall within the historical trend, you have a 66 percent chance of dying if an Aussie great white decides to take a run at you. Compare this to California's relatively tame 10 percent mortality rate, and you have to feel pretty good about your chances should a fifteen-foot-long, two-ton projectile of cartilage and steak-knife-serrated teeth from the Golden State decides to take a nibble.

How they attack is no less forbidding than their appearance. Great whites prefer the element of surprise and most of the time attack by swimming up from below their prey, attaining incredible speed before striking with bone-smashing force. Recent evidence indicates that great whites aren't stupid, either—they do not mistake people (namely surfers) for surface-floating seals, and when they do attack people swimming alone, or on a surf board, much of the time they are simply investigating with the most sensitive tool they have, namely their mouths. This, the popular wisdom goes, explains why so many attacks are not fatal.

This is not to say, of course, that great whites never mistake people for prey; occasionally they do strike humans with the full brunt of a bite, and when they do things seldom work out in the victim's favor. Most of the time, such attacks take place under circumstances that confuse the shark, the most important of which is the presence of sea lions or seals that tend to draw the big sharks and create confusion between the fat-rich pinnipeds and relatively bony, hard to digest human beings.

Let's all thank our lucky stars that, despite the ten or twenty pounds we're trying to lose, to great white sharks, you and I taste like racks of ribs from a malnourished pig—all bones and sinew. Sharks don't attack and eat people very often because their sensitive digestive tract cannot handle our skeletons, particularly given the low nutritional content of what is attached to them. Prey that is low in actual meat runs through the shark's digestive tract slowly, preventing the animal from eating as often as it needs to. This fact explains why most sharks do not come back after the curiosity bite when human beings are concerned; the predator takes a nibble, then moves on to greener pastures. But with a sufficiently savage initial attack, the human victim is in for real trouble.

The fact that most California shark attacks do not end in death is of little consolation to Deborah Franzman, her friends, and her family. The August 2003 death of the fifty-year-old college professor looked more like a mistake than a full-tilt attack, though even an honest mistake by an animal as big as the great white that bit Franzman can still spell tragedy. Franzman taught sociology at Allan Hancock College in Santa Maria, California, and lived in Nipomo, just off the San Luis Obispo coast. She was a lifelong devotee of the ocean, as well as a highly conditioned swimmer and sometime triathlete. She swam in the area where she died—about seventy-five yards off the Avila Beach Pier—several times each week, and she often talked about how much she loved swimming with the sea lions there. She swam with a partner most of the time, which may have lessened her chances of being attacked during previous swims, but the potential danger she faced seemed small, compared to the bliss of being out among the waves and life of the sea.

On August 19, she was swimming in close proximity to a shark buffet—namely a sea lion group—which from the shark's view below her, probably made her look like just another morsel. Just before the attack, the sea lions scattered in flurries of white foam; as they did, the shark breached from the water, grabbed Deborah, and briefly pulled her under. The shark attacked with incredible force and took either one or two bites. In any case, the predator bit a massive chunk out of the woman's side and tore pieces from both of her legs.

Despite her horrible injuries, there is some indication that the attack was a curiosity bite, rather than a full-fledged predatory mistake; for one thing, the location of the attack is not consistent with the method great whites generally use when taking sea lions. (Sharks generally attack the head when they go after seals in order to inflict the most initial damage.) In fact, Franzman might have survived had the shark not severed her left femoral artery, causing her to bleed to death as rescuers were pulling her ashore. Her chances of survival with a less serious bite increase even more considering that just north of where she swam, more than two dozen lifeguards were conducting a training, showing off their skills and generally preparing for just the sort of emergency Franzman faced.

In fact, the lifeguards did their level best—five of them leapt off the pier and into the water as soon as witnesses began screaming that a shark had bitten Franzman. That the guards showed such bravery while the shark undoubtedly camped out nearby would, in a happier story, be the stuff of a heroic close call. In Franzman's case, however, her injuries were far too serious; a severed femoral artery, the major corridor that carries blood to the thighs and legs, will result in death within a few brief minutes, even with emergency medical attention nearby. The guards managed to pull her out of the water and loaded her into the back of a pickup truck, where they struggled to administer CPR and stop the massive bleeding. But the location of the bite dictated Deborah's fate, and she died within minutes.

The attack attracted media attention from quarters both local and national, some more hysterical than others. California had not seen a fatal shark attack in its waters since 1994, when commercial diver James Robinson, while treading water off San Miguel Island, had his right leg nearly bitten off and succumbed almost immediately from blood loss—a scenario strangely similar to Franzman's own. Zealous—or perhaps over-zealous—shark experts and law enforcement authorities used Franzman's death to draw attention to California's great whites and the occasional dangers they pose, each presenting their own theory as to why the shark attacked as well as their own plans to prevent future encounters. Just a week later, on August 23, authorities closed Avila Beach as well as nearby Fisherman's Beach and Olde Port Beach following a somewhat disturbing report from two local fishermen, Joe Dearinger and Deke Wells. The men were bait fishing near Avila Beach pier at around ten o'clock in the morning when a massive great white tore into an unseen pinniped about five hundred yards off the beach. Then, just as Dearinger was about to drop his net, the men saw two harbor seals leap out of the water, followed by another massive shark with a dorsal fin they estimated to be about two-and-a-half feet high. The splash the doomed seal and the shark created soaked the fisherman, who just missed catching the careening shark in their nets. Afterward, Avila Beach, as well as the nearby Fishermen's Beach and Olde Port Beach, were closed until further notice.

More beach closings followed, along with apocalyptic declarations by the press, though none was as well covered and ultimately tragic as the closing of San Onofre Beach. On August 22, the *Los Angeles Times* reported that marine helicopters had discovered great whites swimming in the waters off this popular surfing destination thirty miles south of L.A. The local surfers indicated that yes, the sharks had been making their presence known over the past couple of months, even coming within a few feet of their floating boards (though the lack of seal population in the area may have saved the surfers from mistaken identity bites). In fact, according to the surfers, there were three sharks at San Onofre, and they visited regularly enough to warrant names: Sparky, Fluffy, and Archie. No one could figure out what the sharks were doing in the area, at least not until authorities admitted that they had buried a whale carcass on the beach two years earlier. In any case, the media outlets had a lurid field day, with headlines such as "Sharks Strike California's Coast for Unexplained Reasons" gracing the pages of *USA Today*, along with the following copy:

> After seals and sea lions turned California's Avila Beach into a 'shark smorgasbord,' Paul Schiro shuttered his kayak concession.
> 'We have no control over it,' Schiro said. 'A shark's going to do what it's going to do.'

Which is attack and kill.

Obviously, the effect of such press wasn't a calming of nerves. Beach closings continued through Labor Day, and the paranoia ultimately culminated, the way paranoia often does, in misdirected violence—in this case, toward a five-foot-long juvenile female shark that washed ashore north of San Onofre, its dorsal fin and upper jaw removed. There was also a 1.5-inch hole in the top of its head, first-class evidence of a gunshot wound. Whatever shark or sharks had been seen in San Onofre were certainly not that small, nor were any attacks ever recorded in the area, despite the increased shark activity. Eventually, the hysteria died down, and the surfers got back to surfing the way they always had, the same way that Deborah Franzman did her swimming: fully aware of the savage possibilities, yet still drawn to the beauty and peace of the ocean despite them.

The ensuing chaos did not reflect Deborah's own attitudes toward the ocean, either. She seemed to understand that the danger she faced on every swim didn't amount to more than a fact of nature, one she was willing to face. "Sometimes it takes a big wave to push us to go beyond the wave," she wrote. "Once we get there, it is calm and peaceful and full of energy. Only those that get there understand that life is what you make it. The wave that takes us out to this place is strong, filled with sand with no intention at all. ... It is our own doing that puts us in the way of the wave."

Of course, one could argue that the desire of a shark to fill its belly is a certain type of intention, though not one that comforts us. Even if most—maybe all—great white attacks are terrible mistakes, we must remember that our being in the water, and only that factor, gives them the chance to make such a mistake. Like Deborah and those San Onofre surfers, we all should understand that, as terrible as an animal attack might be, we are still, ultimately, responsible for being in the wrong place at the wrong time, particularly when we are talking about a world as paradoxically inaccessible and enticing as the Pacific Ocean.

Love of the ocean also ran deep in Randall Fry. In August 2004, Fry traveled to Mendocino County to attend a fish fry and fundraiser on Saturday the 14th. He also planned to get in some abalone diving and spend time with his friend Cliff Zimmerman, who lived in the redwoods just off Highway 1. His presence on the coast was no surprise, given his reverence for the Pacific; he practically worshipped the ocean, seeing it both as a recreational haven and a kind of personal responsibility. He worked full-time for recreational fishing privileges across California as the western regional director of the Recreational Fishing Alliance, an organization that fights to preserve fishermen's rights to the same waters the commercial fishing industry has access to.

Fry carried on a love affair with the ocean that began in the longhaired days of the 1970s. Cliff Zimmerman had introduced Fry to diving back then, and the intervening years saw Fry become an experienced diver, traveling to the coast from his home in Auburn, California, on a regular basis. On August 15, Fry and Zimmerman decided to go diving for abalone about one hundred fifty feet off Fort Bragg, in water between fifteen and twenty feet deep. They dove off of Zimmerman's twenty-eight-foot boat *Dolphin*, and though there were sea lions basking on the rocks nearby, the divers had a spotter on the boat who would ostensibly keep an eye out for sharks or any strange behavior from the sea lions that might indicate a shark presence. As experienced divers, they weren't worried—at least not nearly as worried as they should have been.

Abalone divers do not use scuba gear, as it is illegal to dive for these shellfish with any breathing apparatus. Instead, Fry and Zimmerman were free-diving, frequently hitting the surface for breath before turning around and swimming back to the bottom. They had been in the water about half an hour when Fry made his final descent, sometime around four o'clock in the afternoon.

This frequent movement between the bottom and the surface, or the sea lions, or just cosmically bad luck could have brought the shark around; there is really no way to know, as most of the great white's habits are still poorly understood. (Another example: great whites attack people mostly on the surface, according to conventional wisdom, because that is where they usually attack their prey; however, studies by the Pelagic Shark Research Foundation indicate that though observers might *see* attacks on the surface, these are often secondary attacks—follow ups to initial bites that took place deeper in the water, where seals generally spend a lot more of their time. If this hypothesis holds true, then the reason great whites usually attack people on the surface remains something of a mystery unless you chalk it up to curiosity.) In any case, Zimmerman had surfaced and was poised to dive again, kicking his feet at the surface and heading down when he heard and felt a submarine speed by. Within seconds, Fry was gone, replaced by massive plumes of blood.

No one saw Fry again that day, but the Coast Guard found something in the water on Monday: a headless body wearing Fry's personalized wetsuit. Then, three weeks later, a beachcomber walking along Ten Mile Beach just north of Fort Bragg found Fry's head. The type of attack—the fact that the shark had gone after Fry's head and neck—may indicate that the fish thought it was attacking a sea lion. Fry's death had certainly been instantaneous; the location of the bite, as well as the swiftness of the attack, guaranteed that the man felt little or no pain. No one saw the shark coming—not the divers, not the spotter above the water—which is not surprising, given the fact that great whites attack from below to guarantee just this sort of total surprise.

Fry left behind a legion of admirers. One hundred thirty people had come to his fundraiser the night before, in a town of only six thousand people. In his role as fishing advocate, Fry swam in his element that night, pressing the flesh and otherwise charming the crowd who had come to hear a smart guy talk passionately about fishing. They got what they came for; Fry was, by all accounts, a pro completely dedicated to his cause. Which makes his death more than a bit ironic. Oddly, Fry himself joked, "When I go, I bet it'll be a shark." In the wake of the accident, Cliff Zimmerman said, "The odds caught up with him," understating things a bit—considering that the odds of being killed by a shark are roughly larger than winning the lottery.

≋ 光 ≋

The Pacific isn't the only place that people can get those tickets punched by the animal denizens of the West, however. In fact, recent decades have seen more fatal attacks from land predators than from those under the sea; even the great whites of the Red Triangle have claimed only two victims within the last twelve years. On land, the odds might seem a little better—you can, after all, run in zigzags, climb a tree, and otherwise use all those little strategies offered in magazine articles about bear attacks, croc attacks, dingo attacks, etc. But head into the backcountry of Yellowstone National Park, or even into your backyard in parts of Colorado or California, and you could find yourself facing potential death. Even with those long odds, this prospect isn't a lot of fun to contemplate.

Grizzly bears have suffered from a terrible reputation, one often used to justify the abuse they have suffered at human hands. Their scientific name— *Ursus arctos horribilis*—means "horrible bear," a hard moniker to live down when you average around five hundred pounds, hit running speeds of thirty-five miles per hour, and brandish a set of four-inch claws along with massive jaws filled with sharp, short knives. Add a standing height of seven feet and an occasionally nasty attitude, and it is little wonder people and grizzlies generally live together rather uncomfortably.

At one time, grizzlies roamed most of North America, from central Mexico to California and north through Alaska and Canada. Today, however, the bears fill out only about two percent of their original range south of Canada, thanks mostly to a near-extermination in the lower forty-eight states at the hands of human beings.

That extermination was a very near thing, as the population plummeted from an estimated fifty thousand in 1800 to fewer than a thousand by 1975, when the bear made it onto the threatened species list. (Only in the lower forty-eight, however—the Alaskan bear population stands at a healthy thirty thousand, while another twenty-two thousand roam northern Canada.) The bear's slow reproductive cycle compounded the problem; females give birth to two cubs every three years, only half of which survive to breeding age. Among North American mammals, only the musk ox breeds slower, making a population rebound tough to manage without a near-freeze on hunting, poaching, and habitat encroachment. Yet the plan has been a success across much of the board, with populations hitting the target in Yellowstone and the northern part of the continental divide.

This recovery, though, has brought an old problem back into view: with so many more grizzlies running around, human encounters with the big bears are far more likely, and with more encounters come more chances for accidents.

Without a doubt, grizzlies can sport pretty bad tempers, a feature that has made them the stuff of outdoor survival legend for two centuries. Many of us also recall the tragic story of Timothy Treadwell, the controversial bear advocate killed and eaten by an Alaskan grizzly in 2003. Treadwell's case is far from unique, even today; bookstore shelves brim with books full of bear attack stories, mostly from Alaska's bear country and Yellowstone, where man's close proximity to the bears makes contact all that much more likely.

A growing bear population combined with more people using the Yellowstone backcountry has increased the number of bear attacks there in recent years, though they are still freak occurrences. From 1980 through 2002, for example, more than sixty-two million people visited Yellowstone; during that period, only thirty-two people suffered attacks serious enough to injure them, with only two of those resulting in fatality. What's more, during that period, only two attacks took place within developed areas, with the rest happening in the backcountry where the bears are often surprised to see people trekking around, particularly when those people do not follow the very simple rules of the backcountry road.

Yellowstone authorities have taken huge pains to reduce the number of bear attacks in the last three or four decades by promoting safety rules. In the 1960s, grizzly bear attacks averaged four per year, mostly because people were much more free to feed the bears and thus attract them into developed areas. Of course, the bears were not domesticated or trained in any way, so the lure of "people food" simply helped to put massive apex predators into close proximity with people ignorant enough to stick their hands into those predators' mouths. (Black bears, far smaller and less aggressive than grizzlies, still dealt out around forty-six injuries per year before the park got wise and instituted its bear management plan.) Once park managers started cracking down on bear feeding and began educating the camping public about ways to store food away from bears' prying claws, attacks nearly ceased. These education efforts continue today, and they help prevent bear-human interaction that might otherwise spell tragedy for everybody involved.

The rules of bear etiquette—storing food off the ground, never camping alone, wearing bear-deterring bells while hiking, not hiking after dark, talking or singing while you hike—keep surprise encounters to a minimum. Unfortunately, breaking any of these rules at the wrong time, and in the wrong part of the park, could get you killed. In 1984, a Swiss woman named Brigitta Fredenhagen signed the trail register stating that she would be hiking near Pelican Valley, an area extensively used by grizzlies. She then disappeared into the backcountry, where she was found two days later. Though she had hung her food between two trees, she had not hung it high enough, and a bear had managed to get to it. Even worse, the bear had grabbed Fredenhagen, dragged her from her tent, and proceeded to eat her. Outside the tent, rangers found her sleeping bag, as well as "a piece of lip and scalp with hair still attached," according to one report. The rest of her body, found about eighty yards off, had most of its soft tissue missing, presumably transferred to the bear's stomach. No one ever identified the bear in question; fortunately, it must not have developed a gastronomic appreciation for human flesh because no attacks followed closely on the heels of Fredenhagen's unfortunate episode.

In October 1986, photographer William Tesinsky broke another cardinal rule of bear etiquette: he got way too close. Professional wildlife photographers encounter dangerous animals frequently in their quest for fantastic pictures. But Tesinsky wasn't a pro—he was an auto mechanic who loved nature and loved photographing it, and thus may not have had the tools to understand how to approach a cantankerous grizzly. Which is exactly what he did, according to the evidence left; he spotted a subject from the road near Yellowstone's Canyon Village and hiked into the brush toward Bear #59, a young female that had been tagged by the park's staff. The bear dined on roots as Tesinsky approached, and as he pushed closer, she got spooked enough to take a run at him. Though there were no witnesses, the ghoulish evidence indicates a horrific scene: a camera smeared with hair and blood, its last frame a blur of motion; a bent tripod; and Tesinsky's abandoned car, the first thing that gave park rangers an idea that something was wrong.

Rangers eventually found Tesinsky and the bear fifteen feet from his camera and tripod and about half a mile from the scene of the original attack. Bear #59, like the unnamed and uncaptured bear that killed Brigitta Fredenhagen, decided to eat her victim after the attack, and since she was still at it when the rangers showed up, they put her down. Unfortunately, Tesinsky's film was too vague to make out anything about what actually happened, though the autopsies of both the bear and the man seemed to give a pretty clear idea. In any case, Tesinksy, like Fredenhagen, had broken the rules regarding contact with a grizzly bear, and he paid a steep price accordingly.

These terrible stories nonwithstanding, it is fairly hard to get attacked by a grizzly bear. First off, you have to be in the Yellowstone or Alaska backcountry—places most of us do not get to every day. And following the simple rules of grizzly country will keep you out of most potential trouble. Grizzly bears attack the majority of the time because they perceive a threat, or because their victims surprise them, coming through the bush at exactly the wrong time. Contrary to what you might think given these unfortunate events, grizzlies don't generally attack to eat; instead, they attack, find out that what they have just killed is edible, and proceed to eat it.

Mountain lions are not nearly as big as grizzlies; males weigh in between one hundred ten and one hundred eighty pounds, with females around eighty to one hundred thirty pounds. However, unlike grizzlies, these big cats (more accurately called cougars) live in fairly close proximity to human beings across the West, which makes for a lot more contact and, as an unfortunate result, more attacks. The big cats, like Yellowstone's grizzlies, have seen their numbers grow in recent years, thanks to successful conservation efforts and hunting bans in California. (Most western states allow limited hunting of cougars.) And consider this sobering fact: while bears often attack out of perceived self-defense, and great white sharks might just be curiously gnawing at you, cougars most often attack for food. That is, by the time they attack, there is a very good chance they have been stalking their "prey" (i.e., you) for a while, and have decided that your carcass would taste just fine. From the feline predator's standpoint, human beings make excellent prey—we have few natural lines of defense, and our senses are dull enough to allow the cougar plenty of time to stalk before we know what is going on. And, as humans encroach ever deeper into traditional cougar habitats, the cats lose their long-ingrained fear of people, until we become just another prey animal, albeit one far less able to flee or defend itself than most others.

The laws of the jungle being what they are, cougars tend to attack in a disturbing, though fully understandable, pattern. The majority of attacks, both fatal and not, involve the weakest members of our collective pack: children. Of the fifty non-fatal cougar attacks between 1892 and 1997, thirty-five involved children younger than nine, a very good reason to keep your eyes on the tykes next time you hit the backcountry west of the Mississippi. And in California, the statistics are even more sobering: between 1986 and 1993, all five attacks recorded in the state involved kids ten years old or younger, though thankfully none of these attacks resulted in death.

The same cannot be said of the attack Mark David Miedema suffered. The ten-year-old boy was on a three-day camping trip with his family, working the East Inlet Trail to Cascade Falls in Rocky Mountain National Park in July 1997. Mark got ahead of them by maybe three minutes—enough for the cougar to pounce, though no one actually saw the attack. He may have surprised the cat, or been the subject of a prolonged stalking. Whatever the case, his parents and six-year-old sister came around the corner and saw his feet protruding out onto the trail, while the rest of his body was obscured in the brush alongside it.

They thought he might be joking around until they got closer, just in time to see the cat pick up the boy and begin dragging him off. His parents scared the animal off and quickly grasped the horrific situation; there was, however, little to be done by then. Mark's mother Kathy, a registered nurse, tried to revive the unconscious boy with no success. Other hikers on the popular trail attempted to help as well, but to no avail. Mark, who loved to fish and hike in the heavenly Colorado backcountry, died there, victim of an animal that, it was clear, had little of the fear most animals have for human beings.

Without this fear, wild animals take on a decidedly sinister air. A ranger assigned to guard Mark's body shot an eighty-eight-pound female cougar during his watch. According to the ranger, Chris Philippi, the cougar exhibited no trepidation in facing him down—further evidence that the inevitable mixing of cougars and human beings might make the animals a bit too comfortable with us. According to the ranger, the cougar was simply returning to the scene in search of its prey, a natural behavior though one uncomfortable to think about. She stalked toward Philippi, who pulled his 9mm semiautomatic pistol only a few seconds before she leapt for him. His first shot struck the cougar in the right front shoulder. The cougar bounded off into the woods, managing to make it about one hundred fifty yards and up a tree. A few minutes later, three more rangers arrived at the scene and shot the cougar out of the tree, ending what could well have become a developing and ongoing taste for people.

The idea of man-eating wild cats is not terribly far-fetched. Big cats do not start out hunting human beings, but those that do often develop a taste for human flesh. Man-eating tigers in India, African lions like the infamous maneaters of Tsavo, and numerous accounts of jaguar and panther attacks in South and Central America often involve animals that attack and kill humans *more* over the course of time rather than less. The cougar that killed Mark David Miedema seemed capable of doing the same thing again, given her lack of fear when faced with Chris Philippi; I mention this not to sound alarmist, but to illustrate a trend where cougars are concerned. Once they attack a human being, once they get a taste for that particularly defenseless prey, they are less reticent about doing so again when given the opportunity.

The one that killed thirty-five-year-old Mark Jeffrey Reynolds in January 2004 exhibited similar behavior, attacking at least two different people in one day. Reynolds was the first and worst; the avid cyclist was fixing his bike's chain during a ride in Whiting Ranch Wilderness Park when the cougar ambushed him. He was riding alone—never a good idea in cougar country—so there were no witnesses to the attack, but the circumstances must have been unique. Cougars almost never attack full-grown human adults, mostly because human males tend to outweigh them by about one hundred pounds. Why this particular cat chose to attack this particularly big subject, no one will ever know. Perhaps Reynolds' crouched position, bent down and fiddling with his chain, gave him a smaller profile. Perhaps the cougar was just that hungry; the wildfires of late 2003 drove many cougars out of their regular hunting grounds, causing near-starvation across the local population. In any case, here's what we do know: The cougar killed Reynolds and began eating him after dragging him a short distance away from his broken bike, though this was unknown until another attack, involving this same cougar, left Anne Hjelle near death.

Hjelle was riding on a nearby trail when the same two-year-old cougar leapt from the trailside brush onto her back, knocking her down before attempting to drag her off by her head, its jaws clamped down around her face. Luckily, Hjelle was not riding alone, and her friends managed to grab hold of her in a gruesome tug of war that they, to their everlasting credit, won—though not before the cat managed to drag Hjelle one hundred yards into the bush as the other cyclists hung on. It might have been worse, but other bikers on the trail pitched in with some well-placed rocks thrown to the cougar's skull, causing it to give up the fight and take off into the brush.

Luckily Hjelle, a former Marine, was well suited to deal with the trauma. For one thing, she worked as a fitness instructor at a nearby gym and was in peak physical condition at the time of the attack. For another, she had been rescued before the cat could clamp onto her neck, cutting air supply and puncturing her jugular. She hovered along in a bad way for a while, but recovered in subsequent weeks. The cougar tore flesh from her face and neck, ripped her left ear off completely, and cut her left cheek until it flopped over her nose, which was also broken. The bites came within a few millimeters of her spinal cord and carotid artery, all the more frightening considering that they came by way of her face. She is truly lucky to be alive, though multiple rounds of plastic surgery certainly have not made post-bite life any easier.

Reynolds, unfortunately, had no such chance for recovery. Park rangers found his half-buried, half-eaten body farther up the trail where Hjelle suffered her attack. Later in the evening, Sheriff's deputies killed a male cougar weighing between one hundred ten to one hundred twenty-two pounds. It was prowling around about fifty feet from Reynold's body, and a subsequent examination revealed bits of human lung and liver in its stomach, as well as Anne Hjelle's blood on its claws. As time passed, the incident raised more questions: frequent visitors to the park said deer were plentiful, calling into question the reason the cougar attacked in the first place. If, the thinking went, there were so many deer around, why did he go after Reynolds and Hjelle? And why go after a big guy like Reynolds at all, or two victims within hours when the first would certainly have filled the cougar's belly? The unanswerable nature of these questions simply feeds into the mystery I touched on earlier—the unknown of what goes on in the brain of an animal. The cougar simply attacked, killed, and that's the way it went.

≋ 🜏 ≋

Not every creature that prowls the West does so in a bloody, violent fashion. Some of the deadliest killers we have out here crawl, squirm, and wriggle around our ankles, deceiving their victims with innocuous size and near-invisibility. And though they may not attack with the force and theatricality of a great white shark, they still get the business of killing done with nasty efficiency.

Venomous species of every kind populate the American West, mostly in its southwestern reaches. The deserts in particular play host to these dangerous creatures, from snakes to scorpions and spiders. The only poisonous lizard in the U.S., the Gila monster, makes its home in American deserts from southwestern Utah to southern New Mexico and over to California. These lizards don't inject venom very efficiently; in fact, they only get poison into their victims by chewing on them and making the wound big enough to accept it. (Their poison isn't particularly strong, either, so human fatalities from Gila bites are exceedingly rare.) When they do bite, however, they tend to clamp down like pit bulls, so much so that a screwdriver often serves as the only way to get the creature to let go.

Snakes, on the other hand, are built to be living hypodermic needles. They bite quickly, and their fangs mainline venom into their victims with utmost efficiency. Many rattlesnakes—the most common venomous reptiles in the West—also have the ability to control the amount of venom they inject into their victims. Younger snakes have less ability to control their venom than older ones; for that reason, many fatal and near-fatal accidents involving rattlers involve adolescent snakes.

If the West has a reptilian representative, the rattler probably holds the position. No other reptile comes more loaded with lore and legend than this noisy killer of the desert, scourge of a thousand cowboy movies and flip-flop wearing hikers. All manner of rattlesnakes populate the West, sixteen different species in all. Each species owns one of those famous rattles, made of old skin that gets caught on the end of the tail where it dries up. And they slither all over the place, from the northern reaches of California (the Pacific rattlesnake) to the Colorado River (Western diamondback) to, most famously, the deserts of southern California, Arizona, and New Mexico (sidewinders, red diamondbacks).

The good news about rattlesnakes is that, compared to the vipers and cobras of Africa, Australia, and Asia, they are positively nontoxic. The taipan of Australia, an eleven-foot-long nightmare of a predator, is about ten times more deadly than the Mojave rattlesnake, North America's most poisonous serpent, and injects enough venom to kill *one hundred* full-grown adults with each bite. (The creature's formidable fangs occasionally puncture its own lower jaw.)

What the Mojave rattler does have over its more lethal cousins is location, location, location—in other words, a range that encompasses more than six western states. The taipan, for its part, stays stuck out there in the Aussie bush, gobbling down rodents and killing a few people every year. Rattlesnakes in the U.S. inflict around 1,250 bites every year, though the vast majority do not result in fatality. In fact, only about one per year does, out of the total five to ten fatal bites across the whole country. (About 125,000 snakebite deaths occur every year worldwide, most of them happening in the Third World where antivenin is not readily available.)

Luckily for American snakebite victims, not every rattlesnake bite injects the amount of venom necessary to kill. We already know that rattlers can control the amount of venom they put into a bite; but the fact is that some of the time, they decide not to inject any at all. Then there is the quality of the venom itself; most rattlers simply inject their victims with digestive enzymes that begin to break down tissues at the bite spot, hardly something that is going to drop you. The Mojave rattler, or the Mojave green as it is sometimes called, mixes those enzymes with a big-league neurotoxin that goes after the nervous system and can cause paralysis, or even death, under the wrong circumstances.

Getting bit by a snake is not that easy, either. Most snakes—even the relatively aggressive Mojave—do not want anything to do with people unless the person in question presents a threat. The Arizona coral snake, a member of the cobra family that boasts some pretty serious venom of its own, is a chicken despite its lineage; unless you actually pick one up and handle it for a while, you stand pretty much no chance of being bitten.

In fact, a whole lot of people who get bitten by snakes are the very people who know best how to handle them. It's just a question of frequency; these guys give the snakes so many chances at them that, sooner or later, one of them is bound to get lucky. Take Boonreung Bauchan a.k.a. "The Snake Man," who once set a record by spending seven days locked in a room with poisonous serpents. In 2004, he met his end during a routine show in his native Thailand when a mamba finally got its fangs into him. He finished up the show, then collapsed and died.

But for the most part, people get bitten out in the wilderness when the snake takes them by surprise. After all, desert snakes match the color of their surroundings perfectly; it isn't hard to step on one if you aren't careful out there. Near Wilcox, Arizona, for example, a German tourist named Marcus Wolf suffered a bite in September 2005 as he tooled around in the countryside. He was able to drive himself to the local hospital, but lost consciousness on the flight to Tucson; he went into anaphylactic shock on the helicopter and died shortly after. Then there's the case of Ann Avery, a lawyer from Colorado who got bitten as she was hiking around South Table Mountain, near Golden. She didn't hear the snake's warning rattle or see it at all—that is, she didn't see it until she felt "something small and bony hit [her] very hard on the ankle." She panicked at first, but her husband Bill calmed her down enough to get her to the car.

During the ride, she lost her vision, felt numbness in her mouth, had her throat swell shut, and experienced a precipitous drop in her blood pressure. She faded fast on the way to the hospital, to the point that her doctors thought she might not survive. Luckily for all involved, she did eventually recover, though according to her she will be "hiking with hipboots on" in the future.

Then there's Lorain Miller of Tucson. "Bud" Miller belonged to the Huns motorcycle club, and was by all accounts a pretty tough, hard-drinking customer. He kept at least nine Western diamondbacks in his home, including a five-and-a-half footer named Scratch. Miller had a habit of pulling the snake out and playing with him during parties, so it surprised no one when, in March 1992, Miller pulled his slithery buddy out for some drunken hijinks.

Miller had already been bitten a number of times, but never wanted antivenin treatment—he was saving it for "the big one," according to one account of his death. Apparently the big one snuck up on him, because as friends snapped pictures of the man and his snake, the reptile got spooked and bit him. A helpful buddy hit Miller three times with a stun gun attempting to neutralize the poison, but even that novel treatment couldn't save him. He died before even reaching the hospital.

Stupid decisions make frequent appearance in snakebite stories, as Miller's story demonstrates. The plain fact is that ninety-nine times out of a hundred, a bite from a rattlesnake should not kill you. We have the technology, as the Six Million Dollar Man's people used to say. Antivenin and quick access to medical care should pretty much take care of most everybody that suffers a bite. But whether by ignorance or overconfidence or a million other things, people do not always do the right thing. Some of them make truly valiant attempts to get poisoned to death, though more often than not without success—lucky for both of them and their mothers.

Taking in a wild reptile as a pet, for example—or rather, doing that and then treating the creature like a Yorkshire terrier puppy—classifies as just such a stab at mortality. Matthew George nearly died in 2002 when the rattlesnake he picked up in Arizona bit him in the face as he tried to kiss it. Yes, that's right—George was attempting to smooch the young snake when it lashed out and kissed him back, fangs first.

When the paramedics showed up, George was disappointed; after all, he only had a little swelling in his upper lip by that point. But things went south quickly, as the venom in his blood worked through the massive network of vessels in his head. After a few minutes, his cheeks and ears were practically bursting, and his eyes had swollen shut. His lip swelled up to about five times its original size, and his neck swelled out as far as his chin.

According to the paramedics who treated him, he'd gotten a life-threatening dose, thanks mostly to the fact that the snake was young and couldn't control the amount of venom it shot into its hapless owner. For its part, the snake paid for the bite with its life—George's startled friend chopped off its head immediately after the accident, a miscarriage of justice if ever there was one.

Ross Cooke did not pick up the rattlesnake that bit him, though he did seem to forget that its venom would eventually kill him if he did not do anything about it. While walking through a wash in San Bernardino County, California, he stepped on a rattler, which promptly bit him two times on the leg. He then walked back to his car and called his wife and his boss at the refrigeration company where he worked—instead of, say, calling 9-1-1. Then, he proceeded to drive sixteen miles to the hospital, rather than one mile to the firehouse around the corner, where one would assume the firefighters would know how to give temporary medical attention in an emergency.

He got to the hospital and seemed OK for a while, until he began showing signs of neurological problems. According to authorities, he probably suffered from intravascular coagulation, in which a bunch of small strokes eventually build up to a very large one. The doctors transferred him to Loma Linda University Medical Center because of its skill in dealing with bites, but to no avail—Cooke died three days after his bite. Perhaps he had panicked in the beginning and forgotten about calling 9-1-1; had he made the call, there is a very good chance he would have survived. As it was, his long journey to help may have played a part in his death, as movement helps the venom work its way through a victim's system.

Another strange thing about snakes: they will bite you when they are dead. That's right; like zombies from your favorite low-rent horror flick, dead snakes will rear up in a final reflexive flinch and sink their fangs into you. If you doubt this undead behavior, ask Justin Cluff of Queen Creek, Arizona, who lost part of his index finger when a snake *head*—his buddy had just finished blowing it off the rest of the snake with a .22—did just that. According to one 1972 study, snakes are dangerous for up to twenty minutes after they die.

Despite the potential danger our snakes present, though, they have a whole lot more reason to fear us than vice versa. As is our tendency, we have managed to turn a few bites and fatalities into movies such as *Snakes on a Plane*, *Anaconda*, and *SSSSSSS* (though that last one is about a guy who turns *into* a snake, rather than actual snakes themselves). In other words, just as we did with *Jaws*, we managed to scare ourselves into taking out our fears on a whole species of innocent creatures based on their fictionalized misdeeds. People kill snakes for the simple crime of being on their property, or being near the road, or simply being; witness the rattlesnake roundups that still take place all over the western United States, in which gun-toting people who think they're doing their communities a favor drive the snakes together into large public areas in order to massacre them by the thousands. To call this practice stupid degrades stupidity; it's destruction for destruction's sake, as well as a great way to tilt the ecosystem irreparably toward the rats and mice by eliminating one of their major predators.

≋ 𐂷 ≋

Bugs in general, and spiders in particular, spark a recoil reaction like nothing else, not even the big beasts. That's because you will never find a shark, a bear, or a cougar in your garage. You'll never yank your daughter up to your chest just before she touches the mountain lion she has found in her toy box. And unless you are the champion sound sleeper of the universe, you will never, ever experience a grizzly bear crawling into bed with you.

Perhaps the least understood biting bug of the far West doesn't even live there. The brown recluse spider ranges from Texas, Nebraska, and Oklahoma, east to Tennessee, south to Mississippi, and north to Iowa's lower reaches. A few related species live in the massive desert region encompassing southern California, Arizona, and Nevada; these spiders, however, tend to live out in the desert, where there are not a lot of people running around. The brown recluse of urban legend resides exclusively within its range. Yet dozens of bites in California, Arizona, Nevada, Utah, and New Mexico, among others in areas with absolutely no brown recluse population, have been attributed to the elusive arachnid. It is not just crackpots telling stories, either—doctors (and by extension, journalists looking for a lurid story)—have trumpeted the terrible brown recluse problem the West seems to have, even though it absolutely, 100 percent, doesn't.

If there is a bug out there that has a worse—and less deserved—reputation as a potential killer, it is the brown recluse, named not for its aggressive and bloodthirsty nature, but for its—well, reclusiveness. Small, brown, and unassuming, the brown recluse measures only a quarter to half an inch long. A violin-shaped marking on its rear portion earned it the alternate name of violin spider. It infests houses throughout its natural range on a regular basis, to the point that people can pick up a dozen or more in minutes from the nooks and crannies of their very own homes. In fact, one family of four, in a study run by Rick Vetter of UC Riverside, lived with upwards of two thousand brown recluses in a Kansas home. That family never registered so much as one bite, a testament to the generally benevolent nature of these little guys.

However, they do occasionally bite. The spiders do not seek out humans to nip; pretty much all bites happen when people roll over on them in bed, or when they put on clothes that the spider has decided to curl up in. Ninety percent of the time these bites do not cause symptoms any more serious than those of a wasp or bee sting—just a little red bump surrounded with white. That other ten percent, however—the ones unlucky enough to get a solid dose of venom in their bites—experience effects ranging from mild discomfort to a breakdown of the tissue around the bite, known in the medical profession as necrotizing and to the rest of us as utterly terrifying and horrible-looking. After a day or so, the wound goes purple, and the tissue around the bite starts to die. After that, the local tissue turns black and begins to slough away, leaving a sucking wound with a hole at its center. In the worst cases, brown recluse bites look as if the biter must have been about five feet across, sporting mandibles dripping with viscous black poison. The hole that is left is deep and ugly, to say the least, a cavity with a soggy-looking black residue ringing its inside. What is more, the wound takes months to heal to an even level with the rest of the surrounding skin; the scar never goes away, though it does fade some. You would not want one, no question about it.

The thing is, the bites look an awful lot like an awful lot of other things. Cutaneous anthrax, Lyme disease, some cancers, and that crazy "flesh-eating bacteria" all mimic the advanced symptoms of brown recluse bites, resulting in a lot of wrong diagnoses by doctors who, just like everybody else, get caught up in the spider paranoia. The downside, for those who are misdiagnosed, can be dire—up to and including amputation, or even death. In fact, a significant portion of the deaths from such diseases get attributed to brown recluses, despite the fact that, according to all the best medical opinions, no one has ever died from such a spider bite.

But don't try telling that to the Californians who have been "bitten by the brown recluse," where brown recluse paranoia is especially pronounced and incredibly misinformed. In fact, you would be hard-pressed to find another place where more people get attacked by something that, as a scientific certainty, is not there.

Stranger, and perhaps sadder, a number of supposed bites in California result in death, indicating that somewhere along the line, scared people and their doctors are making bad decisions that might end in unnecessary tragedy. The following accounts come straight from California newspapers, publications a little too eager to run with the "killer spider" headline:

From a June 2000, Associate Press wire article with the headline "Spider bite contributes to woman's death": "A 62-year-old woman has died from complications following a spider bite, possibly from a brown recluse spider."

From a May 1993 article in the Riverside *Press Enterprise*, titled "Officials investigate spider bite in woman's death": "The concerns are prompted partly by the events that left Valerie Slimp, a 39-year-old Mira Loma mother of two, on the verge of death last June. By the time doctors learned Slimp may have been bitten by a brown recluse spider, an extremely rare species in California, much of the tissue in her extremities had been destroyed. Portions of each limb had to be amputated."

Again in the *Press Enterprise*, this time in a 1996 article "Death points to spider bite; 85-year-old waited 2 days before getting help": "Audrey Needham noticed what appeared to be a spider bite on her left hand January 22. ... Two days later, Needham's left arm was black, her speech was slurred and she was sluggish, apparently as a result of the venom entering her blood. ..."

In all fairness, however, the *Enterprise* published an article a week or so later about the "bum rap" brown recluses have gotten. But the same article refers to brown recluses in California as "uncommon," which is true, after a fashion, if in fact the author meant completely and utterly uncommon, as in you will never, ever see one unless you are out in the middle of the desert under a log, and certainly never, ever in Riverside.

Black widow spiders, unlike brown recluses, actually do live in California, as well as every other western state, and actually *can* kill you. Female black widows are, if you've never seen one, the Scary Spider Prototype—thin, sinister legs attached to a compact mass that blows out into a bulbous black abdomen, painted with a red hourglass meant to symbolize the ticking clock of life the spider seeks to end in you. Add to that eight eyes, fangs, the ability to get just about anywhere they want to, and a venom fifteen times more lethal than the prairie rattlesnake's. Here's a little taste, via Gordon Grice and his excellent treatment of these tiny carnivores in *The Red Hourglass: Lives of the Predators*:

> Besides pain, several other symptoms appear regularly in widow victims. ... a rigid abdomen, the "mask of latrodectism" (a distorted face caused by pain and involuntary contraction of muscles), intense sweating (the body's attempt to purge the toxin), nausea, vomiting, swelling. A multitude of other symptoms have occurred in widow bite cases, including convulsions, fainting, paralysis, and amnesia.

Not a pretty picture—in fact, if you scare easily, it's downright terrifying. All the worse considering that this passage does not mention the drop in blood pressure, the spike in heart rate, or the itching.

But don't be scared. For all the things that can happen if you do get bitten, the chances of your doing so are pretty low, and even lower if you take some elementary precautions. That lethal venom? The black widow, for all its intimidating features, is above all a very small creature. Thanks to that fact, it does not inject much venom at all when it bites. And the female spider—the one with the poisonous bite—rarely leaves her web to seek victims, instead preferring to wait around and bite what she plans to eat. Sometimes they do not inject any venom at all when they bite, preferring perhaps to take in the look on your face when they nip you. Once you take into account these little tidbits, the whole package becomes a little less frightening.

The elderly and little kids have most to fear from the black widow, as their immune systems have the least weaponry in the arsenal. In addition, the very symptoms of a widow bite—the high blood pressure, for example—can aggravate a preexisting condition and trigger strokes or heart failure in elderly bite victims. Nevertheless, death occurs only in about one percent of people bitten; in fact, not one documented case of fatality via black widow bite has happened in the West, or in the rest of America for that matter, in about ten years, though Europe saw fatalities in 2001 and 2003. And even if you are bitten, there is an antivenin for black widow bites, which means that a healthy adult's only real shot at a fatal experience with this particular spider is to be bitten and not seek treatment.

≈ ♯ ≈

The West is host to a few more venomous creatures, though not one has caused a verifiable human fatality within the last few decades. The legendary tarantula, for example, subject of a thousand horror movies and creepy TV moments, is about as poisonous as a honeybee.

And those scary Africanized killer bees that are invading the nation from Mexico, threatening to end forever the fine American traditions of cooking outside, mowing the lawn, and whacking the weeds? Well they are here, scattered from Louisiana to California. And they do kill, unfortunately, though not necessarily for the reasons you might think. First off, they are no more venomous than the honeybees we already had; the principle difference is their aggressiveness. While the average honeybee colony will station around two hundred "guards" in the vicinity to protect the hive, killer bees will designate around two thousand soldiers for sting duty. And they are a lot more persistent than their mellow domestic relatives; you can run up to a half-mile after disturbing an Africanized bee hive, and they will chase you all the way.

More than any creature here, these bees will come after you, which explains why they end up killing a few people every year. This kind of aggressiveness in a more venomous or toothy creature would be downright terrifying. Imagine black widows chasing you out of your shed, intent on sinking their fangs into you; or a bear guaranteed to attack you for entering the range of its senses. A whole lot of us would be toast under either one of these circumstances, but the bees, thanks to their non-lethality, don't score the kind of kills a more inherently deadly creature would. If not for their tenaciousness, bees would mostly kill only the exceptionally allergic. But the fact that they will follow, keep stinging, and bring lots of their buddies along for the chase makes them dangerous, particularly if you happen to be very old or very young.

Africanized bees landed in the New World in 1956, when Brazilian scientists brought some African bees over to breed with domestic varieties and produce a more heat-resistant, honey-rich bee. The imported bees promptly escaped and started breeding in the wild, instilling their bad attitude into the local population. The rest is hysterical, though occasionally dangerous, history—bees with the African blood arrived in the U.S. around 1990, and their reputation spread largely via overwrought press coverage.

That being said, the immigrants do exhibit some truly scary behavior. They will wait for you if you jump into a body of water. Their stingers continue to inject venom even after they are embedded in your skin. And they live mostly in ground-level burrows, rather than visible aboveground hives the way their European brethren do.

And they do attack, to be sure. Somewhere between forty and one hundred fifty people die every year from bee attacks, though most of the attacks bear some extenuating circumstance—allergies or age—that the initial report of death tends to gloss. Take Lino Lopez, for example, a Texas rancher living way down near Harlingen along the Mexico border. He died of a forty-sting bee attack in 1993. But get a load of these extenuating circumstances: he was eighty-two years old at the time, and he had a heart condition to go along with his emphysema. The bees that attacked him were probably Africanized, but forty stings from regular honey bees probably would have done the same thing, according to Ruben Santos, a forensic pathologist interviewed by *USA Today* about the attack.

Mary Williams was the first Arizonan killed during the Africanized bee invasion, back in 1995. Though she was eighty-eight years old, and thus had some extenuating circumstances herself, the details of her attack are still chilling; she was walking home from her sister's house when a massive swarm living in a nearby abandoned house came after her and stung her more than one thousand times. She was conscious the entire time, as every square inch of her body was covered with stings; she'd even been stung inside her mouth and nose. At the hospital, stingers littered the floor as nurses pulled them out, but in the end they couldn't save her.

Lorenzo E. Castaneda also succumbed to Africanized bee stings, but in a different way: he was only stung twice, but his own physiology betrayed him. The stings brought on an allergic reaction, which soon led to a series of massive heart attacks. His heart, according to his son-in-law, "stopped three or four times," and paramedics used shock paddles over fifteen times to bring him back. Still, in the end it was all for naught; his organs began to fail at the hospital, and the damage to his heart was just too much. Like the sting victims mentioned above, Castaneda was no spring chicken—he was sixty-six at the time of the attack. And the outcome would likely have been the same if the bees were European, since the venom in both species of bee is roughly the same (and the European honeybee, in fact, carries a bigger supply). But his death seems far more accidental, less savage and deliberate, than the other two mentioned above. The colony of forty-five thousand bees living nearby didn't emerge to envelop their victim; exterminators didn't even find it until afterward. The incident feels a lot more like an accident, an unfortunate result of a scouting mission gone bad.

So bees kill, no question. But again, the press overshadows the reality where these little guys are concerned. Truth is, the West's smallest killers present far less a threat than its biggest—and even those big boys stand less a chance of getting you than a bolt of lightning, or a wall of mud, or another person.

CHAPTER FOUR

Mayhem and Murder
Attacks from the Human Animal

Obviously there's nothing very special about murder in general, outside its overall ugliness. We read about murders and murderers every day in the paper, and think nothing of them. Some killings, of course, manage to attract our attention; Ted Bundy, Charles Manson, and their ilk capture our interest with their heinous nature and savagery. Other slayings attract notice via their wanton meaninglessness, the foolishness of the act when it involves a pair of sneakers, or an empty wallet.

Other murders stay with us thanks to their association with a particular place, or set of circumstances. Such is the case of Kris Eggle, a former ranger at Organ Pipe Cactus National Monument. Organ Pipe offers a fairly incredible slate of natural phenomena; for one thing, it features more than twenty-five different types of cacti, most notably the towering organ pipe. This cactus, branched like fingers pointing skyward, doesn't generally appear north of the border. In fact, Organ Pipe National Monument encompasses pretty much all of the organ pipe cactus range in America.

These botanical gluttons for punishment situate themselves in as much sunlight as they can, which in the Sonoran desert is potentially quite a lot; they cluster on the southern slopes of small, rolling sand berms, in order to avoid the dangerous frosts that come in winter. When the spring hits with the force of a furnace, the organ pipe waits until the sun goes down and reveals dainty white and lavender flowers, providing a ghostly show that few people ever get to see. Few, that is, except those people who put themselves in the middle of the desert's desolate expanse at that time of year, out of desperation or blind greed.

The park, while presenting a pristine Sonoran desert environment—covered in the thin layer of beautiful, fragile life that makes Arizona's deserts a national treasure—also happens to be one of America's least hospitable human environments. Brutally hot, sun-blasted, devoid of anything remotely resembling comfort, it might not be so bad if it were located near a large city. A few signs to warn hikers to bring enough water, and that would cover it. But Organ Pipe runs along the U.S.–Mexico border for some thirty miles, with a total area approaching five hundred square miles of isolated, open ground. As you might imagine, this location makes for a few tragic complications.

According to the U.S. Border Patrol, about one hundred eighty thousand illegal immigrants and seven hundred thousand pounds of illegal drugs make their way over the border into the States via this naturally vital corridor, resulting in big problems for both the park and those trying to cross it. For the flora and fauna, traffic like this spells catastrophe; at its high point, one thousand people per day cross the delicate landscape. One thousand pairs of feet every day, all of them compacting soil, eroding natural land features, and spooking the bighorn sheep, jackrabbits, kangaroo rats, and various reptiles that call the park home. The crossers trample young cacti that take years to grow a few inches, and leave trash, both physical and biological, in their wake. (Dripping Springs, an ancient oasis for desert travelers, now suffers from E. coli infestation, while other desert passes smell like New York City sewers.) The backcountry, so well preserved in other sanctuaries all over the country, suffers more off-trail traffic here than almost anywhere else in the national park system. All those tramping boots—along with the vehicles that often wend their way through the fragile desert—are killing the land.

As for the people crossing the border in the middle of the Sonoran summer (or anytime from late April through October), the potential problems aren't hard to imagine—namely dehydration. Simply think of crossing a few hundred miles of shadeless desert in which the daytime ground temperature regularly pegs at one hundred sixty degrees or higher, and you have a pretty good idea of what makes traversing Organ Pipe such a terrible idea.

Unfortunately, the people attempting to make the cross don't have too many choices in avoiding the dangers. Immigrants and drug runners, two groups very eager to avoid contact with any authority, bet their lives on their ability to cross Organ Pipe's merciless real estate, and they congregate there *because* of its very isolation. Thus a vicious pattern has developed: more border crossers, heading into punishing and life-threatening territory, doing more damage and requiring more border control, making the region even more dangerous for everyone involved as the ante goes up and the number of dangerous criminals who choose to cross there increases. The result: everyone gets bolder, both the criminals and the authorities charged with catching them, and disastrous results are just a matter of time.

It's no surprise, then, that Organ Pipe National Monument holds the title of America's most dangerous national park. And perhaps it's also no surprise that Kris Eggle, a law enforcement ranger at Organ Pipe, found himself chasing a group of Mexican drug runners through the desert on August 9, 2002. Rather, he thought they were drug runners; the Mexican police had reported two armed fugitives crossing the border into Organ Pipe, and Eggle responded to the call. He couldn't have known about the sordid complications involving the two men, Panfilo Murillo Aguila and Dionicio Ramirez Lopez.

Some details of Aguila and Lopez's journey across the border are shady still. On Thursday, August 8, a commando-style assault team attempted to carry out an execution over an unpaid drug debt. The result of this attack: four dead men, beaten and brutally executed in a small house southwest of Sonoyta, Mexico. (The two men who sped over the border on August 9 may have had some role in this execution, either as escaped targets or members of the assault team, though no one knows for sure.) Murillo and Lopez entered the scene definitively when they took part in a carjacking, taking a Blazer from a Scottsdale man on his way to Rocky Point, Mexico. From there, the three or four carjackers headed to the local prosecutor's office, where suspects from the quadruple homicide were being held. Officers there recognized the carjacked vehicle and sighted an AK-47 inside, and the men (who may or may not have been there to spring the offenders from jail) took off for the U.S. border and Organ Pipe National Monument.

Aguila, believed to be the driver, sped through a twenty-foot hole in a border fence before abandoning the vehicle and scattering, along with his passengers. U.S. border agents apprehended Lopez soon after; he had dropped his weapon in order to run faster. Aguila, however, held on to his as he fled and hid not far away.

A surveillance helicopter notified Eggle once it found Aguila, and directed the ranger to the fugitive's location. Mexican agents, who pursued the Blazer all the way to the border, weren't far off, but Eggle reached Aguila first.

Eggle was one of five law enforcement rangers at Organ Pipe in 2002. This number in and of itself portends trouble, as studies of the park demonstrate that the volume of illegal activity requires at least sixteen rangers to handle adequately. On top of the chronic understaffing he had to deal with, Eggle had little experience—he'd been out of training only a few months—and the massive disconnect between a park ranger's traditional job and the extreme circumstances Organ Pipe presents.

Park rangers enforce a wide array of laws as a rule, everything from hunting and fishing regulations to drug laws and health codes; but they don't get tactical, weapons, or field training the way Customs and Border Patrol officers do. Controlling dangerous drug smugglers does not fall into their job description. When Eggle found himself barrel-to-barrel with a hardened drug runner who may have also been a hitman, it was a situation certainly not discussed at length in the classrooms where Eggle got his training, and he had never prepared for anything resembling it. In short, he was the wrong man at the wrong time, trying bravely to fulfill a role he had never signed on for.

But there he was regardless, rifle drawn, working with at least one Border Patrol agent to apprehend Aguila about two miles east of Lukeville, a frequent point of passage between Mexico and the U.S. The men in the helicopter heard two shots ring out, after which Eggle fell to the ground, and the Mexican officials began firing on the crouched form that had pulled the trigger. From their side of the border, they brought down Aguila, who died after efforts failed to keep him alive for a helicopter transport to a hospital. Eggle, shot in the lower abdomen, died soon after he was hit.

At first, Eggle's death didn't raise too many hackles outside the Southwest, but those it did raise were of a high profile. Rep. Tom Tancredo of Colorado called for congressional hearings into park ranger training practices, drawing attention to the rangers' plight at Organ Pipe. Eggle's family also became active in the immigration debate, and today runs a Web site dedicated both to border issues and to memorializing Kris. In November 2003, by order of the U.S. congress, the visitor center at Organ Pipe National Monument became known as the Kris Eggle Visitor Center, ensuring that the man's sacrifice would have a public acknowledgment. In addition, a long-delayed anti-vehicle wall received funding in the wake of Eggle's death; the eighteen-million-dollar, thirty-mile barrier runs through the park, preventing vehicle traffic while impacting wildlife relatively little. Consensus is that funding for this wall only came at the expense of Kris Eggle's life.

In many ways, Eggle's murder turned up the volume on the debate over illegal immigration and its costs, both in human terms and in the less visible, but no less devastated, calculus of the natural world. This debate continues, and will continue, to be a part of the West's heritage as well as its future. The border crossings continue, as do the debates over what they mean and how to deal with them effectively. And rangers like Eggle still find themselves on the front lines, holding a line in the sand.

But the sand that line is drawn in, perhaps, bears more scars than any of the people involved in the border struggle. No environment so fragile can withstand one thousand passages every day, and as they continue, a part of the West's natural heritage comes closer and closer to permanent ruin. Think of an oil pipeline into the ocean off Big Sur, or a parade of garbage trucks dropping their loads into the Grand Canyon by the ton every day. The destruction of the desert paradise just one hundred twenty-five miles south of Tucson falls into the same league, minus the outrage such extreme examples would elicit. Kris Eggle is the most visible and obvious casualty in Organ Pipe National Monument's slow and painful death, but he is far from the only one.

※ 𝍢 ※

The desert isn't the only pristine western environment to play host to our worst impulses. In 2003, for example, at least thirteen people died on Colorado's pristine and lovely ski slopes. In California, 2006 brought the most ski slope deaths in a generation—ten, according to the *Chicago Sun-Times*. From 1991 through 2004, about four hundred seventy people died in ski slope accidents, the vast majority of them by running into things. Ten percent of those, however, died by running into other people, which raises the question: is it murder when you run somebody over as you burn down the slope far faster than you should be going?

Take the case of Robert Wills, an Englishman who killed fellow skier Richard Henrichs by running into him at an incredible rate of speed—so fast that the impact knocked Henrichs clear out of his skis and into a tree. Wills was ultimately exonerated of any wrongdoing, and the whole thing was chalked up to a terrible accident.

This is what happens most of the time when two people collide on a ski mountain and one dies: the death is ruled accidental, and everyone moves on as best they can. This was not the case, however, for the famous Nathan Hall—the only skier ever to be tried and convicted for killing another person while skiing.

Hall wasn't the first to see criminal charges brought for homicide by reckless skiing. That dubious honor goes to Howard Hidle, who killed eleven-year-old Kari Meylor while skiing at Winter Park in Colorado. He decided to ski into a designated "slow" area in a full racing tuck, and slammed into the little girl as she took off her skis at the bottom of the mountain. Hidle eventually copped a plea and served thirty days in jail, sixty days in work release, and four years on probation. He also paid for a memorial built at the spot where he killed her. (And, in a bit of sad irony, he killed himself in the accident's aftermath.) Most criminal cases involving reckless skiing end the same way whether someone dies or not—the violator takes the plea, acknowledging his wrongdoing, and everybody goes home. In Colorado, four to ten of these criminal cases happen every year, with little fanfare.

Hall, however, chose to fight his charges for years, providing some interesting insight into a person who will drunkenly careen down a mountain, kill someone, and then deny he did anything wrong.

In 1997, Hall was working as a lift operator at Vail—not a bad gig for someone who enjoys skiing the snowy mountains of the West. And Hall, a member of his high school ski team back in Chico, California, and all of eighteen years old, was probably living his version of the American Dream up there in Vail. It was the end of the season, the last day in fact, and Hall had eagerly clipped into his skis and started down the mountain after finishing off a celebratory beer. At the bottom of the Riva Ridge slope, one of the resort's best-known trails, he lost control of himself. Hall had his skis pointing straight down the mountain, blowing down with as much speed as he could muster and taking a straight line on the hill—two things that all skiers know will guarantee endless and burning acceleration.

But he wasn't just skiing fast. He was bouncing off the tops of moguls without paying attention to what was below him, a dangerous practice that ensured, by dint of his speed, that he would not see whoever might be obscured by the moguls until it was far too late. He also leaned back on his skis, completing a trifecta of idiocy: skiing too fast, not paying attention to what was out in front of him, and getting in a back-leaning position. On top of all this, he had alcohol in his blood stream.

On the same day, Alan Cobb, a thirty-three-year-old cabinetmaker and father of two, was enjoying a day on the slopes with his fiancée. He'd only skied three times previously, having just moved to Denver eight months before. Hailing from Ipswich, England, Cobb had just ordered materials and gotten a bank loan to begin pursing his passion: building guitars.

Hall, predictably out of control given his speed and form, came up and over a mogul and launched into the air. Now a pair of skis in contact with the snow will seldom injure anybody; at head-level, however, moving through the air at thirty or forty miles per hour, they will do a load of damage if they happen to hit you. Hall's ski dislodged itself from his foot and rocketed into Cobb, hitting him just below his right ear and cracking his skull all the way down to the top of his neck. He dropped to the snow in an expanding gush of blood.

Cobb's fiancée Christie Neville found him afterward, already close to death. Rescue crews arrived at the scene soon after, but their efforts to revive Cobb proved fruitless. At Hall's preliminary hearing, one doctor would testify that Cobb's injuries were consistent with "someone who is thrown out of an automobile or a moving vehicle," giving some indication as to just how fast Hall must have been going. The authorities charged Hall with manslaughter that same day, a charge that carried up to sixteen years in prison and half a million dollars in fines. The decision to go after Hall set the stage for five years of legal maneuvering, as well as a debate on whether or not skiers should be held accountable for any mayhem they cause as they speed down the mountain.

The first two judges to hear Hall's case dismissed it outright. The first judge said that Hall's "conduct in skiing too fast for snow conditions does not rise to the level of dangerousness required under the current case law," a decision the first appeal judge agreed with. The conditions on the mountain—it hadn't been groomed in a while, and the snow was pretty wet that day—got the blame for the accident, rather than Hall's reckless skiing. Christie Neville, among others, saw this ruling as the right to act the fool without consequence; the other people who saw it that way were the prosecutors of Eagle County, who went ahead with an appeal. They got the same result at the district court: Hall hadn't really endangered anybody, even though he was moving so fast that he couldn't come to a stop until he'd gone another eighty feet down the mountain after hitting Cobb.

When the case reached the Colorado State Supreme Court, however, the legal tune changed. Almost three years to the day after the accident, that court unanimously decided that Hall would have to stand trial for killing Alan Cobb, deciding that skiers like Hall presented a "substantial risk" on the slopes, and that someone skiing as recklessly as Hall could certainly have guessed that his actions might hurt or kill somebody.

The trial held implications for ski areas everywhere. What happens in Colorado, one of the world's ski Meccas, tends to reverberate throughout the rest of the snowbound world. In November the trial started, revealing more details of the incident. Christie Neville told the jury that blood had soaked into the snow a foot deep, and that Cobb was bleeding from his eyes, mouth, nose, and ear; another witness revealed that Hall ran into another skier after hitting Cobb, knocking that person's skis off and breaking a pole. The same man, J. Cyrus "Buck" Allen, also testified that after the collision with Cobb, he saw a ski fly twelve feet into the air. Ultimately, the jury found Hall guilty of negligent homicide, a lesser charge that carried a three-year maximum prison sentence and one hundred thousand dollars in fines. The jury decided on the fact that Hall was clearly a good skier, an expert even, and that he should have known what he was doing out there.

Throughout the entire affair, for the whole three and a half years between the accident and the trial, Nathan Hall never attempted to contact Alan Cobb's family. When the case was finally decided, Hall angrily and arrogantly told Mike Goodbee, one of the district attorneys prosecuting the case, that he would never win. Hall did sob upon hearing that Cobb had died back in 1997, and he finally apologized during a *Dateline* interview the day before his sentencing, proving that he wasn't completely unaware of the consequences of what he'd done. Still, the sentencing itself brought more drama: as he was sentenced to ninety days in jail, three years' probation, and two hundred forty hours of community service, he announced his intent to appeal, inciting disgust and anger from the people Cobb left behind. Hall's words, given that development, rang hollow: "I know I am guilty ... I think about it every day, about the emotional devastation to you. I'm ready to accept responsibility for my action." Or not.

Hall decided to serve his ninety days right away, but eventually lost his appeal and had to do the rest, too. Over the next few years he paid late on the restitution, failed to perform his community service, and finally got picked up for probation violations in April of 2004, almost exactly seven years after the accident. The whole ordeal came to an end the next day, when a judge dismissed the violation and announced Hall's sentence officially fulfilled. Hall didn't appear in court to hear the good news.

Nathan Hall's behavior after the accident made the whole thing worse—a lot worse. Had he simply accepted responsibility right off the bat, he could have saved a lot of people seven years' worth of pain and frustration. The bottom line is that his actions caused Alan Cobb's death, and he fought for years to avoid taking responsibility for it mostly because of where it happened— namely, out on the mountain, where apparently skilled people have the right to do whatever they want regardless of the consequences.

Now, people choose to recklessly endanger their *own* lives everyday—what are hang gliding, cliff diving, and any number of other questionable activities *but* that? Unfortunately, some among us have the idea that everyone else wants to take part in their little experiment in havoc. While their assumption often leads to inconvenience and irritation for the rest of us, in the worst cases it can mean serious injury and even death. The worst part, of course, is the fact that when these boneheads pull their stupid human tricks, they usually end up hurting someone else, rather than themselves.

Even worse, a lot of them—particularly the ones who act up on ski slopes—end up hurting children. In 2003, for example, Texan Michael Wolff got drunk, went snowboarding, and proceeded to slam into a kids' ski school class at Sunlight Ski Area, three of whom were five or six years old. He then kept on going, and when the ski patrol finally caught him, he said the children were in his way. Luckily, none of the kids died in the accident, but Wolff did manage to score the longest jail sentence yet handed down for recklessness on a ski mountain: two hundred forty days, almost three times longer than Hall's ninety-day sentence.

Reckless boaters are the summertime equivalent of reckless skiers. The western U.S. features some of the most picturesque boating in the country; head to the California Delta, Lake Havasu in Arizona, or Lake Powell on the Arizona-Utah border, and you're in for major fun in the sun buzzing around on the water vehicle of your choice. Unfortunately, the same kind of reckless people that may mow you down on the slopes can also be found when the mercury's up. Although speedboats are the most common watercraft involved in deaths on western lakes and rivers, smaller craft, such as jet skis and fishing boats are often the culprits.

Boats seem to bring out the worst in us. In some minds they don't even classify as vehicles with moving metal parts; they make people forget the most elementary laws of nature and physics, demonstrated by the sheer number of cosmically absurd things that people do while boating. Behind the helm of even the smallest, slowest water vessel, people will take actions that result in injury and death without an apparent second thought, never quite grasping the most basic fundamentals of boat safety—things like, don't breathe in the exhaust fumes or mistake a fishing rod holder for the gas tank.

The vast majority of boat owners also don't seem to appreciate that to properly operate a boat requires some training. According to California's 2003 review of boating accidents, almost eighty percent of all boating fatalities involved boaters with "little or no boating safety instruction." They may have borrowed or rented the craft and didn't really know that waterways feature their own set of rules, just as the highway does. Thirty-eight percent of the accident total involved alcohol, proving once again that driving under the influence probably will not work out for the best no matter what the vehicle in question.

Lake Havasu, straddling the California-Arizona border, sees numerous accidents every year, thanks both to big-time overcrowding and incompetent boating. Between 1995 and 2003, fifteen people died on that lake, while 484 total accidents took place. While some of those accidents were certainly of the purely coincidental kind, a disturbing number of others happened because the people involved were simply too drunk or ignorant to have any business behind the wheel of a large motorized vehicle.

Robert Padilla was one such person. On June 16, 2004, Padilla was tooling around in his twenty-three-foot speedboat the *Magic* late in the day, around 6:00 p.m., with five other passengers. And apparently, he was tooling around very fast. Whether he saw the catamaran bearing Tyler, Stephan, and Steven Patchett is unclear, though what happened next is not. There is little doubt that Padilla was driving his boat drunk and in no condition to be blazing through the water in a speedboat. Few boats were on the water at that hour, being a weekday, which makes the whole thing even more senseless.

The two boats, trying to avoid the collision, swerved to get out of each other's way. Tragically, both drivers guessed wrong each time, like two people trying to anticipate each other's trajectory until the inevitable bump. They ended up mirroring each other's movements, and maintaining their collision course even as they struggled to avoid it. The speedboat struck the thirty-two-foot catamaran in a "severe side swipe," with disastrous consequences. Ten-year-old Tyler, who was wearing a lifejacket, launched into the air and landed in the water. But he sustained profound head injuries in the crash itself, and may have even been dead before he hit the lake. Steven, the boy's father, was also thrown from the boat, while Stephan took a direct hit from Padilla's boat on the right side of his face, smashing the bones there. He wasn't wearing a life vest, but somehow he managed to stay aboard and survived as a result. The six people in Padilla's boat suffered only minor injuries. Steven's body turned up six days later near the crash site.

Padilla admitted to being drunk once he was charged with vehicular homicide and faced prison time. He pled no contest, and eventually got three years' probation for his recklessness. Upon hearing the sentence, Sheila Patchett, the boys' mother and Steven's ex-wife, said, "It's better than getting a not guilty. … It doesn't change the fact that they're both gone."

≋ 𝕶 ≋

Boat owners, to be fair, have to deal with a few vehicular quirks out there on the water, from increased turning radii to slow-reaction steering. Not compensating for such particulars of water travel can spell big trouble, particularly at high speeds. But the deadliest of those little concerns isn't even visible, and ironically it becomes a lot worse the longer you sit still.

People regularly succumb to carbon monoxide fumes while tooling around on their boats, so much so that the Coast Guard regularly releases admonitions for boaters to beware of its dangers. On its face, the issue sounds like another problem related to lack of thought and bad decision-making; and much of the time, it is. But death by emissions just isn't something we worry about much on dry land, so it's hard to fault people too much when they don't consider it out on the lake, either.

Boat engines aren't subject to the same emission standards that cars are. As a result, marine motors, which don't generally have catalytic converters, produce a lot of carbon monoxide that can, on calm days, linger on the surface of the water where people can easily breathe it in. According to Sonoma Technology, an air-quality research firm in Petaluma, the average boat gives off as much CO as 188 cars, making for big problems if you happen to be breathing the air blown from a running boat engine. And it accumulates quickly; during a test by the Sacramento Metro Fire Department, the CO level around an idling boat engine jumped to two hundred parts per million within the first thirty seconds. After nearly a minute, the level hit nine hundred ninety parts per million. Given more time, that concentration can increase to twenty thousand parts per million. (The World Health Organization says that eighty-seven ppm, with exposure over fifteen minutes, is dangerous.) Breathing clouds of carbon monoxide will bring on dizziness, along with drowsiness, loss of consciousness, and worse—all things that don't bode well for anyone who happens to be hanging off the back of the boat.

You read correctly—hanging off the back of a running boat, right where that nasty exhaust belches forth—was classified as a good time in some circles until quite recently. The activity, known as "teak surfing," enjoyed a brief run of popularity before people caught on to how dangerous it is. Surfers simply grab hold of the boat's swimming platform, get towed along as the boat builds up a bit of speed, and then let go when the wake is sufficient to let them body surf it, thus keeping them up with the back of the boat. The effect is sort of magic, being pulled along as if by invisible, watery cables. Sounds fun, except for two slight problems: your face, right at the water's surface, is exactly level with the boat's exhaust pipe, which puts out lots of poisonous carbon monoxide. And just in case you aren't hip to boat engineering, here's a primer: the sharp, fast-moving array of blades that propel a surface vessel through the water is known as the propeller. This device sits a few feet under the water at the back of the boat—in other words, right around the place your feet might be dangling if you decide to go teak surfing. What's more, you can't wear a lifejacket and teak surf properly, so if something does happen to you back there, chances are you'll be sinking.

The first mention of teak surfing fatality in the western U.S. occurred in 2001, when eighteen-year-old Chad Ethington drowned in Lake Powell while teak surfing behind a boat that had been weighted down to increase its wake and make for better surfing. Park rangers said at the time that they didn't know "if this is an emerging new trend or not." Unfortunately it was; apparently, enough people had done it enough times to deem it a safe activity, despite the insane levels of CO the participants breathe in while being dragged behind the boat.

A lot of people who have died as a result of teak surfing are kids, as they are a little less prone to realize that something they cannot see or smell might be killing them. Or it could be that the sheer concentration of CO renders them unconscious so quickly that they don't have time to react. Whatever the case, eleven-year-old Anthony Farr's final teak surf ended under the lapping waters of California's Folsom Lake, and finally focused attention on just how dangerous the activity is.

On May 28, 2003, Anthony, his father Mike, and seven friends set out on a ski boat belonging to Sean McKune, Mike's friend and neighbor. It was he who taught his friends how to bodysurf on the wake of a moving boat, and after some begging the adults agreed to let the kids give it a shot. It seemed an innocent activity, to say the least—downright tame, really. "We had easily done this 200 to 300 times with nobody getting hurt," McKune told the *Sacramento Bee* in the accident's aftermath.

In any case, there was certainly nothing to worry about from the propellers on McKune's boat; they were tucked up underneath it, out of reach particularly when the boat was moving. And no one smelled anything peculiar as Anthony clung to the swim platform behind the boat. Anthony wore no life jacket—the better to ride the waves—so nothing held him up as the fumes overtook him with incredible quickness. He went from laughing and clowning around to unconsciousness in about thirty seconds, according to McKune.

Mike Farr dove into the water as soon as his son went under, but he couldn't locate him no matter how deep he swam. As his father searched, the boy, massive amounts of CO running through his bloodstream, succumbed to the lake. The first day of Folsom Lake's watersports season would be the last of Anthony's life.

After his son's death, Mike Farr did his level best to ensure that it would not be in vain. He began by campaigning down at the lake, handing out pamphlets warning against the activity that killed his son, and portraying it for what it is: a dangerous, stupid idea. He also tried to spread the gospel regarding CO poisoning in general, and how much of the dangerous gas unregulated boat engines produced. But his efforts were strictly local. Six months later, however, California Assemblyman Paul Koretz's office called to ask Mike if he would support a bill banning teak surfing statewide. It seems his chief of staff had read about Farr's tragedy in the *Sacramento Bee*, and passed on the article to her boss. Farr was "blown away," and began working tirelessly to support the bill and make people aware of the danger.

In the end, his efforts bore fruit; California became the first state to ban teak surfing in January 2005. Farr also took his fight to the boat companies themselves, holding them accountable for continuing to make engines with so little in the way of CO and pollution control. He eventually sued Calabria, the manufacturer of the boat Anthony died on, and accepted an eight hundred fifty thousand dollar settlement from them in 2006. The company, along with other boat makers, told the press that they would try to find cleaner alternatives to their current engine designs. Anthony's death, ultimately, had come to mean something, and his name became literally synonymous with the reform he inspired: the California anti-teak surf law is called the Anthony Farr and Stacy Beckett Boating Safety Act, named after Anthony and a fifteen-year-old girl from Ontario, California, who died under the same circumstances.

Anthony's death, and the subsequent triumph of his father in raising public awareness, stands as one of the more inspiring examples of the fact that sometimes terrible tragedies can amount to something good in the end. But there's still a long way to go on the CO front—boats still belch out all that nasty gas, and a lot of people still don't know how dangerous it can be, even if you're not trailing behind the boat on a gas-drenched wake.

In fact, boat exhaust might just be one of the leading killers on American lakes and rivers, though the idea didn't even occur to anyone until very recently. Only in the last five or six years have people become acutely aware of the danger, as a result not of foolish practices like teak surfing, but of innocuous deaths that usually happen when the victims aren't doing much at all.

And they are tragic. A nine-year-old girl drowned under three feet of water as she played near generator exhaust; two brothers, ages eight and twelve, died as they swam in Lake Powell, the percentages of CO in their blood at fifty-nine and fifty-two percent (fatality can occur at twenty-five percent); and in August of 1998 at Lake Powell, two fatal poisonings took place within weeks of each other. These kinds of deaths happen fast and with no mercy; the gas, so concentrated and deadly, simply overwhelms the victims, most of whom are children unaware of just what's going on.

And despite the fact that the dangers inherent in teak surfing came to public attention in 2004, and the California law went active in January 2005, unwary teak surfers continued to die. In August 2005, twenty-two-year-old Jenda Jones died while teak surfing in Lake Tapps, two years after Denise Colbert died in the same lake doing exactly the same thing.

≈ ⚔ ≈

One thing to remember about the stories above is this: no matter what their specifics, death came accidentally in each one of them. Even when some other person's negligence caused the death, the fact is that no one had planned to kill anyone—no maliciousness, outside of a general disregard for other people, was at play, even in the worst case of negligence on the ski slopes or the lakefront.

But nature and the human capacity for destruction do intersect on occasion. The reason: murderers commit their crimes no matter what the view is where they happen to find their next victim. Cary Stayner, otherwise known as the Yosemite Killer, stands out as a prime example.

Carole and Juli Sund, Silvina Pelosso, and Joie Armstrong were four women who, like Chris Eggle, found themselves in the wrong place at the wrong time. The location, Yosemite National Park, holds a revered place in the West's hierarchy of natural wonders. The time was 1999, two years after Cary Anthony Stayner became handyman at the Cedar Lodge motel in El Portal, a town just outside the park.

Stayner had himself been touched by tragedy at a young age. A few weeks before Christmas 1972, Cary's little brother Steven took a ride from a local church minister who offered to take the boy home. Unfortunately, the man was no minister; his name was Kenneth Parnell, a convicted child molester who would abduct Steven and proceed to rape the boy on a regular basis for the next seven years while passing him off as a son. When Parnell brought home another boy, five-year-old Timmy White, Steven finally got up the courage to get away and did so, hitchhiking into Ukiah and finding the police station there. The tale saw its share of true-crime books and articles, and a TV miniseries called *I Know My First Name Is Steven* attracted around twenty-two million viewers when it aired in May 1989. Just a few months later, Steven died in a motorcycle accident. And, as if this sequence of events weren't bad enough, Cary Stayner maintained that he'd been sexually abused himself by an uncle when he was just eleven years old.

In fact, Stayner's mind is and was, for all intents and purposes, thoroughly broken. During his trial in 2002, witnesses described a whole slate of illnesses, beginning with a compulsion to pull out clumps of his own hair that started when he was only four years old. Stayner exhibited symptoms of pedophilia, obsessive-compulsive disorder, even mild autism, according to the defense team's experts. This terrible culmination came together in Stayner's tortured head, ultimately leading him to room 509 at the Cedar Lodge, where Carol Sund, forty-three, was staying with her fifteen-year-old daughter Juli and Silvina Pelosso, a sixteen-year-old exchange student from Argentina.

Stayner did not look or act like a raving lunatic. He was similar to so many people infected with these impulses. Those around him saw a nice, law-abiding man who took profound interest in hiking the breathtaking Yosemite countryside and who also enjoyed nude sunbathing, which he did regularly at Sacramento County's Laguna Del Sol nudist colony. In every way, he pulled off the prototypical "quiet guy next door" that Jeffery Dahmer, John Wayne Gacy, and so many others like them were purported to be; but like those better-known killers, Cary Stayner's outwardly placid demeanor was simply a curtain, behind which horrors bubbled.

Stayner knocked on room 509's door after spotting the women and marking them as easy fodder for a fantasy he'd harbored for thirty years: Cary Stayner wanted to kill women. (Once caught, Stayner blamed many of his problems on his brother's abduction and death, and claimed those events took part in twisting his mind. However, by his own admission, his murder fantasies started in 1969, three years before Steven was even abducted.) He often fantasized about rape, sometimes participating in the act and at other times rescuing imaginary victims. During an FBI confession, he said, "One minute I'm thinking great thoughts and world peace and the next minute it is like I could kill every person on the face of the earth." When he walked into the Sund's room on February 15, 1999, the latter impulse must have been ascendant.

He entered on the pretext of fixing a water leak. Initially, Carol Sund wouldn't let him in, so he consented agreeably, and told them he would go find a manager. His ambling, nonthreatening demeanor must have swayed Carol, because within a few minutes he was standing on the toilet removing the fan to "make it look authentic," in his own words. At some point after that, he felt comfortable enough to pull the .22 revolver he kept in his backpack—the same bag in which he kept a roll of duct tape and a large knife, a collection he referred to during his confession as his "kit."

He tied up the women, then led Juli and Silvina into the bathroom. Stayner went to his backpack for some rope, and "kinda sat on [Carol's] back and wrapped the rope around her neck and nonchalantly strangled her to death." He then went into the bathroom, collected the girls, and proceeded to molest them for the next few hours, shredding their clothing and leaving small pieces of fabric all over the room. He told them that Carol was in another room, but Silvina wouldn't stop crying, pleading with him to stop. So he strangled her, too, and stashed her body in the trunk of their rented car next to Carol's, which he'd put there after murdering her. Stayner then turned his attention to Juli Sund, abusing her for seven hours. He'd been impotent for most of his life, however, and that may have led him to his next act—wrapping Juli in a blanket and driving her to Don Pedro Lake, a pretty little recreation area huddled in the Sierra Nevada foothills east of Modesto.

Once there, Stayner drove to a beautiful spot overlooking the lake, and carried Juli to a grass hillock nearby, holding her "like a groom carrying a bride over the threshold." He attempted to rape her one more time, again with no success. Then he told her he loved her, and cut her throat.

No one missed the Sunds and Silvina immediately. Jens Sund, Carol's husband, was to meet them in San Francisco before flying on to Arizona, where the ladies were set to tour the Grand Canyon. They didn't come, and he assumed they must have gone ahead to Arizona without him. He took his own flight and even played golf the next day, still believing that his wife and the girls had made their own way. After his round, however, with still no word from them, he called the police; soon after, he learned that the women never returned the Pontiac Grand Prix they'd rented, nor had they contacted the rental agency to extend their rental time.

During the next six weeks, intense search efforts were organized in the Yosemite area. At one point a red herring planted by Stayner—Carol Sund's wallet—turned up in Modesto with all of its contents. As all evidence pointed toward violent crime as the reason for the women's disappearance, the brave souls eager to experience Yosemite in its snowbound winter glory felt a pall settle on the park. Jens Sund ultimately offered three hundred thousand dollars for information about his family, and Carol's parents Francis and Carole appeared on *Good Morning, America* to plead for the lives of their daughter and granddaughter.

As the Yosemite community shuddered and the Sund family searched, Cary Stayner played the prototypical serial killer to a tee: quiet and dependable at work, unassuming and solitary, the farthest thing from the deranged killer his acts revealed. He was, in that way, not unlike the inviting but occasionally deadly Yosemite backcountry, wilderness that attracted visitors from around the world—people who often stayed at the Cedar Lodge while taking it all in. The same 2001 report that named Organ Pipe National Monument the most dangerous national park in America "awarded" Yosemite second place, thanks to staff cuts and the resulting inability of the park rangers to properly do their jobs across the board—whether fighting fires, catching criminals, or saving lives in the backcountry. As the third most popular national park in the country, it attracts between three and four million visitors every year. With this influx of humanity comes all the problems crowds bring, including tight accommodations, congested roads, general frustration with the press of people all around. Add the possibilities of natural disaster—a rockslide here, unexpected blizzard there—and you've got what one park official called, according to the *Christian Science Monitor*, a "pressure cooker."

The vast majority of people who have died in Yosemite over the last two decades either met their fates while hiking and getting lost, subsequently succumbing to the elements, or from getting a little close to Yosemite's spectacular waterfalls and ending up in the water and over the edge. One thing that probably won't kill you in Yosemite, however, are the animals—in fact, the only person ever killed in Yosemite by a wild animal was actually killed by a mule deer. Cary Stayner killed four times that number by himself, in the span of a few months.

Not that anyone realized it until March 18, when the Pontiac's charred remains turned up in a secluded part of the Stanislaus National Forest. It had burned with Carol and Silvina's bodies in the trunk. Then the FBI received an anonymous letter detailing the location of Juli Sund's remains. (Saliva tests on the envelope proved inconclusive, since Stayner had paid a kid five dollars to spit into a cup so he could use it instead of his own.) On March 25, searchers found Juli's remains near Don Pedro Lake, and all worst fears were confirmed: someone had murdered the women, brutally and right under the noses of thousands of tourists and the people charged with taking care of those visitors. The FBI sifted through the area looking for suspects, and in doing so interviewed Cary Stayner before letting him go, never even naming the quiet, unassuming nudist as a suspect.

That mistake cost Joie Armstrong her life. Armstrong, age twenty-six, worked as a naturalist at the Yosemite Institute, a private nonprofit dedicated to teaching students about the environment. She lived a few miles from Cedar Lodge, in a primitive pine cabin she and her boyfriend Michael Raffaeli called the Green House. On July 21, she was planning to spend the night alone in the cabin, as Michael and her other roommate were out of town. She'd mentioned the fact to colleagues at the Institute, and had even said she was nervous about spending the night alone in the Green House. Apparently she decided not to stay the night, since she was packing her car for a trip to Sausalito when Cary Stayner, on his way to Foresta, spotted her around dusk.

During his FBI confession, Stayner told the agents that he'd seen Bigfoot in the area around the Green House in the early 1980s, and that he was "walking around just checking it out" when he saw Armstrong. He got out of his blue and white International Scout, said hello, and asked her if she'd ever seen Bigfoot in the area. She said no, stepped back up on her porch, and turned around. At that moment, Stayner pulled his .22 (having brought his "kit" along with him) and ordered her to come outside again. He got her into the front seat of his car and began driving, but she started to struggle mightily and eventually jumped from the vehicle in a nearby parking area. She got up and began running through the brush toward a friend's house a few hundred yards off. Stayner pursued her, and eventually caught up about one hundred fifty yards later. Unlike Juli, Joie Armstrong didn't suffer long, but she most certainly suffered—Stayner grabbed her from behind and slashed his knife across her throat again and again. He didn't stop until he'd decapitated her.

Stayner deposited her body in a nearby drainage ditch, and stashed her head forty feet from there. He then tried to leave the scene, but his Scout broke down on the way back to Cedar Lodge. The Yosemite ranger Stayner flagged down for a ride sensed nothing amiss; his easygoing demeanor hid any possibility that something was wrong. Again, Stayner evaded detection, though this time it wouldn't last.

On July 24, FBI agents picked up Stayner for questioning at the Laguna Del Sol nudist resort as he was eating breakfast (fully clothed, for the record). When they walked into the restaurant, Stayner stood and put his hand up, a strange but suspicious gesture, so the agents clapped handcuffs on him and led him away. During the ninety-minute ride back to FBI headquarters in Sacramento, Stayner began talking to agent Jeff Rinek, an FBI veteran who, ironically, had worked on the Yosemite case in the months previous. Rinek talked with Stayner about his brother Steven and the effects of his awful fate, and Cary began opening up, so much so that when they reached the station Stayner confessed to all four murders. But not right away; he first tried to negotiate with Rinek, asking to be housed in a federal prison close to his parents and for a "good-size stack" of child pornography. He believed that because he'd never seen such material, he had been pushed to kill. Rinek denied these requests, as might be expected, but persuaded Stayner to stick with his confession anyway. Cary Stayner received the death penalty for his crimes in 2002, and he sits on California's death row today.

Though Cary Stayner may be the best-known killer to have murdered in the national parks of the West, there's no shortage of stories involving the murderous overlapping of natural wonder with human depravity. At the Grand Canyon, for example, Sandra Marie Elizondo died after a suspicious push from the South Rim in 2001. The pretty eighteen-year-old traveled from Phoenix to the Grand Canyon on February 19; she fell into the canyon the evening of February 20, plummeting three hundred sixty feet to her death.

The questions surrounding her death outpace the answers: why was she even up there, when she was set to begin training as an America West Airlines ticket agent that same day? Why did she have a clump of her own hair in her hand when investigators found her? And most intriguing of all: how did she even reach the canyon? She was in Phoenix for her ticket agent training, having come from her home in California. She didn't have a car to drive, since the airline had flown her into town. Why would she have taken off for the Grand Canyon, anyway, since she had to be in the classroom the next day?

Two couples, some of the last people to see Sandra alive, said that they saw her walking alone on the Rim Trail hours before she died. The same people reported her missing after finding some of her personal articles—namely one of her shoes, its strap broken, sunglasses, and her purse—at the top of the canyon. She wasn't obviously depressed; she was all smiles in her ID photo taken the day before her death, and she was, by all accounts, excited to join America West and work her way up to flight attendant. Signs of a struggle in the area where she fell also lent credence to the foul play hypothesis, but no one knows much of anything for sure.

Nothing about Sandra Marie Elizondo's death makes any sense, and five years later it makes even less. The chances of determining why she died diminish all the time, and at this point they have to be close to nil. The canyon simply grabbed her, with a little help from somebody else.

Something similar happened to Japanese tourist Tomomi Hanamure on the Havasupai Tribe's reservation, located in one of Grand Canyon's many side gorges. The area might be one of the most beautiful in the entire West—three waterfalls drop into spectacular pools there, making for perfect swimming after a long day's hike. The canyon walls don't enclose so much as embrace the whole scene, which attracts around thirty thousand people every year. The Havasupai, for their part, take care of the travelers passing through, and remain one of the most isolated groups of people in the whole nation; in fact Supai, the tribe's largest village, lies in a three-thousand-foot-deep canyon, reachable only by foot or helicopter.

Tomomi reached the area on May 9, 2006, having hiked in earlier that day. She rose at 4:00 a.m. to reach her destination, and hiked into the canyon alone once she'd made the drive to the trailhead. Tomomi checked in at the Havasupai tribal lodge in Supai, then set out for a little more hiking around the waterfalls nearby. (By all accounts, she was completely at home in the backcountry, which would explain her traveling alone.) She took a daypack with her and then disappeared into the wilderness. The next time anyone saw her was four days later, when she was found less than a mile away. She'd been stabbed twenty-nine times, mostly in the head and neck, with a blade that left wounds over three inches deep. In fact, her face was damaged enough to require a dental records check to confirm her identity.

She'd never slept in her room—the bed and surroundings were pristine. She was also traveling alone, so there were no suspects who might have known her. Her clothes were intact, which eliminated the sexual assault motive. Investigators did find that her money, credit cards, and cell phone were missing, however, suggesting a far more base motivation than revenge or psychotic urge. Someone with a nasty violent streak robbed her, apparently. Police picked up a few "people of interest" in the murder's immediate aftermath, and recently they charged a local resident of Havasupai with the murder.

The Havasupai living in the canyon took the incident particularly hard; since they're so isolated geographically, they don't tend to have much contact with the outside world, and the crush of Japanese journalists flocking to cover the sensational story overwhelmed them. Worse, the tourist industry the tribe relies on—which represents the only local employment outside of the government—suffered a massive setback. After all, Japanese tourists visit Grand Canyon in general, and the Havasupai in particular, with some regularity; in the wake of the incident, according to the *Arizona Republic*, some were wondering if Arizona was, in fact, safe to visit at all.

Tomomi, however, was traveling under somewhat unique circumstances; any change in her plans might have saved her life. First off, she was traveling alone—never, ever a good idea while traversing backcountry, even for a seasoned outdoorsperson like her. Second, Tomomi set off for her little day hike without so much as (from the looks of it) stopping in her room. She set out without telling anyone where she was going, into a very, very isolated environment. Given this fact, it is small wonder that the search party, which eventually grew to fifty people or so, couldn't find her even though her body lay less than a mile down the path.

Still, traveling alone in breathtaking backcountry shouldn't be a capital offense, no matter how ill advised it might be.

≋ ⚙ ≋

Southern California's roadways might be the most famous asphalt in the world outside of the German autobahn. Route 66, the Pacific Coast Highway, the Santa Monica Freeway, Interstate 405 where O.J. Simpson took his scenic tour with police entourage—all of these highways, instantly familiar, run wholly or in part through California's southern reaches. Motorcycle culture saw its birth in southern California, as Marlon Brando frightened the locals in *The Wild One* and the Hell's Angels made that celluloid a reality; *Easy Rider* begins in California. And the epic westward journeys of the Great Depression and later inevitably involved pilgrimage to the Elysian fields of Los Angeles and San Diego. More than any other part of the country, pavement has made southern California what it is today.

Those same roads to salvation also encourage anonymity, disconnection, and loneliness. As easily as one can take the highway and get somewhere, another can use the same road to disappear, or to make someone else do so. Southern California, with its grand infusion of famous asphalt, has always played host to misfits who plied the highways not to get somewhere, but to go nowhere. Some of our most famous cultural touchstones—the aforementioned *Easy Rider*, as well as *On the Road* and *The Grapes of Wrath*—involve just this type of drifter. There aren't many stereotypes as American as the rootless highway wanderer, though most don't leave a big dent in the world around them, if they leave any at all. But some malevolent wanderers strike terror into the roadways they travel, and fear in everyone who shares them. In 1979, for example, California's hidden byways played host to William Bonin, otherwise known as the "Freeway Killer." In a few brief months, this monster and his accomplices killed dozens of people and practically shut down the southern half of America's second-largest state. Without a doubt, Bonin is the most vicious serial killer you've never heard of.

William Bonin, born in 1947, grew up in Connecticut, the son of compulsive gamblers that began neglecting William soon after he left the womb. His father once gambled away the family's house, while his mother, addicted to bingo of all things, would forget to feed William and his two brothers, who lived in a constant state of hunger, thirst, and filth. She would often leave the boys in the care of their pedophilic grandfather while she played, and it took the man no time to begin abusing them regularly the way he'd abused her. Young Bonin never had a chance from that point; he served his first stint in juvenile hall at age eight, where older boys began subjecting him to tortures including forced restraint and submersion in freezing water. When he returned home, he began molesting children in the neighborhood, including his own brother. He then served a stint in Vietnam as an aerial gunner, and logged more than seven hundred hours in hot zones. (Only after his honorable discharge did the military learn he'd found time to sexually assault two members of his unit at gunpoint.) The post-war years brought him to California, where he really began to explore his dark, abusive tendencies.

At first, it didn't involved murder. In 1969, Bonin went to jail for sodomizing five boys, having picked each of them up in his van while driving around L.A. County. That first arrest only got him sent to a mental hospital, where doctors—as one might expect—declared him a "mental disordered sex offender." They found brain damage in addition to ample proof that—surprise—Bonin's history of sexual abuse has damaged his mind irreparably. Despite this diagnosis, Bonin left the hospital within five years. The state put him on probation until 1975, when he violated that probation by assaulting David McVicker, a young hitchhiker. Bonin went to prison for the first time, and stayed there until 1978, when he was, inexplicably, released again.

Less than a year later, he was once again picked up for almost the identical crime—assaulting a young male hitchhiker. This time, Bonin walked because of a paperwork mix-up, and then he vowed that he would never leave a witness to his crimes alive again. He was horrifically efficient to this end.

The Freeway Killer unleashed himself for the first time on May 28, 1979, when Bonin and his friend Vernon Butts picked up Marcus Grabs, a seventeen-year-old German exchange student. (Vernon Butts had his own load of baggage—a sexual predator as sick as Bonin himself, he maintained that he was a wizard and that he slept in a coffin.) Bonin and Butts beat and sodomized Grabs, then stabbed him more than seventy times before dumping his body in Malibu Canyon. After this first "success," Bonin began cruising the highways around Los Angeles looking for victims. Butts often accompanied him on these trips, as the younger man had picked up a taste for violent, sadistic sex during one of his many stays in prison. Together the men started abducting, assaulting, and killing young men at an alarming pace, striking seven more times before the end of 1979.

By 1980, the denizens of L.A. were understandably terrified. A murderer roamed among them, killing at will, and police were baffled by the seemingly random attacks. Bonin punctuated the unease the New Year brought by abducting and killing sixteen-year-old Michael McDonald on January 1. A month later, on February 3, he and Gregory Miley, another sexual psychopath, would kill two boys in one day: Charles Miranda, fifteen, and Bonin's youngest victim, twelve-year-old James McCabe. McCabe was waiting for the bus to Disneyland when Bonin and Miley snatched him off the street. As Miley drove, Bonin killed the boy in the back of the van. The killers bought lunch afterward with the six dollars James McCabe had in his pocket.

As 1980 rolled on, Bonin accelerated his murderous schedule, killing three boys in March, another three in April, and two more in May. He discovered the vast majority of his victims on the road, picking them up as they hitchhiked, rode their bicycles, or simply stood there. The feverish pace stoked Bonin's homicidal impulses; once police brought him in, he admitted that every murder became easier, and that had he not been caught, he would certainly have continued stalking L.A.'s young men. He certainly gloried in the attention, as demonstrated by the folder of Freeway Killer clippings in his van, and the fact that he talked about the murders on a regular basis. To his friends, authorities learned later, he said, "This guy is giving good gays like us a bad name." Meanwhile, he allowed others in on the secret, recruiting like-minded criminals such as Vernon Butts and Gregory Miley.

Actually, Bonin's desire to involve others in his crimes eventually ended his deadly spree. In May 1980, the police arrested William Pugh, a young car thief who, they eventually found out, had accepted a ride from Bonin on March 20, the same night he killed young Harry Turner. Bonin had bragged about being the Freeway Killer, and killed Turner with Pugh in the car. Police put Bonin under surveillance, and picked him up on June 11 in the middle of another assault. Bonin's last victim had died only nine days before, on June 2.

The sordid, horrific road show ended with Bonin confessing his crimes matter-of-factly, showing far more enthusiasm than remorse. Sterling E. Norris, the DA who prosecuted Bonin, said that he "was impassioned about what he did. He loved it. … Listening to his confession was like sitting in a room of horrors. Here we are talking about killing kids, killing one and throwing him out like a piece of trash, then going back to get another. It made me sick." Such lack of remorse probably played a part in his eventual punishment: in 1980, after a blessedly short trial, a jury convicted Bonin and sentenced him to death.

Bonin ultimately killed twenty-one men and boys, though he's suspected in another seventeen deaths. At no time did he ever express the least bit of sympathy or regret for his acts, though he did admit being embarrassed about getting caught. He also capitalized on his infamy by publishing a book of short stories, and having his art displayed in a few galleries. He corresponded with his victims' survivors, at times commenting on how their loved ones faced death. ("He was such a screamer," he jotted to one victim's mother.) Bonin himself died by lethal injection in 1996, seventeen years after his initial arrest.

Putting Bonin's crimes in perspective demonstrates just how scared the people of southern California must have been. Ted Bundy—another California killer—is thought to have killed thirty-five or forty women between 1974 and 1978; John Wayne Gacy killed thirty-three boys between 1972 and 1978. Bonin, by contrast, killed twenty-one people between May 1979 and May 1980, his reign of terror lasting almost exactly a year. Of the other seventeen or so deaths he might be responsible for, some took place during the same period of time. Evil doesn't require ranking, but Bonin certainly takes the cake for quickest work by a psychopath during a killing spree.

≋ ⅄ ≋

Both Stayner and Bonin did their deeds in California. While the Golden State is certainly part of the American West, it is also something unique, its own animal. A multitude of reasons lead to this conclusion—the sheer size of the state, its huge population, the presence of Hollywood, the many natural wonders, the Pacific, etc. Perhaps more than any other state, California has its own specific identity, a part of which is the presence of more serial killers than anyplace else in the country.

Why this is remains a mystery, but the fact is undeniable: Charles Manson, the Nightstalker Richard Ramirez, the Zodiac, Charles Ng—all of these murderous men plied their chosen trade in the Golden State, many of them coming from elsewhere to do so. Whatever the reason, terrible people seem to choose California for their playground more often than anywhere else, much to the horror of the people who vacation and live there.

But human depravity knows no boundaries, either geographic or psychic. In fact, one of the West's most horrible sadists didn't hail from California; he called the New Mexico desert home, and in that isolated, primal environment, he created a house of horrors, a macabre base to rival not only the Golden State's worst offenders, but the worst anywhere.

Horror movies about strange backwoods clans claiming hapless victims abound—*The Hills Have Eyes*, *Deliverance*, and *The Texas Chainsaw Massacre* leap immediately to mind. These films get made for a reason: because the idea of a psychotic tribe murdering dozens of people in places where no one can hear them scream is just plain creepy. These fictional characters, crazy as they are, revel in taking their time, and utilize their isolation as just another sharp object with which to cut.

The New Mexico desert might be the most isolated real estate in the United States. It has certainly seen some events that people have a solid interest in hiding; after all, this is the land of Roswell and Alamogordo, site of the world's first nuclear explosion. Unlike the California desert, which sees traffic from travelers between Phoenix, Los Angeles, San Diego, and Palm Springs, the New Mexico desert is essentially on the way to nowhere— the great void between larger cities in Texas, Phoenix, Albuquerque, and points north. "Flyover country" never described any place so well.

Truth or Consequences, New Mexico, located smack in the middle of that great belt of nothing, is the sort of place that might appeal to someone like David Parker Ray. With a population of only eight thousand permanent residents, the town doesn't attract much attention for anything other than its strange name. (Which it acquired after changing its name from Hot Springs. Back in 1950, game show host Ralph Edwards offered to broadcast his show—

Truth or Consequences—on location if the town changed its name. By a vote of 1,294 to 295, it did.) For the most part, despite the area's reputation as a nice place to retire and vacation, T or C, as the locals call it, doesn't stand out on anybody's radar for much of any reason.

This isolation makes the desert around the city nearly uninhabited and capable of holding terrible secrets among its dunes. David Parker Ray took advantage of this remoteness and created a personal dystopia built on suffering. Ray had been born in New Mexico back in 1939, but in subsequent years he traveled far from his desert home. He joined the Army and went to Korea around 1959, where he learned to repair just about everything. He was married three times before the end of the 1960s. His third wife came with a stepson, and the same woman bore Ray another son in 1967. He spent the next two decades bouncing around throughout the Southwest, from southeastern Texas to Phoenix, where he worked as a mechanic at a used car dealership. He eventually returned to New Mexico, though, and began living near Elephant Butte Lake around 1989.

Nothing from this stage of his life would reveal much about his proclivities; he was never arrested for anything, much less a sex crime, and he was nothing but gentle with his children, even "mellow" according to his stepson. The only indication was an intense interest in talking about sex with his friends and colleagues. He also moved a lot, changing jobs over and over, while keeping to his area of expertise: fixing mechanical things. He even opened up his own auto repair business from about 1991 to 1994, calling it "Dave's Emergency Roadside Service." His specialty: rescuing stranded motorists on the dark desert highways around T or C and bringing them back to town.

There were strange things happening, though, things that might indicate what was to come. Ray's third wife Glenda, for example, supplemented their income when they lived in Tulsa through prostitution. He himself began supplementing their income by growing marijuana in 1983, driving from his home in Phoenix to Fence Lake, New Mexico, where his children were running the family farm. People who knew Ray also revealed his devious nature, not above criminal acts. He stole parts from one of Elephant Butte's park trucks on one occasion, resulting in a month-long suspension without pay. And though he traveled extensively between the five state parks in which he worked, he always got back to town for the holiday weekends, when T or C's population would explode from six or eight thousand to over one hundred thousand as New Mexico's citizens would flock to the town's nearby natural wonders. He took his daughter's friends out on his sailboat, and talked about them afterward. According to Byron Wilson, a state park officer and acquaintance of Ray's, he "always seemed like the old pervert who was screwin' his daughter's friends."

These warnings registered as nothing more than blips to anyone who knew him in passing. But his inner circle—his daughter, his girlfriend, and a man named Dennis Roy Yancy—knew exactly what the man was capable of. The sadistic, psychotic mind slithering around in Ray's skull didn't fully reveal itself until the 1990s, when his activities took a decidedly sordid turn. The same decade saw little T or C go through a little identity crisis of its own; crystal meth users began a beachhead assault on the town, turning the evening streets into a junkie bazaar. According to a 2006 article in the Los Angeles Times, even the town's chief of police acknowledges the town's "high meth rate, and extremely high homicide rate."

That's not to say that Ray didn't have some earlier problems controlling his impulses; in fact, there's good evidence that, despite the fact he was never arrested, Ray might have been indulging himself all along, moving around the West in order to keep ahead of suspicion. In 1988, for example, Ray was working in Phoenix with a man named Billy Ray Bowers at a used car dealership. The two men hated each other, by all accounts. Then, on September 22, Bowers disappeared without a trace. Without a trace, that is, until a year later, when a fisherman found his body in Elephant Butte Lake—quite a coincidence. Unfortunately, no one could identify the body at that point; it was decayed beyond recognition, having spent all that time under the water with two eleven-pound anchors lashed to its feet. Only when Ray got arrested for his later crimes did dental records reveal the corpse as Bowers'.

In March 1999, Ray's neighbor Darlene Breech stood in her kitchen pouring herself a glass of water. Suddenly, a young, hysterical woman wearing nothing but a metal collar burst into her house, screaming for help. According to Breech, "Her wrists looked like hamburger meat. She had beautiful long brown hair and it was matted with blood. She was dirty all over and it looked like she had pooped her pants." The girl, twenty-two-year-old Cyndy Vigil, then told Breech her story: David Parker Ray and Cynthia Hendy, Ray's girlfriend, had kept her confined for three days and nights, torturing her the entire time in the most ghastly ways. Cyndy somehow managed to get a key to her bonds as Hendy sat close by watching soap operas; Ray was out at work. Hendy slammed a lamp over Cyndy's head trying to prevent her escape, but Cyndy had fought back, sticking an ice pick into the back of Hendy's neck. Then she jumped out a window and took off.

Police came and picked up Vigil, then found Hendy and Ray driving about a block from the Breechs' trailer. As authorities began searching Ray's Elephant Butte property, the story assumed chilling dimensions: Ray had tortured and killed a number of people—fourteen by his admission to Cynthia Hendy, perhaps far more than that. (Some estimates run as high as sixty.) Perhaps more disturbing, he'd done most of this killing in his self-described "toy box," a literal torture chamber so disturbing in its contents that one of the first FBI agents to penetrate its depths, Patty Rust, shot herself after four days of cataloging its contents and sketching them for the evidence team. That trailer, and Ray's horrible acts, proved more than she could take.

The "toy box" showed an uncommon degree of regularity—of ordinariness—in Ray's practices. Like a workplace supervisor, he posted instructions to his accomplices on how to handle pleading victims, as well as directions on how to use the torture device he'd built. A large, handwritten sign named the place—SATAN'S DEN—and provided further evidence of an occult, Satanist angle to the whole affair. (Ray often dressed in black robes as he tortured his victims, and wore a black mask flecked with gold sparkles.) A gynecological chair, surrounded with tools of torture, sat toward the back of the trailer. Additional devices—whips, clamps, electrical prods, and sexual devices of all deviancies—hung on hooks and wall, like so many tools in an evil handyman's workshop.

These physical items, if you can believe it, weren't even the worst thing the investigators found. Ray made graphic videos of his torture sessions, capturing every horrific detail via multiple cameras. He recorded messages on tape to his victims, briefing them on the ordeal to come. He kept a running tally of the women he had abducted since 1993 on a clipboard next to his devil robe, separating them by date abducted and keeping track of the frequency with which he'd tortured them. (The largest number: fifty-three, on a woman abducted May 8, 1995.) He raped, hurt, and violated his victims in the vilest ways, with help from Hendy and his daughter Jesse, who helped him procure victims from among T or C's drug-addled lower rungs. And he did it all in that trailer, over and over again, without anyone finding out. The sheer volume of paraphernalia resulted eventually in fifteen hundred pieces of usable evidence.

Over the next few months, more details and victims emerged. His accomplice Roy Yancy confessed to killing Marie Parker, a woman he abducted from a nearby bar, back in 1997. For his part, Ray was never actually convicted of killing anyone, though he did take pictures as Yancy strangled Marie Parker. In addition, two more torture victims came forward to say that they'd spent time in Ray's torture chamber. In February 1999, just a month before Vigil's ordeal, Ray and Hendy had Angelique Montano in their "custody" for five days. She spent three of them chained to a bed in their trailer before Ray told her she was "going to the toybox." (Ray and Hendy never got the chance to take Cyndy Vigil out to their shed, luckily for her.) Out there, Montano suffered hours of electrocution, among other horrors too terrible to describe. On the fifth day, she somehow convinced Ray to let her go, promising she would never tell anyone of the ordeal. They dropped her off on a nearby highway, where she was eventually picked up by an off-duty sheriff. Montano told him the story, but he didn't believe her. Only later, once Ray and Hendy had been picked up, would she receive a properly attentive audience.

The other victim, Kelli Van Cleave, came to light after her mother saw a TV story on Ray and notified the FBI. Van Cleave disappeared for three days and nights back in July 1996. She knew Roy Yancy, knew of his violent reputation and willingness to hurt people; he repeatedly told Kelli that he belonged to a Satanic cult. She also knew David Ray's daughter Jesse, who dealt drugs in T or C. That particular acquaintance eventually got her into big trouble; on July 25, 1996, Van Cleave hopped on the back of Jesse's bike, thinking she was getting a ride home. What she got instead was a ride to Ray's compound and a three-day stay in his toy box. Eventually, Ray let her go, too, driving her to a friend's house. Van Cleave, scarred by the nightmare, didn't tell anyone what happened, particularly since most of the people around her at the time thought she was simply "partying" during the days she'd been missing. "I guess I've got lousy friends," she told investigators.

Once all these incidents came out in court, Ray's fate was sealed. He received two hundred twenty-four years in prison, to be served consecutively. Roy Yancy got twenty years for killing Marie Parker, while Jesse, Ray's daughter, got only five years probation for delivering Kelli Van Cleave to her father, as part of a plea deal. (In fact, Jesse had tried to report her father to the FBI way back in 1986, but the Bureau closed the case due to insufficient evidence.) Cynthia Hendy made a deal, too, and testified against Ray; in exchange, she revealed that Ray told her he'd killed fourteen people, disposing of them in the remote desert they lived in, as well as in Elephant Butte Lake's depths. According to her account, he sliced open the bellies of his victims so they wouldn't surface again.

No additional bodies were ever found nearby, however. (The statute of limitations had run out on Billy Ray Bower's murder.) And unfortunately, the true extent of Ray's crimes will have to remain a mystery forever—he died in 2002. But even if he were only responsible for the things we know for a fact he did, his place among the West's worst examples of evil would be solid. Knowing that he probably killed more people only moves him closer to the top of the list. But he certainly has some competition. In fact, all three of these murderers—Cary Stayner, William Bonin, and David Parker Ray—killed in western places that, under other circumstances, represent all the best things about the region. Yosemite, obviously, remains a symbol of the West's rugged beauty; the California highways still call forth their fair share of meanderers; and the desert towns of New Mexico, like their counterparts in Arizona, Nevada, and California, represent a everything good in the western character: work ethic, self-sufficiency, and the uncanny ability to build something from nothing. That Ray exhibited all these traits, albeit in horrible, perverted ways, makes him perhaps the most stereotypically western of the killers included here.

Ray was a cowboy, a frontiersman who worked with his hands to build and fix things. He felt at home in the deepest reaches of the New Mexico desert. That he brought such horror and suffering to those otherwise beautiful, lonesome landscapes, that he used his frontiersman's skills to such evil ends, doesn't make him any less a product of the West—not a fun thing to contemplate for those of us who love the place and its people.

CHAPTER FIVE

Out of Our Element
Death in Strange Places

The human body, to put it lightly, isn't built for some of the things we do to it. Sure, we jump out of airplanes, dive to three-hundred-foot depths, and hang off thousand-foot rock faces. But it's the plane that does the flying, and the tanks that permit the breathing, and the ropes that allow the climbing; by ourselves, without all that gear, we're pretty miserably equipped to do any of these things. And those are just the extreme examples. —we commonly jet all over the world in metal tubes with wings, sail the seven seas on massive steel islands, and every day, nearly every person in America, from triathlete to couch potato, travels at speeds faster than any but a few elite members of the animal kingdom, thanks to our beloved automobiles. Such feats seem innocuous, but think about it for a second: we human beings spend a lot of time doing things that, when the system breaks down, get us splattered all over the pavement in a big hurry.

We aren't *supposed* to do these things, biologically speaking; we don't have clinging claws or paws, or the ability to hold our breath for sixty minutes, or flaps under our arms that allow us to glide from cliff to cliff. We don't have many useful tools, really, except for the massive precision instrument inside our skulls and the capable digits on our hands. Luckily for extreme athletes the world over, our ingenuity is enough; it lets us get ourselves into nearly every conceivable state of physical distress, positions that—without the stuff we bring along—we would stand nearly no chance of surviving.

The West doesn't lack for environments of the alien variety. Scuba diving off the California coast, flying over the Rockies, hiking through a barren desert, or simply sailing the ocean blue—when things go wrong in any of these circumstances, they get bad quickly, and generally leave the unlucky victims in terrible, fatal lurches. People just don't come back from scuba tank failure at depth, or an equipment malfunction at twenty thousand feet elevation. And when the very air you breathe gets a dose of ancient gasses from beneath the earth, wherever you happen to be—in a cave, even skiing a picturesque western slope—the environment you know and love can get unlivable with sickening speed.

≋ ⅄ ≋

The Professional Association of Diving Instructors (PADI), scuba diving's largest certification organization, issued somewhere around 946,000 certifications worldwide in 2005, more than half of them to new divers. (PADI also certified experienced divers in specialized disciplines such as cave diving, deep-water diving, rescue, etc.) Surprisingly, this number represents a decrease in new scuba divers versus other years; in 2001, for example, almost forty thousand more new divers earned their underwater wings than did four years later. The fact remains, however, that scuba, though not as popular as it once was, still attracts a lot of people eager to explore the other two-thirds of the Earth's surface.

In the United States, the undisputed capital of scuba recreation is Florida. Technical divers get off on diving the caves and sinkholes of the state's central and northern reaches; spearfishermen and wildlife watchers check out massive groupers and other tropical fish off the Gulf Coast; and everybody takes a long look into the crystalline waters off the southern Atlantic coast, site of the clearest water and best visibility most divers will ever see.

California, however, doesn't lag very far behind in terms of diving popularity. Most of those who live west of the Mississippi get their first dose of ocean diving in California, either in the kelpy waters off San Diego or in Monterey, the Golden State's best-known diving destination. Cannery Row marks one of the more active scuba beaches in the entire world; though the water's a little cold for some divers, the climate remains fairly steady all year, with temperatures never swinging much above eighty-five degrees or below forty-five. The visibility's not too bad, either, and the exploding population of sea life due to cold water that wells up there, bringing tons of nutrients up from the briny depths, makes Monterey Bay prime ground for a nice, big food chain complete with a legendary apex: the great white shark.

But you don't have to meet up with Jaws to die diving the Pacific. In fact, scuba diving itself will kill you just as dead as a twenty-foot shark if you don't do it right. After all, it does involve toting around an artificial breathing system in a radically hostile environment. One little hang-up is all you need to find yourself breathing vapors.

If the phrase "hostile environment" seems a bit extreme, please keep in mind the plain and simple fact that you cannot *breathe* down there without help. After one minute in that circumstance, your lungs are on fire, at best. At worst, you're already on your way to passing out, or gulping water into your lungs. After two minutes, most people are unconscious, and after three almost 100 percent are, except for a couple of navy SEALs and magicians locked in glass boxes for obscene lengths of time (and those guys are probably cheating anyway). Anywhere you go that lacks the most basic requirement for human sustenance certainly qualifies as hostile, even if you can get there with relatively little trouble.

About one hundred people die every year in American scuba accidents; since California draws so many divers, an inordinate number of those deaths happen in that state's waters. And most of them, while tragic, involve little things that could have been prevented or dealt with by cooler heads. Getting hung up in underwater obstacles—fishing line, kelp, caverns—gets people killed most frequently. And some obstacles are bigger than others; in June 2005, scuba instructor Steven Donathan died after getting trapped in the *Yukon*, a 366-foot warship the city of San Diego sank to the bottom of Mission Bay in order to create an artificial diving and wildlife reef.

Steve Donathan, like so many proficient outdoorspeople before him, suffered from one fundamental problem: too much faith in his own abilities. He must have, since he disregarded some of diving's most sacred rules as he wound his way into the wreck until he couldn't get himself out again.

Scuba diving comes in a number of different varieties. Perusing pretty reefs and taking fish photos in tropical locales is probably the best-known, and most accessible type. Diving shipwrecks, on the other hand, falls firmly into the "technical diving" category, which covers those dives that require a bit more training, more specialized gear, and attention to detail. Forget or neglect any of these things, and a technical dive will just as soon kill you as look at you.

Technical diving includes wreck diving, cave diving, diving deep with different mixtures of gases, using various tools at depth, and a number of other skills that go beyond simply swimming around and looking at the pretty fishes. At its root, technical diving teaches its adherents to delve ever deeper into alien realms, to places where one false move can mean life and death. Think, for example, about this nightmare scenario: you've got ninety minutes' worth of air in your tanks for a sweet little wreck dive in pretty shallow water—let's say, fifty feet, so there's no problem with the bends. You get into the wreck a ways, and before you know it, sixty minutes have passed. No problem—it's only twenty minutes back out to the surface. Plenty of time. Nonetheless, you turn around to leave, just to make sure you'll get up in time, and suddenly realize that you don't remember whether you swam in through the left-hand passage or the right. You eventually figure things out at the fork, but it takes you fifteen minutes. Twenty minutes to the surface, and only fifteen left in your tanks. Five minutes with no air is about three minutes too long for most everyone who has not had training in holding their breath for extended periods. Throw in the near-certain panic, along with the effort of swimming for an hour and a half, and it becomes clear that underestimating a technical dive has seriously fatal consequences.

Technical divers get around snafus like this one by planning every minute detail of their adventures, accounting for every breath of air and building double- and triple-redundancies into their gear. Run out of main-tank air? Go to the secondary tank. Regulator not working properly? Grab the backup. The worst-case scenarios have all occurred, and the best divers hit the water with all the bases covered. Occasionally, though, a sense of invincibility afflicts technical divers just as it afflicts people who jump out of airplanes a lot, or hikers as comfortable in the wilderness as they are in their living rooms. Lots of experience can make you lazy; after so many difficult dives done so well, the urgency of preparation begins to wear off. "How bad can it get?" they begin to think. "I've been on this exact dive a thousand times before, and it always goes off without a hitch. Maybe I don't need my third backup tank/guideline/ extra diving knife this time, since I didn't need it a thousand times before." As you might expect, thinking of this variety has some tragic consequences when circumstances line up against the cocky, unprepared diver in question.

Unfortunately for Steve Donathan, he was a very good diver, and an exceptionally cocky one. His skill, according to an investigation by the San Diego police department, made him complacent. The result: a slew of errors and omissions that ended with Donathan stranded inside a sealed boiler room eighty feet underwater, becoming the first fatality inside the *Yukon* since its sinking in July of 2000. According to Donathan's companion Vicky Samuel, he would have been embarrassed to die on such a simple (for him) dive.

Ships like the *Yukon* are a scuba diver's paradise—purposeful wrecks placed on the ocean floor to entertain both the fish and the people willing to descend for a visit. These "artificial reefs" lie all over the California coast, most predominantly off Mission Beach near San Diego. Wreck Alley consists of five separate wrecks in close proximity to each other, four of which were sunk on purpose to augment the underwater environment. Only the NOSC tower, plowed over by a storm in 1988, hit the ocean bottom by accident; the *El Rey, Shooter's Fantasy, Ruby E.,* and *Yukon* all met their final fate after long careers plying the world's oceans, and now have a guaranteed lifetime run as tourist attractions and wildlife sanctuaries.

Not that everything went exactly as planned in the *Yukon*'s case. The ship started its life as a Canadian destroyer in 1963, and served well for the next thirty years. San Diego bought the ship for $235,000, in order to expand its artificial reef. The *Yukon* itself would become the largest artificial reef off the West Coast, after a thorough cleaning and removal of all toxic substances in the old vessel.

On July 13, the cleaning job completed, tow ships pulled the *Yukon* into position almost two miles west of Mission Beach, where explosives were to sink the ship over the next day or two. Much fanfare accompanied the upcoming sink; the city had planned a fireworks show and party to coincide with the event, complete with a ceremonial button—pushing to blow the eight putty charges on the ship's hull. The point of the controlled sink was to put the ship rightside-up on the sea floor and allow easy access via massive holes in the ship's hull. But for some reason that no one could quite figure out, the ship began sinking a bit early, all by itself, as five hundred gallons of water rushed into its belly every minute. The bow went down, the stern levered thirty feet up out of the water, and the big tilt began.

Before it was over, the *Yukon* dropped down to one hundred feet and rested on its left side. Instead of leaving the top of the ship just thirty feet below the surface, it crested at sixty feet or so, complicating the wreck and cutting down its accessibility. The whole thing turned out to be something of a black eye for the San Diego Oceans Foundation, the organization that brought the ship to San Diego, but ultimately it did little to scare people off the wreck, and the *Yukon* remains one of the most popular dives in the country.

Steven Donathan had dived the *Yukon* many times before June 25. He was certainly comfortable underwater, even going so far as to say that he had gills, not lungs. He came to diving relatively recently, in 1999, but wasted no time getting into the swing of it. Over the next two years he accumulated an impressive twenty diving certifications, becoming so proficient and passionate that he opened a dive shop and began instructing other people. He didn't make a lot of money doing it, but enthusiasm carried the day. He even discovered a wrecked B-36 bomber that crashed off Mission Beach in 1952, and led a History Channel film crew to the wreck 267 feet under the ocean. Steve was a technical diver—most interested in deep, difficult dives such as wrecks and caves. When he taught, however, he drilled his students on safety and mental preparation—two skills that, over a ton of technical dives, had served him well.

On June 25, Donathan struck out for the *Yukon* with his eighteen-year-old student Joseph Dangelmaier. They hit the water with eighteen other divers and four crewmembers, one of which listed Donathan as a "basic skin diver" on the dive roster as a joke. Trouble started once they reached the wreck, and Steve decided to penetrate—that is, swim into the ship's bowels—deeper than

Dangelmaier was comfortable going.

The *Yukon*, pitched over on its side, presents a number of unique and dangerous obstacles to divers. First off, it sank completely intact; whereas many wrecks burn before they go down, leaving prominent gaps in their structure, the *Yukon* is still riddled with passages, doors, and rooms to get lost in, its internal structure still mostly undamaged. What's more, the sideways orientation of the ship is liable to throw a diver off kilter, as the floors are the walls, the walls are the ceiling, etc. Add the warren of passages to this potential for disorientation, and you have a very real possibility of getting lost down there, no matter how many tough wreck penetrations are under your belt. Good divers—both beginners and experts—avoid this fate by using guidelines, run from the diver himself to the wreck's entry point. Following the line back like a trail of bread crumbs, divers are able to get themselves out safely and quickly, thus allowing for safer exploration and longer dives, as you don't have to spend any time at all deciding how to get yourself back out again. On this particular dive, for reasons that defy comprehension, Donathan neglected to use his line even though he had one on him. His confidence in his abilities probably made the line seem unnecessary; after all, he had been on the wreck a ton of times, and thought he knew its ins and outs.

He swam into the wreck, and for a while Dangelmaier followed him in. But Donathan seemed intent on finding something deep inside the *Yukon*, something that neither Dangelmaier nor anyone else knew was down there for sure. Dangelmaier turned around and headed back the way he came, while Donathan continued to swim deeper into the ship. Anyone who has ever been diving is probably sensing a big violation here: recreational divers rely on the buddy system to get through their dives safely, and one of the biggest no-nos of the underwater world is to leave your buddy hanging. But technical divers often set out alone, thanks mostly to the tough nature of what they are doing. If everybody turned back when one diver had an equipment issue, few technical dives would ever find their way to completion. Thus Donathan, a technical diver himself, continued to delve into the wreck after his ostensible diving buddy turned around.

What happened after the two split up isn't completely known, though scuba observers have a few ideas. Foremost among them: Steven Donathan was headed toward an off-limits boiler room, which he had managed to access despite the fact that the door should have been welded shut. The room, judged too cluttered for safe exploration, had actually been sealed before the *Yukon* ever hit bottom. But someone—possibly Donathan himself, though there is no way to know—pried the door open again soon after the sinking.

Dangelmaier waited outside for his teacher about fifteen minutes, then headed for the surface. He waited up there for another hour, and when Steve still had not surfaced he called the Coast Guard. Though some area divers criticized the subsequent rescue effort—technical divers did not start penetrating deep into the wreck until the next day—the chances are pretty good that Steve was already gone when the search started.

Somehow he got tangled up in the boiler room's debris, or could not find his way back out, or had some technical issue; whatever the case, he remained in that room until he died. Subsequent investigation revealed that his tanks were indeed empty, proof that he'd almost certainly drowned; the lifeguards who found him thought he may have kicked up some silt lying on the pipes and debris, then become disoriented enough to lose his way. They found his body pinned between the wall and the pipes that crisscrossed the room, and brought it back to the surface the next day.

The really tragic thing about Donathan's death—its preventability—drives home the point that accidents underwater, like outdoor accidents above water, usually result from an intersection of bad decisions and lack of preparation, made all the worse by bad luck and lack of cooperation from the environment. Accidents like his are blessedly rare, given the number of people out there doing the same thing, even taking the same chances and making similar mistakes. But not preparing, not treating the natural world with the respect it deserves, removes the safety net that years of human experience has taught us we need to survive under those circumstances. Sometimes that net doesn't come into play; when it does, embarrassment and maybe some discomfort might come to pass. But terrible fates like Donathan's generally don't.

Sometimes, however, this safety net breaks down through no fault of the victim. Outdoor accidents, particularly accidents involving a lack of oxygen, require a quick response—after all, people who have scuba accidents generally haven't been breathing for a few minutes already. Ten minutes spent waiting for an ambulance, for example, will make an emergency situation far worse; throw in a few more snafus on top of a time crunch, and a simple accident can mutate into tragedy double quick.

Such was the case for Mollie Suh Yaley, a dive instructor from Aptos. Yaley had just finished conducting a diving lesson near Cannery Row during the summer of 2002, and somehow managed to slip under the water. Stranger still, she went under only five yards away from the student she was instructing, who began calling for help. Other divers found her after a few minutes, meaning she had enough time down there to go unconscious and come within a hair of death. Her rescuers rushed her to the beach, where police and firemen were waiting. Unfortunately, the paramedics hadn't arrived yet.

No one really knew why Yaley went under, which is the case in most scuba diving accidents. Visibility underwater isn't very good to begin with, and since her only dive companion was an inexperienced student, she didn't have the benefit of an immediate response to her plight. Once some problem does happen, even a momentary lapse in concentration can mean too much time under the water and empty air tanks. Whatever happened to Yaley, ironically enough, happened in only fifteen feet of water—only a bit deeper than your typical diving pool.

Yaley had no pulse, so the personnel on the scene started giving her CPR. Unfortunately, they would have to do so for about fifteen minutes, as it took paramedics Bruce Faucett and Al Martorella that long to get there. Part of the problem stemmed from the fact that just that day, American Medical Response, the local ambulance company, was doing some maintenance on its system. The 9-1-1 operator who took the call, according to the *Monterey Herald*, tried to send the call in via the off-line computer system first, and didn't realize that the computers were down until eight minutes later. After calling for the ambulance on the phone, another five or six minutes passed before the paramedics made the scene—despite the fact that they were stationed only two miles away, at the Pacific Grove Fire Department.

When the paramedics did arrive, they proceeded to spend a little more than twenty minutes trying to revive the driver. When this didn't work, the paramedic in charge—Faucett—declared her dead, a strange thing to do given that he had not checked with any doctor at any hospital before doing so. If he had, he might have been told that patients who suffer from hypothermia—as Yaley, who'd just spent all that time in the cold Monterrey water probably suffered from— often recover from life-threatening drowning episodes, as the body's drop in temperature helps keep things stable until the victim warms up. Despite this fact, the paramedic declared Mollie dead, and stopped CPR. When he called that information in to the hospital, the doctor on the other end, not surprisingly, told him to get his posterior in gear and resume lifesaving techniques. Unfortunately, this admonishment came four or five minutes after he had stopped his efforts— an insurmountable time gap in terms of saving a life.

Predictably, the situation reached a terminal point, and Mollie never did recover. She died four days later in the hospital. In subsequent years more depressing details emerged, chief among them being that the paramedics who attended to her were both doing heroin at the time, and that their delay in reaching her, along with their horrendous handling of the situation, might have had something to do with the horse shooting around in their veins.

In 2005, Yaley's family sued American Medical Response for the litany of mistakes and outrages that day, and settled out of court. The settlement's amount remains secret, but state law decrees that the most they could have received was two hundred fifty thousand dollars.

≋ 𝄃 ≋

Diving wrecks or diving open water—either of these activities can kill you if you forget to show proper respect and take care. Cave diving, however, might just get you regardless of how much you try to avoid catastrophe, and how much planning goes into the endeavor. Under all that rock and water, when things go wrong, the implications are generally, not occasionally, fatal.

Cave diving doesn't have organizations like PADI out there promoting it. In fact, the people who do it often try to talk other divers out of following in their footsteps. With good reason—according to some estimates, every cave diver with at least five years' experience has helped to pull at least one body from the dark depths. Sheck Exley, the best-known cave diver ever, said he made thirty-six such recoveries, before he himself died in a thousand-foot Mexican pit during his bid for the deepest cave dive record. Cave divers pursue their craft with an obsessive combination of worst-case scenario planning and controlled recklessness, constantly moving deeper and deeper as their surface support crews prepare for disaster. Not that there's much those topsiders can do in the event of a problem; even getting to the diver in trouble without getting another diver stuck can take too long. Mostly, cave divers rely on a set of rules and practices that resemble those regular scuba divers do, but that differ in their number and importance.

The number of things that can go wrong during a cave dive numbs the mind. You can get lost in a million years' worth of silt, lose your orientation and start swimming up for down, or have rocks fall from loose ceilings onto your head. Hypothermia can set in from the bone-chilling water. Nitrogen narcosis, which happens when divers move too deep for the gas they're breathing, can occur, causing a sensation akin to drunkenness. If any of these things happen, the expedition will probably end badly. To make sure that it doesn't, cave divers run lines to the surface, carry backups to their backups of light and air, and generally take their time to keep from lifting silt or collapsing rock.

The result is a surprisingly decent safety record, considering the number of cave divers out there. In fact, the cave-diving community likes to compare their sport's safety record to that of bowling, though with tongue planted firmly in cheek. Still, the standard warning posted at underwater cave entrances includes a picture of the Grim Reaper standing over a skeleton wearing scuba tanks. The text above the Reaper's head reads: "STOP! PREVENT YOUR DEATH! GO NO FARTHER!" Bowling alleys generally don't require such signage.

But the rewards of cave diving almost justify all its insane risk. For one thing, penetrating grottoes that maybe five or ten people have ever seen provides a sense of adventure that not too many other activities can match. Not to mention that divers blazing trails in new caves are liable to find relics from ancient civilizations, hidden fossils, even brand-new life forms in those murky depths. And the fragile, gravity-defying formations down there, formed over thousands, if not millions, of undisturbed years have no equal in the surface world. That rush of discovery is enough to get quite a few people into the water, who defy the inherent risks in doing so.

When people meet their maker down there, more often than not, they are woefully unprepared for what they face. In fact, according to a report by the International Underwater Cave Rescue and Recovery Team, the vast majority of people who have died during subterranean excursions did so in serious violation of the activity's most basic tenants. The huge majority had PADI's Open Water certification—a wholly inadequate level of training for getting into technical dives—and very few had any cave certifications whatsoever. More than half didn't use guidelines at all, while eighty-five percent of them carried only one light or, in a highlight of stupidity and lack of preparation, no lights whatsoever.

The Channel Islands, a geologic oddity located just off the Los Angeles coast, happen to contain some of the longest cave networks on earth. The whole place has an otherworldly sheen to it, thanks to its relative isolation and wildness; of the two thousand species of animals to be found there, about one hundred forty-five make their home nowhere else. The eight islands lie at the point where nutrient-heavy cold waters from northern California smack into warm water from Baja, resulting in the huge and varied animal populations.

As far as the caverns go, Santa Cruz Island boasts the best of them, including Painted Cave, one of the largest sea caves in the world. The entrance vaults up one hundred sixty feet above the water's surface, while the cave itself drills about a quarter-mile into the island. Kayakers seek out the grotto to bask in its otherworldly beauty, while divers flock to it and Santa Cruz's other caverns to experience the best—actually, some of the only—cavern diving on the Pacific coast.

Unfortunately, since cave diving isn't well represented in California, California divers are not well acquainted with its dos and don'ts. As a result, people get into serious trouble under circumstances that do not really warrant it, by getting involved in dives that they have no business trying. It doesn't take long for the mistake to become fatal, either; in December 1997, an assistant principal named Peter Yan died after heading off by himself during a thirty-passenger dive expedition near Diablo Point. He went missing around two thirty in the afternoon, and turned up about fifteen minutes later on the floor of a nearby cavern. He died when his tanks ran out of air. He had no dive buddy with him, so the exact circumstances of his last dive will remain unknown; the evidence at the scene, however, painted a grim, familiar picture. Yan was diving for lobster, a common activity among California's better divers; that search probably brought him into the cave. Silt filled the cavern, which lay fifty feet under the surface. Those two factors would have made visibility virtually nil, even though Yan carried two flashlights with him and, according to his brother James, knew how to handle himself under stressful circumstances.

But another familiar theme shows up here, too: Yan had more than five hundred dives under his belt, which might have been enough to breed the fatal hubris that killed Steve Donathan in the *Yukon*. However well he might have handled himself in a tough situation, Peter Yan may not even have admitted to himself that a critical situation existed until it was too late to do anything about it. The autopsy showed no profound medical event, so the best explanation is that he just ended up somewhere he probably shouldn't have gone, and paid for it with his life. A terrible price to be sure, and yet more evidence that even the thinnest safety net is better than none, no matter how good you think you are.

Yan was not the only diver to die in the Channel Islands that year, either. In fact, he wasn't the only one to die that holiday season. On December 15, an urchin diver named Timothy McFadden died off San Clemente Island as he searched for his quarry some one hundred feet below the surface. And two weeks before that, a forty-five-year-old man named Oscar Urzua died in Channel Island waters. Not a good month for diving among those caves, seals, and sharks, to be sure.

≋ ⚶ ≋

Though diving in caves will certainly take you into a foreign environment, those subterranean spaces don't need water to be alien worlds—nor do they need water to kill the unwary.

As far as strange places go, they don't get much stranger than the nooks and crannies right under our feet. Cave networks run under many parts of the American West, some of them huge—Carlsbad Caverns National Park in New Mexico, for example, encompasses more than one hundred limestone caves, running beneath 33,125 acres of rugged, largely untouched backcountry. If any word properly describes a cave system like Carlsbad, it's "pristine"—only under such circumstances can the delicate, intricate formations common in caves develop. Being out there in the middle of the desert certainly kept people out of the way for a long time, allowing those amazing features to build at a glacial pace for millions of years.

Cave formations resemble nothing so much as coral—spindly, delicate, and wondrous in their variety. These structures—officially known as speleothems—form as water makes its way down into the earth, pulling soil down with it. In limestone caves, that mixture becomes acidic as it travels, carrying tiny bits of calcium carbonate away with it and depositing it elsewhere. The result: accumulations in all sorts of fantastic shapes, depending on the flows of water and what random action the drips take when they arrive at their final destination. Some structures resemble popcorn; others collect in bristling pincushions that reach confounding dimensions. "Dripstone" describes the formations that occur when the water flows along cracks, slowly building into stalactites and stalagmites. And weird, bush-like collections of thin mineral fingers can grow to six feet in height when left to their own devices. Nowhere in the natural world are geologic forces left to work in such isolation; as a result, you will see things in caves that you will see literally nowhere else.

Many, if not most, western caves lie in backcountry regions away from easy access. This fact makes caving accidents all the more dangerous, as help isn't generally a hop, skip, or jump away. In the best cases, cave explorers can overcome this isolation with quick thinking and quick action, even when the situation seems dire. In March 2006, for example, David Shipman fell into a fifty-foot pit while exploring an unnamed cave in Arizona's Huachuca Mountains near Tucson. The cave's entrance, a three-foot tall, fifteen-inch wide cut in the rock, lies at the end of a thirty-minute climb, which can only be reached after a twenty-minute drive over a dirt road. Yet even with all this extra travel, around one hundred seventy people turned out to rescue Shipman once his friends called out for help.

Not that the rescue was easy. Shipman, who had been searching for a camera memory card lost during a previous trip, separated from his two friends and hiked back into the cave and through a couple of rooms, until the fifty-foot shaft he fell into opened up at his feet. Once he was found, it took the rescuers about twelve hours to extract him on a gurney, keeping him immobile. But they did succeed, and Shipman pulled through.

Charles Johnson wasn't so lucky. In fact, nearly every aspect of Johnson's story lies in direct opposition to Shipman's. The cave he died in while exploring back in November 1993 wasn't some backcountry hole; rather, Utah's Logan Cave is a fairly open cavern, not far from the road he and his Boy Scout troop used to reach their destination. It burrows about four thousand feet into the mountain above it, and rises to seventy feet in height at some points—hardly the tight-squeeze danger zone that David Shipman took on.

Johnson didn't fall a tremendous distance, either; the ledge he fell from stood only six or eight feet above the cavern floor. Unfortunately, that distance proved enough. His head and stomach struck the stone-strewn ground, and he never woke up. Amid the screams of the youths he and brother-in-law Robert Ashton brought on this spelunking lark, Charles Johnson died. The poor man's *son* was even there, and witnessed the whole thing.

Strangely, it wasn't the first scouting-related fatality in the Johnson family—in 1986, Charles' brother Marc died when his canoe pitched over on the San Rafael River. For his part, Charles didn't seem to let this previous incident get the best of him; he continued to enjoy the outdoors until the freak accident that claimed him. Today Logan Cave is closed to spelunkers, ostensibly to protect the Townsend big-eared bats that roost up in those high caverns.

Utah boasts its share of caves, as do most western states. Colorado's mountains bear hundreds of old mineshafts, popular among cavers looking for underground access, as well as a host of tourist caves open to the public and set up for easy access. Timpanogos Cave National Monument, located up in Utah's Wasatch Mountains, is a three-cavern system decorated with a ton of delicate spindles and spirals, known as helictites. Utah also holds its share of old mineshafts, remnants of a rockhound past in which Mormon pioneers pulled silver, coal, and iron from the earth. These shafts and spaces present a temptation both to those who take caving seriously and to amateurs, who often don't know exactly how much trouble you can get into down there. The four young, would-be adventurers who stripped to their swimsuits and dove into the "Cave of Death," as it was known locally, fell firmly into this latter category.

Blake Donner, Scott McDonald, Jen Galbraith, and Ariel Singer all planned to make it big. They were all musicians; Blake had managed the most success thus far, at the helm of the up-and-coming punk band Parallax. He wrote lyrics and manned the lead mike, helping to bring the band a national fan base during the summer of 2005. They had already toured California and the Pacific Northwest, and the band's first full-length album was due out soon. Jen Galbraith, Donner's girlfriend, was a gifted photographer attending Utah Valley State College, where Donner and Scott McDonald also took classes. Singer, fresh out of high school at eighteen, had decided she wanted to be a chef. They had big dreams; and unlike so many of their drifty peers, they were making those dreams real.

They also shared that occasionally tragic flaw of the young: perceived indestructibility. Maybe they went into the cave hoping to journey into the unknown and find something spectacular. Or maybe they were looking for a cool place to hang out for a couple of hours. Whatever it was, the impulse led them to the Cave of Death, just outside Provo, at about three in the morning on August 18, 2005. Parallax had finished playing a show earlier that evening, and as the band and its fans milled around afterward, someone suggested the cave.

Police and rescue personnel didn't even know the Cave of Death existed; the local kids who did tagged it with the forbidding moniker. After crawling into a small entrance, explorers moved about seventy feet through a cramped passage, until they came to a small pool. Under that water, a fifteen-foot passage led to a small cavern, a hidden place ripe for exploration. On August 18, the four friends crawled down, dipped themselves into the chilly water, and prepared for the short swim and that little thrill on the other side.

Blake had probably been there before, as the cavern was a well-known destination among the area youth. One of the girls, too, had been there, according to Steve Hundley, a friend of the group who had dinner with them the night before. In fact, her previous experience had been a frightening bit of foreshadowing: she passed out from the cold, yet still made it out safely. Another local, Brian Lamprey, had journeyed into the cavern with a few experienced friends, yet still managed to overshoot the exit on his way out and end up at a wall of rock. He eventually managed to find his way out, but only after smacking his head on the cavern's ceiling a few times and coming close to panic.

They had one flashlight between them—an unfortunate start, given that cave divers, as a rule, carry three light sources each on their dives to ensure proper illumination. They also misjudged the temperature of the water; rescue divers went in with wetsuits to stave off the cold. (Most underground water is chilly enough to take your breath away—forty-five degrees Fahrenheit isn't uncommon.) What happened after they entered the water is, predictably, unknown. They probably reached the hidden room they sought, as they were all found facing the cave entrance, rather than the hidden cell. They may have become disoriented and lost their way; the passage might have been too tight, pinning the four of them together for the crucial seconds it took for one or all to panic; or maybe the cold water simply took their collective breath away and disoriented them just long enough. Then there is the question of the cave's air quality; at its highest point, the hidden cavern was only six and a half feet high, with only enough room for two people to stand and another few to crouch in the dark. At that size, the amount of air inside must have been pretty small. Whatever the case, none of them surfaced again.

A fifth member of the party, Joseph Ferguson of Reno, decided not to enter the cave with them. He sat outside in the darkness, waiting and wondering as time drifted by. After about forty-five minutes, he began calling friends who were familiar with the cavern, probably wondering what his friends were facing down there. Around six thirty, he was worried enough to call 9-1-1.

The search and rescue team arrived quickly, though by the time they got there the four were already in the cave about four hours, and had probably died long before. The rescue team crawled down into the cavern and began pumping water out. Before long the first evidence of disaster surfaced: one of the girls, bobbing in a six-inch airspace between the water's surface and the tunnel ceiling. Some rescuers speculated that she was the first to succumb and that her body blocked the way for the others in the tight waterway, which was only two and a half feet wide. From that point—around 9:45 or so—more bad news followed. Ironically, the officials said that had they known about the passage they would have closed it off to avoid just such an accident. As it was, they had to settle for walling it off in the wake of these four deaths.

None of the victims had any drugs or alcohol in their systems, though it is possible they were looking for a high of sorts. Previous visitors described entering one at a time, breathing the limited, stale air in the cell cavern until they felt light-headed, then returning through the passage via a rope that led from the waterway's entrance through to the smaller cave. Later study of the cavern also indicated that a couple of the victims had, in fact, stayed in the cavern for a while—not a fantastic idea when breathing stale cave air. "Bad air," as this type of oxygen-deprived, subterranean atmosphere is commonly known, can mean very bad news for cavers and spelunkers who find themselves faced with it. (To people who spend a lot of time underground, "spelunkers" are amateurs who are probably not doing things right down there. To differentiate themselves from these novices, experienced subterranean explorers call themselves "cavers.")

Bad air will make you light-headed and a lot worse under the wrong circumstances. Carbon dioxide is the most common culprit when underground air turns foul, thanks mostly to a complicated soup of water, rotting vegetation, and soil that works its way down into the earth and releases gas in the cavities it finds. In very bad air, there isn't even enough oxygen to keep a candle burning, let alone keep all a person's vital functions up and running. In very, very bad air, usually found near volcanic features, methane or other flammable gases can accumulate and make those candles—along with everything else that happens to be in the cave, including the person holding the candle—burn to a blackened heap.

Most often, however, bad air leads to other problems, rather than outright death from asphyxiation. On the National Speleological Society's list of cave-related fatalities and injuries for the last twelve years, bad air accounts for some injuries, but not one fatality. This is not to say that, as may have been the case at the Cave of Death, some of the other fatalities on the list—falls while rappelling, people getting lost or stuck underground, etc.—might not have come about as a result of breathing bad air. The four who died on August 18 most likely breathed some bad air in that cave, possibly on purpose. That air might very well have drowned them.

Bad air doesn't always stay underground, either. In 2006, three people died at Mammoth Mountain Ski Area in California, that state's biggest snow hill and a great place to put ski to powder, as a result of gas venting from the mountain's gaseous, belching interior.

The 2006 snow season at Mammoth Mountain was deep—the deepest in the resort's history, with a record fifty-two feet of snow falling through April 6. The season was set to extend all the way through July 4, with twenty feet of snow on the ground and more falling from the sky every day. To skiers around California, however, that year proved one of the deadliest on record—

by the end of it, thirteen people died in various accidents around the state, with eight of those fatalities happening at Mammoth Mountain. Most, as you might expect, involved avalanches or collisions—the unfortunate events that typically afflict an unlucky few on the slopes every year. At Mammoth Mountain on April 6, however, a different kind of scourge stalked the slopes: massive concentrations of carbon dioxide and other volcanic gases collecting via a vent under the snow blanket.

These vents, otherwise known as fumaroles, pop up through the ground all over Mammoth Mountain, venting subterranean vapor from miles below the surface. This particular vent had been working overtime during the record-breaking snows, so much so that the gasses formed a massive pocket beneath the powder as the underlying snow melted. The six-foot vent lay just off the Christmas Bowl, one of the more popular runs on the mountain. Gaseous heat melted the snow all the way up to twenty-one feet off the ground, creating an airtight envelope filled to the brim with unbreathable gas.

"Unbreathable" might even be too mild a word for that particular gas pocket. What lurked down there came from deep within the earth, places that would instantly kill anyone unlucky enough to find themselves there. And the main offender: simple, everyday carbon dioxide that accumulated into a mega-dose as the fumarole leaked.

Breathing too much carbon dioxide brings on a host of symptoms that get worse as CO_2 concentrations increase. When concentration reaches two percent, the lungs start working harder, trying to pull in more oxygen; at three percent, those lungs pump twice as hard as normal, and other symptoms—headaches, dizziness, spots before the eyes—begin. From there, it gets worse quickly: 10 percent will cause total exhaustion and spastic panting, with potential death after prolonged exposure; at 25 or 30 percent, convulsions and coma begin within a minute, and death is a certainty. The air in that snowy cavern had to be at least that concentrated, if not more, as the only air in it came from deep inside Mammoth Mountain, a dormant volcano with a reputation for spewing carbon dioxide. In fact, at its southwestern edge, the mountain is actually killing stands of trees with CO_2 emissions. The soil in these areas contains between twenty and ninety percent carbon dioxide, while soils elsewhere on the mountain have less than one percent—a tough state of affairs even if, like those trees, you happen to "breathe" carbon dioxide from the atmosphere.

The ski patrol at Mammoth had set out to rope off the Christmas Bowl fumarole, also known as "the stinkhole," and prevent skiers from getting too close. People familiar with the mountain knew about the hazard, but the recent snowfall had buried the fences surrounding it under dozens of white feet. Two patrollers, John (Scott) McAndrews and James Juarez, were helping to position fencing fifty feet up the slope when the snow under them gave way. They plunged twenty-one feet down into the well of gas.

The whole accident demonstrates just how quickly the earth can kill when it has a mind to, and how capricious it can be in the process. Neither McAndrews nor Juarez saw it coming, nor could they have. Nor were they simply incompetents who stumbled headlong to their deaths; McAndrews joined the patrol only a year before, but had just taken Rookie of the Year honors for the season. Juarez, a five-year veteran, had moved north from San Diego, and by all accounts thrived in the high country, both on duty and off. In fact, he loved his job so much that he kept working even after breaking his back in a ski accident, and after his girlfriend—also a ski patroller—was killed in an avalanche earlier in the year.

The massive cavern under the snow simply swallowed them up before they knew what was happening. Witnesses heard the two men calling for help at first, but in just a minute or two they stopped, having been overcome that quickly. But within those few seconds, fellow ski patroller Charles Walter Rosenthal decided to leap down into the pit to rescue his comrades, carrying a small oxygen tank just in case. More than anyone there, Rosenthal probably knew what was going on; he had been working for the Mammoth ski patrol almost thirty years, and served as an assistant specialist at the University of California–Santa Barbara's Institute for Computational Earth System Science. He also held the head avalanche forecaster's post at Mammoth. By all accounts having a gifted mathematical mind, Rosenthal studied snow hydrology, or how snow behaves in its various states and formations. Unfortunately, he didn't account for just how toxic the air would be down there, and succumbed nearly as quickly as the men he was trying to save.

As the gas billowed up into the air, seven more members of the ski patrol breathed the toxic cloud and eventually had to go to the hospital for treatment. Another patroller, Jeff Bridges, put on an oxygen mask and dove into the six-foot hole to rescue his comrades, but quickly felt the effects of the carbon dioxide poisoning him. Luckily, his comrade Steve McCombs managed to hook himself to a line, jump down, and pull Bridges to safety before the mountain claimed a fourth victim. But Juarez, McAndrews, and Rosenthal were lost, their fates determined too quickly even for the brave action of the other patrollers.

Subsequent investigations revolved around whether the accident could have been prevented. Had Mammoth Mountain declared the site a hazardous space, there would have been additional rescue gear stashed there just in case, including tethers and breathing equipment. But the strange circumstances— the deep snow, the gas carving a trap underfoot, the incredible toxicity of that gas—seem to indicate that even if there had been emergency gear available, it wouldn't have made much difference. Within a few short minutes the three victims died; when nature is working that quickly against you, there's very little to do about it. The men were unlucky enough to stumble into one of those deadly pockets of the environment that man just is not meant to venture into without the tools of his ingenuity—whether they be breathing apparatus, wings, or rappelling gear. Without those protections, in a place like that, death is a near certainty.

≋ 🏋 ≋

But alien worlds don't have to be tucked deep under tons of earth or water. In fact, one of the environments we are least equipped to deal with—and that, ironically enough, we manage to spend a lot of time in—spreads out right over our heads. I'm talking about the sky more than fifteen feet or so over our heads. I say fifteen feet because that is about as high as you can get before you really, really do not want to fall.

Gravity pulls down all the time and everywhere at around thirty-two feet per second. At that rate, it doesn't take very long for a falling human to reach max speed—about one hundred twenty miles per hour. So, if you happen to find yourself plummeting through the air after, say, your hang glider folds up on you or your ultralight runs out of gas, you will hit the ground moving as fast as a Lamborghini on the autobahn, unless you happen to reach it before peaking your speed. The good news is, you won't move any faster in your journey toward pancakehood—air resistance will slow you down. The bad news—well, that's pretty obvious.

If there is one factor that unites every air accident, it's the terrible speed with which everything happens. From the initial hang-up until impact, the most time that is ever going to pass midair is two minutes. And that's at the high end—often accidents happen only a few hundred feet off the ground, and they are over inside of twenty seconds. That's all the time we're good for up there without our ingenious inventions.

Despite its potential for trouble, the air out West has its own special charm, and attracts people from all over the world who want to recreate in it. Paragliding, soaring, hang gliding, skydiving—all of these activities see some of their best, most avid practice in the western U.S., thanks to a whole slew of factors that vary from state to state. Arizona, with its calm, dry, and sunny weather, makes for great year-round flying with incredible visibility. Ditto for large parts of New Mexico and southern California. And the Owens Valley, up near Bishop, California, might just be the best spot for motorless flying in the Americas, as well as one of the world's best-known. The valley lies bound between two of the lower forty-eight's most imposing mountain ranges, the

Sierra Nevada to the west and the Inyo and White Mountains on the east. The amazing aerial feats accomplished there owe themselves to Owen's powerful, lifting airwaves, generated by winds coming off those massive peaks. The air currents create massive and sky-stretching lift, and have been known to push gliders, paragliders, and hang gliders to heights unheard of elsewhere. (The altitude record for a two-seat glider—44,255 feet attained in 1952 during a study of these waves—still stands today.) Conditions in the Owens Valley vary all year, but the experts flock there during the summer when long, cross-country flights of one hundred miles or more become possible. As the valley is wide-open and devoid of much on the ground, landing is relatively easy, even if you end up flying quite a distance from where you take off.

Other parts of California present ideal flying conditions, too, among them the region around Lake Elsinore, in southern California's Riverside County. In August 2005, paraglider Mario DeLuca took off from a 2,300-foot perch above Badger Canyon, and began rocking his "wing" as he drifted along, a common practice also known as a wingover. The day, sunny and temperate with decent wind, rated perfect for paragliding, a fact Deluca reveled in during the hour of soaring he got in before his final launch.

Paragliding involves flying a modified parachute, using air currents to stay aloft and move through the air. The sport appeals to all sorts of people interested in motorless flight, since it requires less physical strength than hang gliding and is a lot cheaper than buying a sailplane. It's also a bit less extreme than hang gliding, at least in terms of speed, but once something goes wrong with the wing—it is, after all, just a nylon canopy—the outcome is usually pretty dire.

DeLuca, an intermediate pilot according to the U.S. Hang Gliding Association, lost control of his rocking about two hundred feet above the ground. The paraglider folded under itself, and he began spiraling toward the earth at about fifty miles per hour. The man who taught him to paraglide, Marcello DeBarros, tried to tell DeLuca how to recover, but it was too late—within fifteen seconds, Mario had hit the ground. He died on the operating table about three hours later.

Such accidents don't happen frequently, but they are certainly a part of paragliding and hang gliding even at the uppermost levels of those sports. Walt's Point, located in the Owens Valley, towers nine thousand feet above the valley floor, just off the Horseshoe Meadows Road. Kari Castle of Bishop set the women's long distance record in 1991 after launching there, sailing for two hundred miles to Austin, Nevada. The 1983 men's record, since broken, was also set there, along the same route Castle took. By all accounts, this launch site is for experts only—experts like Bruce Wallace, who took off from Walt's point with two other gliders on September 20, 2002.

Wallace loved to paraglide. According to his friend, Kate McLean, "He was enthralled by it. His whole face would light up." He wore a number of other hats, too, most notably as the self-proclaimed "first employee" of biotech behemoth Amgen, a company best known for its work in recombinant DNA and molecular biology, as well as numerous big-name medicines. Wallace had worked in a number of positions with the company since 1980, and he had just retired from his position as manager of environmental health and safety.

Wallace took off from Walt's point around 12:45 into somewhat "active" air. Conditions were not hazardous by any means, so it is hard to know exactly what went wrong up there; none of the people Wallace flew with had any problems that day. But within fifteen minutes their driver—the person assigned the task of following the flyers on the ground and picking them up as they landed—couldn't raise him on the radio. After another half hour, she was concerned enough to call the local sheriff's office, though the search didn't begin in earnest until the next morning, when the search and rescue helicopters could get in the air with proper visibility. (Paragliders often lose radio contact for periods of time and cover a lot of ground; getting lost for a little while isn't unheard of. This might explain why the sheriff's office didn't rush out that day with both barrels blazing.)

That Saturday, September 21, the helicopters got off the ground, setting up a search perimeter. Wallace's friends also joined the search, chartering a private plane and broadcasting radio calls throughout the area. The effort simply grew from there—by Sunday, there were three helicopters in the air searching hundreds of square miles.

Unfortunately, they found their quarry on Sunday morning, at about 11:30. According to Brendan Pegg, a friend who had been flying with Wallace that day, "He was not deep in a canyon, or too far back in the mountains. From his position he could have easily made the glide out, even against a headwind." Why he crashed remains a mystery, but crash he did, and hard. He still had his wing attached to him; it was on a rocky spire, draped, without the reserve parachute deployed. His water bottle was still full, and all the medical evidence indicated that he had died instantly upon impact.

≋ 𝕵 ≋

Paragliding and hang gliding accidents kill a few people every year—in fact, 1998 was one of hang gliding's deadliest seasons, with nine fatalities reported to the U.S. Hang Gliding and Paragliding Association (USHGPA). From 1997 through 2003, however, the USHGPA only reported twenty-seven total fatalities, with only two in 2003 and one in 2001. In 2003, nine people died in paragliding accidents, the most in the last fifteen years. In all, accidents do not seem all that prevalent, but consider this: the nine fatalities in 2003 represented one and a half deaths per one thousand pilots. Among automobile drivers that same year, that number was around 0.022. So much for flying being safer than driving.

I'm being facetious here, of course; flying is, by and large, much safer than driving if you stick to doing it in a plane. That covers planes of all varieties, as the safety record is pretty good across the board considering the astounding number of flights that take off every year from American airports of all sizes. Whatever method of flight you pick, your chances are pretty good. Even if you choose to fly in a plane with its motor missing.

Gliding (or soaring, as it's sometimes known) involves riding a motorless plane on the crests and waves of the atmosphere. The sensation of flying unaided, *sans* engine noise, is like no other experience; watching the tow rope fall away from the nose of the plane and not falling away with it will make you believe in nature's power like very little else. But, then again, so will a prop plane flying through your airspace and lopping one of your wings off, sending you into an unstoppable drop towards Mother Earth. Gravity's pretty powerful, too.

Fortunately, when things go wrong in a glider, they do not *always* go extremely, horribly wrong. Since 1990, the National Transportation Safety Board accident database recorded 576 glider-related accidents across the country. Of those, eighty-five involved one or more fatalities. That's a 15 percent fatality rate—not wonderful by any means, but far less deadly than you might think given the fact that you are thousands of feet in the air with no engine in your plane when disaster strikes. By contrast, from January through August of 2006 alone, there were 159 fatal airplane crashes in the United States, most of them private pilots crashing their small, planes.

So flight is fairly safe, and among flying machines the glider is a bit safer still. But the worst still happens fifteen percent of the time. Like when Keith Coulliette was demonstrating some acrobatic flying for passenger Matthew L. Broadus near Peoria, Arizona, above the Turf Soaring School's runways. Coulliette worked at Turf, the company his father Roy owns, and was a crack glider pilot, proficient in flying difficult aerial acrobatics, also known as aerobatics. Glider aerobatics rely on the pilot's use of wind and air, rather than the sheer forces of horsepower. The results, however, are largely the same as what happens in high-energy jet plane shows—thrilling dips and dives, moves that don't even look legal by the laws of physics.

Carl Remmer and Bob Schaff had also taken off from Turf, though they flew in a Piper J-3 Cub single-engine plane rather than a glider. Remmer was over eighty years old, and had extensive flying experience, while Schaff had about twenty years in the air, and was training with Remmer that day on some advanced flight techniques. Unfortunately, the men never saw Coulliette's glider until it was too late. Just as the sailplane was coming out of a loop, the Piper Cub struck it, shearing three feet off of the prop plane's left wing. The glider took the hit on its tail, and immediately began to drop toward the ground.

The glider plummeted into the earth below at a high rate of speed. The Piper Cub, also mortally wounded, spun down more slowly, but the end results were the same. All four men died in their respective crashes, ending the lives of three very experienced pilots who ended up occupying the wrong space at the same time. As the planes were only about six hundred feet off the ground when they collided, people on the ground heard the sickening crack, then watched as both planes slammed into the ground, spreading debris over about two hundred yards.

Obviously there were a lot of potential trouble factors up there. Aerobatic flying is tough, precision work—one mistake will leave you in the wrong piece of sky, or send you spinning out of control even without other planes in the area. And though there is no need for age-based prejudice, the idea of an eighty-year-old pilot seems a little outlandish. Reflexes slow, vision deteriorates, and muscles freeze a little more in people that age—there is just denying the fact. And according to the accident report from the National Transportation Safety Board, both pilots bore responsibility for the accident; it seems neither one had properly scanned the sky for other planes. The safety report cited this failure to see each other as the accident's main cause.

Perhaps the saddest part of the whole incident, though, was the fact that everyone involved not only had flying experience, but scads of it. Keith Coulliettes took his first solo glider flight at age fourteen, and had more than five thousand flights under his belt when he died. Carl Remmel was a retired Marine Corps pilot who owned his own plane, and had flight instructor level licensing. Robert Schaff, with twenty years' flight experience of his own, may have been manning the Piper's controls at the time—he was, after all, taking advanced flight lessons from Remmel—but there is no way to know for sure. Regardless, three good pilots and one other person died as a result of those good pilots not paying enough attention, an example of the same disease of expertise that killed Steve Donathan on the *Yukon*. The end result: the deadliest glider-related accident in the last twenty years.

These ostensibly experienced pilots flew with blinders on, and it ended up killing them. Donald Engen's fate, however, classifies as irony of an even higher order: a former director of the National Air and Space Museum, former chief of the FAA itself, and retired navy admiral who received the Navy Cross during World War II, Engen died in the Nevada desert when the high-tech glider he was riding in smashed into the ground as a result of pilot error.

Aviation careers don't get much more storied than Mr. Engen's. He volunteered for service during the Big One as a dive-bomber pilot on the aircraft carrier *Lexington*, and flew missions during the battles for Iwo Jima, Okinawa, and Leyte Gulf. He helped to sink the *Zuikaku*, a Japanese carrier that assisted in the attack on Pearl Harbor. After the war he commanded the *America*, a one-thousand-foot-long Kitty Hawk-class carrier and the first of that class to be retired, in 1996. (The *America* is perhaps best known as the largest ship ever sunk intentionally, via explosives tests in 2005.) He eventually rose to the rank of rear admiral, and retired as a vice admiral in 1978. Ronald Reagan named him to head the FAA in 1984, and he held that post until 1987. The same organization would end up investigating the accident that killed him.

That event took place on July 13, 1999, about fifteen miles outside of Lake Tahoe. The pilot that day was William S. Ivans, seventy-nine years old and an officer in the Soaring Society of America, a post Engen also held. (Apparently pilots don't count old age as a reason to hang up their wings.) Like Engen, Ivans had an extensive background in flight, including more than 3,300 hours piloting gliders, at least 100 of those hours logged in the Schempp-Hirth Nimbus-4DM the men were flying in that day. The Nimbus, a German glider meant for high-performance flying, was no peach in the air, however; the ATSB report of the accident reveals that the Nimbus series is "particularly sensitive to over input of the rudder control during turns due to the eighty-seven-foot wingspan, with a resulting tendency for unwanted rolling moments." In layman's terms, yanking too hard on the controls can flip the plane over and cause a ton of trouble. These potential problems kept the glider's classification as experimental, to be used in racing and exhibition only (though in Germany the sailplane does hold a standard rating).

Everything seemed to be going well, according to eyewitnesses. The Nimbus was climbing upward on the excellent thermals common all around the desert West, when it began a hard downward spiral at about forty-five degrees. Sailplanes are by no means sturdy pieces of equipment; made of light, flexible materials, they are the kind of vehicles in which you have to take the maximum tolerances seriously. Too much airspeed will rip your wings right off, leaving you with nothing but a fuselage and a long, steep drop in which to think about what just happened. Same goes for aerobatic maneuvers; of course you can do them in a sailplane, but you'll only be able to handle so many g's in a vehicle that is flimsy in the extreme. Just consider these specs: the Nimbus Engen and Ivans flew in had a wingspan of about eighty-seven feet. A Piper dual prop plane, by comparison, has a wingspan of about forty feet, and weighs three and a half tons upon takeoff. The Nimbus the men flew that day weighed just 1,300 pounds total, despite its huge spatial dimensions.

Witnesses in the air described the plane's wings as bowed as it spiraled downward, its nose dropping into an almost-vertical line with the ground.

Apparently Ivans managed to stabilize the plane somewhat, pulling back up to forty-five degrees, but by then the damage had been done—the glider's wingtips began to break up as the wings pushed unnaturally upward, coming up in a bird-like, slow motion flap before debris started to come off them. Immediately after that, both wings simply sheared off, and the remainder of the plane plummeted to the ground from about nine thousand feet. Both Engen and Ivans died either on the way down or once their plane hit the ground.

It may be a bit alarmist to let these stories scare you off of gliding—after all, it is quite hard (statistically speaking) to get killed while gliding, despite the tales told here. But if you simply must get as close as possible to zero risk, perhaps ballooning would be a better fit. Giant balloons float thanks to the superheated air shot up into them, which makes the air contained inside lighter than the atmosphere outside, thus creating gentle, controlled lift and a quite pleasant aerial experience. If you've seen a hot air balloon up close, you know just how much hot air is needed to float a wicker basket with a couple people in it—those envelopes, as the professionals call them, can tower up to one hundred feet high and measure just as big around their middles. As is the case with gliders and other motorless aviation of every stripe, the ballooner finds perhaps the best conditions possible in the dry, sunny climes of the American West.

Ballooning is nearly as safe as sitting still; it's literally next to impossible to die as a result of a hot air balloon accident. From 1990 through 2006, for example, the NTSB reported just twenty-four fatal balloon accidents in the U.S., resulting in thirty-nine deaths. Given the hundreds of thousands of flights that went up during that same period, you should feel pretty good about your chances next time you board a balloon basket.

But under the wrong circumstances, even the most innocuous activity becomes deadly. Thus even the annals of recreational balloon flight have their share—small though it might be—of tragedies. The worst of these happened in 1993 over Aspen, Colorado. In fact, two major accidents that same day, within a few minutes of each other, demonstrate that even when you're floating along on the breeze, it's the breeze that ultimately decides where you're going to go.

Conditions were calm, if a little drizzly, the morning of August 8, 1993. Two Aspen-based balloon companies, conducting business as usual, were running tours about twelve miles north of Aspen, drifting lazily over Roaring Fork Valley at about one hundred feet or so. The two companies—Unicorn Balloon Company and Aspen Balloon Adventures—both had years of safe and successful operations behind them, a fact that would unfortunately change that morning when a freakish wind gust whipped through, grabbing both massive envelopes and tossing them like carnival balloons.

The wind turned one hundred eighty degrees, then picked up speed until it was blowing around forty miles per hour—dangerously quick air for balloon flight. The unruly gust struck the Aspen Adventures balloon first. The craft lurched suddenly, according to eyewitnesses, and crashed into some high-tension lines. The static lines sliced through the sixteen cables securing the gondola to the envelope, dropping four passengers and two crewmembers to the rocks one hundred feet below. It happened so fast that the pilot, Deborah S. Hodgden, never had a chance to avoid the worst. One minute she was flying her charges on a lazy, ninety-minute lark, and the next all six were plummeting to their deaths in the worst ballooning accident in American history.

The passengers in the Unicorn balloon saw the entire horrific incident. As they watched in shock, Pilot Suzanne Prendergast told them, "That's not going to happen to us," just as the same wind gust slammed into her balloon. The impact drove it backward, forcing Prendergast to find a landing spot quickly. She screamed commands to her ground crew, working hard to get her balloon down safely and avoid resigning her ten passengers to the fate she and they had just witnessed.

Luckily, the extra seconds of preparation Prendergast had, along with her own skill, averted a second, even more horrific disaster that day. She first blasted air into her balloon to make sure she cleared a house directly in her path, then proceeded to vent it off again. As she did, she shouted at her passengers to assume a crouch position to avoid injury. She herself stood as she guided the craft toward a nearby field and smacked into the ground about six times faster than she would have during a normal landing. As they came to the ground, Prendergast was thrown from the balloon, courtesy of a fence across the chops. But in one last bit of good piloting, she managed to open the envelope's top vent and release the hot air inside before getting tossed, bringing the craft to a quick standstill as it deflated.

The impact threw her passengers all over the place, but the only serious injury came when one of her charges, mother Denice Reich, tried to pull her kids, ages eight and twenty-three, out of the still-bouncing basket. The whole thing ran her over, resulting in major injuries—though she, like everyone else in that fortunate basket, lived.

Authorities hailed Prendergast as a hero, which she was. Deborah Hodgden, unfortunately, never had the chance to prove herself one. The wind was just too quick, and the power lines were just too close.

Major airline accidents are, thankfully, even more rare than recreational air tragedies. In fact, the annals of plane crash lore leave the American West practically untouched; there have been no horrific, massive tragedies along the lines of Pan American flight 103 over Lockerbie, Scotland, or the Tenerife disaster of 1977, a horror of massive proportion. In that tragedy, two 747s collided when one of them, in the process of taking off, slammed into the other, which was still taxiing on the runway. The accident ultimately killed 583 people, making it the worst disaster in aviation history.

For some reason—maybe good weather, maybe luck, maybe something else entirely—big passenger planes just don't crash out here very much. Smaller planes go down in a regular trickle, but the big airlines just seem to keep their planes in the air where the West is concerned, despite the heavy traffic. The last plane crash out West that involved more than one hundred casualties was the 1985 Delta Airlines crash in Dallas, which took 135 lives. California has seen only one crash of a similar magnitude—the 1978 crash near San Diego that killed 144 people. Arizona hasn't seen a major crash since the 1956 collision of a United Airlines DC-7 and a TWA Constellation over the Grand Canyon, which resulted in 128 deaths. Colorado had a relatively minor crash in 1991 near Colorado Springs, which killed twenty-five people.

California has seen its share of more serious accidents recently, although things could have been a lot worse. In March 2000, for example, a Southwest Airlines 737 arriving at the Burbank airport from Las Vegas accelerated off the end of the runway, smashing into a blast fence and a wall around the airport's perimeter before coming to a stop out on the street just shy of a gas station. The plane hit the ground 2,150 feet beyond where it should have landed on the runway, at around 182 knots, or 209 miles per hour. Luckily for the pilots who messed up their landing big-time, no one died in the crash, though two people did sustain some serious injuries. The worst-case scenario, 142 dead on the plane, plus whoever would have felt the effects of the exploding gas station had the plane reached it, incites a shudder.

This is not to say, of course, that fatal, catastrophic plane crashes have not happened out West recently; they simply are of a less spectacularly fatal variety, at least in terms of the numbers involved. Take Pacific Southwest flight 1771, for instance. "Only" forty-three people died in that crash, though its story shows, in tragic detail, how tenuous our hold on control really is in the air, and how easily one factor—in this case, one disgruntled airline employee—can disrupt our airborne passage.

David Burke moved to California from Rochester, the son of Jamaican parents. He had worked for USAir—Pacific Southwest's parent company—for fourteen years by 1987, and though he had been by all accounts a fairly solid employee, there were suspicions that plagued him, like the hunch Rochester police had that he was involved in drug dealing. He'd even been investigated for an alleged part in a local narcotics ring, though nothing came of the charge. Nor was an auto theft accusation borne out. But it wasn't as if David Burke didn't attract attention—he did, after all, own a house in the suburbs and an expensive Mercedes supposedly shipped from Germany. His brothers maintained that Burke did favors for "important travelers," who rewarded him with favors of their own, and said their brother sometimes ran with a bad crowd who naturally gravitated toward him.

Burke had a bit of family history to deal with, too. His younger brother Joseph had died of a heroin overdose seven years earlier, which dealt a mighty blow to the entire family. Then there were the work issues—like the promotion he'd been gunning for that went to a white woman with only a third of his experience. To him, racism seemed a possible motive for his not getting the position, though of course there would be no way to know for sure. It all made David Burke bitter, though before he was through he would become much more than that.

He got fired on November 19, 1987. Two weeks before, he had been caught stealing sixty-eight dollars from an employee drink fund, and had been on unpaid leave since. Burke's hearing before the Board of Appeals took place that day, during which Burke pleaded with the members of the panel for lenient treatment. He lamented that his seven children would have no one to support them, and that he was sorry for the theft; his appeals, however, fell on deaf ears. Burke's supervisor Raymond Thompson fired the man, turning him out that very day.

From there, Burke spiraled further downward. On Friday, December 4, for example, he held his girlfriend Jacqueline Camacho and their six-year-old daughter at gunpoint during a six-hour drive. He also expressed rage toward his former supervisor for costing him his job. Burke's imbalance ultimately brought him to a fateful decision: he bought a one-way ticket for flight 1771, the short L.A.-to-San Francisco flight that Thompson took every day from USAir's headquarters at LAX to his home in Tiburon. Then Burke borrowed a .44 Magnum from a friend, and used the airline employee route through security checkpoints. In those days, aircrews were not scrutinized closely as they passed through security, in order to save time and money. Additional metal detectors, according to the airlines, were a bit too expensive. And, as a "familiar airline employee," Burke breezed through despite the facts that he didn't show ID and wasn't in his uniform. In the end, he managed to get on the plane with his gun without raising any suspicion, and without being searched at all.

He waited until the plane was about halfway to San Francisco before acting. At some point during the flight, Burke pulled the airsickness bag from his seat pocket and wrote: "Hi, Ray. It's kind of ironical, isn't it? I asked for leniency for my family, remember? Well, I got none, and now you'll get none." He got up, walked toward the rest room, and dropped the bag in Ray Thompson's lap as he passed. What Thompson must have thought at that moment, whether he'd even known Burke was on the flight beforehand, we will never know.

We do know, however, what came next: just a few seconds after entering the bathroom, Burke re-emerged with his weapon drawn and shot Thompson dead. The on-board flight recorder picked up the sounds of the shot, as well as the sounds of Burke forcing his way into the cockpit, where he fired two more shots after a brief exchange with the flight crew:

> Flight Attendant: We have a problem.
> Pilot: What kind of problem?
> Burke: I'm the problem. (Two gunshots heard.)

After this, another gunshot rings out, and the pilot's groaning becomes audible. Then there is another shot—the one Burke saved for himself—and a loud, high-pitched whining the rest of the way down, probably caused by a bullet through the windshield or the wall through which the cabin's pressurized air rushed. It all took about twenty-five seconds from beginning to end, the end being when the plane began a dive so steep and fast that it hit the ground at around seven hundred miles per hour.

The remnants of the plane resembled oyster shells, they were so pulverized. Even so, Burke's note, the Magnum (complete with Burke's fingerprints), and six spent shells pretty much revealed what happened up there. The pilots, after they'd been shot, may have slumped forward on the controls, or Burke himself may have planned to crash the plane regardless of what happened and pushed things along himself. Whatever the case, Burke's revenge plot exploded well beyond the man he was ostensibly targeting, as forty-one other people besides him and his former boss perished in the accident. It was, and remains, the worst case of workplace-related violence in American history; in addition, David Burke is sometimes regarded as the most prolific African-American killer in history, despite the fact that he did all his killing in a few merciless, rapidly accelerating seconds.

Though the casualty count isn't especially high in comparison to many other airline crashes, the fact that one angry man brought down flight 1771 shows us how fragile an airliner can be. It's a lesson we have a better handle on now, of course, but it helps sometimes to see that all those security lines do not serve simply to protect us from terrorists. Sometimes the people most willing to kill are motivated by the simple thirst of revenge. Mix that ancient, bloody impulse with a human pocket in a hostile environment, and killing dozens is not just simple—it's almost a guarantee. Survival is just too fragile when everything depends on that plane staying aloft and functional, just as it is when your whole life boils down to the amount of gas left in your tanks.

CHAPTER SIX

A Record of Death
Historical Deaths in the West

ll of the events documented here so far have happened fairly recently—over the last twenty years or so. That is, they've all happened in a modern world full of convenience and comfort, seemingly removed from our wilder frontier days.

But what of those "good" old days? Just how bad were they? Did the San Francisco earthquake and fire of 1906 do that much more damage than the one that interrupted the World Series in 1989? The fact is, there's no way to know—they were both terrible and both did their own kind of damage. In death's terms, the famously destructive 1906 quake claimed seven to eight hundred lives, though some research suggests a figure closer to three thousand. In terms of physical destruction, only Katrina has destroyed an American city of such size so completely—the San Francisco quake demolished 28,000 buildings, left 225,000 citizens homeless out of a city population of 400,000, and did $400 million in damage (1906 dollars—in current dollars, that's somewhere around $8.2 billion). By comparison, the 1989 quake only killed 63 people, and ended up doing $5.9 billion in damage. Not that the latter quake was a slouch of any kind (7.1 on the Richter scale is certainly plenty), but that earlier quake—now *that* was a disaster, coming in around 7.8 and responsible for biblical damage.

The NOAA has kept track of all the serious (one billion dollars in damage or more), weather-related disasters that have afflicted the U.S. since 1980. During that period, ten events—four floods and six wildfires—have caused around $23 billion in damages across the West. In the same period, two hurricanes—Katrina in 2005 and Andrew in 1992—caused more damage and killed more people all by themselves. So did the 2004 hurricane season (four storms, $44.9 billion). As the East Coast continues to see ever-more destructive weather year after year, the West carries on in relative peace, spared major catastrophe. Further, of the serious non-weather disasters the West has seen lately—namely that 1989 earthquake and Mount St. Helen's— neither one qualifies as anything close to a seriously murderous event. The worst volcano eruption that the nation has ever seen, Mount St. Helen's, killed fifty-seven people and did a few billion dollars' worth of damage. Those floods and wildfires mentioned earlier, according to NOAA, caused just over one hundred fifty deaths combined. Tragic, to be sure, but certainly not in the league of Katrina, responsible for more than 1,300 dead, or the 1993 Storm of the Century that caused tornados and yard-deep snows along the eastern seaboard while killing 270. Compared to atmospheric horror shows like this, the West is having a pretty good run.

It was not always so. In fact, the old West got downright murderous at times. The casualty counts for some of these historical cataclysms pushed into the multiple hundreds; a few even got close to the thousand-casualty mark, a scale of bloodshed that would incur screaming headlines and massive relief concerts today. The largest of these is, of course, that famous San Francisco quake of 1906. But the rest, the vast majority in fact, are largely forgotten, relics of an era in which the West was a far more dangerous place to live than it is today.

Not all of the dangers came courtesy of Mother Nature, either. In fact, one of the West's most violent forces during the nineteenth century wasn't a weather system or seismic apocalypse; it was a religious movement, one that today enjoys a reputation for goodwill, charity, and all-around tranquility. That movement—the Church of Jesus Christ of Latter Day Saints—committed acts and engaged in violence that rivals the worst atrocities of fundamentalist Islam, Crusade-era Catholicism, or any other religious extremism you can name. And it all took place on western soil, mostly in and around Utah's Great Salt Lake Basin, where the Saints made their Zion in 1847.*

Early Mormon history is crowded with persecution and attack against the faithful. Founder Joseph Smith died in 1844 after a mob of one hundred fifty men tracked him to the Carthage, Illinois, jailhouse where he and his brother were being kept. American authorities from New York to Ohio to Missouri had issued threats and warnings to Saints throughout the 1830s and '40s, and

---

* *I feel it necessary to reiterate: the LDS church has moved past their early history and its violence, at least for the most part (though Jon Krakauer's* Under the Banner of Heaven *demonstrates that it isn't quite gone among some extreme practitioners). But there's no denying its presence in western history or its violent streak, as the stories here show.*

the violence directed toward them was often shockingly horrible. Such violent persecution raised a defensive streak in these early Saints, one that eventually found its response in kind. Smith called it "blood atonement," though it would take his own death for the blood to really start spilling.

According to Smith, there were sins so serious as to be unforgivable, even by Jesus's sacrifice on the cross. Such sins could only be erased, and the sinners saved, by those transgressors having "their own blood shed to atone," since the Savior's blood alone wasn't enough. Early Mormons—and some fundamentalist sects still in existence today that are not affiliated with the official LDS church—saw a literal element to this doctrine. LDS icon Brigham Young verbalized the doctrine of blood atonement again and again in his sermons; his statements leave little doubt that Young meant a literal bloodshed, rather than a figurative or symbolic one.* In fact, according to Young, blood atonement benefited those who had their blood spilled, as their sins could then be wiped clean. "I know, when you hear my brethren telling about cutting people off from the earth, that you consider it is strong doctrine; but it is to save them, not to destroy them."† "Cutting people off from the earth" seems difficult to misinterpret, especially given Brigham's other statements about taking lives to save souls.

The violent streak didn't last long. By the early twentieth century, the LDS church was already moving into the mainstream, and within a few decades the huge majority of church members abandoned the blood atonement doctrine except as a theological concept. While it lasted, however, Mormonism's violent impulses gave rise to one of the West's bloodiest episodes, as well as at least one brutal outlaw.

Orrin Porter Rockwell bears a striking physical resemblance to an Old Testament avenger. One of Mormonism's earliest adherents, he acted as Joseph Smith's bodyguard and as the faith's "Destroying Angel" through much of the mid-nineteenth century. On Christmas day 1843, Joseph Smith told Rockwell that while he kept the faith, he would fear no enemy; in fact, like Samson, he was told never to cut his hair, and no "bullet or blade" would harm him as long as he kept his locks long. And none did—Rockwell lived until 1878, when he died in Salt Lake City while awaiting trial on murder charges. Before that gentle end, though, Rockwell accumulated a reputation as a frontiersman, scout, lawman, and religious zealot through decades of combat against those who would attack the Mormons and invade their lands.

Rockwell's deeds remain shrouded in conjecture and legend. He may or may not have killed John and William Aiken, Californians who were moving

---

* *Young's sermons frequently mention blood atonement, and do so very literal ways.*
† *This quote comes from The Journal of Discourses, a twenty-six-volume collection of LDS sermons from 1852 through 1885.*

through Utah when Rockwell and the rest of his party attacked and killed them along with four others. He may or may not have attempted to assassinate Missouri governor Lilburn W. Boggs. He probably did fire the shot that killed Frank Worrell, the commander of the troops who killed Joseph Smith in Nauvoo, Illinois. Regardless of how true these stories are (or aren't), he certainly killed on a number of documented occasions, almost always to further the Mormon cause. His extreme methods elicited this description from writer Fitz Hugh Ludlow in 1870: "Porter Rockwell was that most terrible instrument that can be handled by fanaticism; a powerful physical nature welded to a mind of very narrow perceptions, intense convictions, and changeless tenacity."

Not that he didn't have good reasons to do some of the things he is purported to have done. Take Missouri governor Lilburn W. Boggs, for example—in 1838, Boggs signed an order to drive all Mormons from his state, by whatever means available. It read, in part: "The Mormons must be treated as enemies, and must be exterminated or driven from the State if necessary, for the public peace—their outrages are beyond all description." Fighting words to be sure, guaranteed to rouse ire in one like Orrin Porter Rockwell.

A year to the month later, on May 6, 1842, an unknown gunman sprayed buckshot over Bogg's neck and head as he sat in his study, two balls of which entered the left side of his brain. He somehow survived the attack, but his assailant was never positively identified. State authorities hauled Rockwell into custody in March 1843, though they failed to convict him in the attempted murder. According to Rockwell's biographer Harold Schindler, he never refuted the charge; in fact, some contemporaries said that he bragged about the shooting and regretted its failure to kill Boggs. Whatever the case, the Boggs shooting is simply the highest profile attack in which Rockwell most likely participated, though most of the other ones took place closer to the Mormons' Utah Zion.

Joseph Smith's death triggered something in Rockwell. "He boasted openly," according to Harold Schindler, "that with Joseph's death, the Gentile mob had eliminated the only man who could control him." (Gentiles, in the LDS lexicon, are non-Mormons.) During the migration to Utah, he fought Indians regularly, killing an unknown number; he also kept the Mormons eating antelope and buffalo on the trail with his crack shooting and tireless hunts. As years passed and the Salt Lake settlement became less a frontier outpost than a gold-rich magnet for the faithful, stories of Rockwell's exploits became more lurid. In one, he and two other Saints chased down an immigrant he thought might have been in the mob that killed Joseph Smith. According to the story, Rockwell, "without trial, judge, or jury," chopped off the man's head. He was also blamed for killing Almon W. Babbitt, even though the local Indians had actually attacked and scalped him.

Rockwell almost certainly took part in the Aiken party's demise, though just how much actual killing he did is an open question. In October 1857, six men from California entered Utah carrying gold and gambling paraphernalia, wearing fancy clothes, and riding beautiful horses. They were, according to Harold Schindler, professional gamblers looking for marks—in this case, the Utah Expedition, an army President James Buchanan had put together to keep the Mormons in line. The Aikens and their partners sought to reach the force and take their money; they would not get the chance to do so.

Instead, they wound up getting arrested and questioned by the Nauvoo Legion, the large Mormon army charged with defending Utah territory. They remained in custody for two weeks, after which the Mormons gave them a choice: go back to California, or stay in Salt Lake. They decided to get out, and on November 20 four of the six Californians set out for home with a small escort. One of the escorts was Orrin Porter Rockwell.

Everything seemed fine until November 22, when Tuck Wright, one of the Californians, stumbled out of the woods near Nephi, another Mormon settlement. He had a bullet in his back, as well as two profound head wounds "such as a dull hatchet would make." Later on John Aiken emerged too, covered in blood and sporting similar head injuries. The other two men who had been traveling with Rockwell, Tom Aiken and one Colonel Eichard, never turned up. According to witnesses, Rockwell and his men attacked the Californians as they sat around the campfire, clubbing them and throwing their bodies in the river.

What they didn't account for was Wright's and John Aiken's survival. But Rockwell and his associates soon fixed the error; a few days after the injured men turned up, they left for Salt Lake City. Between the two settlements, at a place called Willow Creek, the Californians stopped for water; as they did, two double-barreled shotguns began firing from a shack close by, killing both men. Their various possessions started turning up the very next day— local men were somehow riding their horses, wearing their coats, and using their saddles.

Rockwell's exploits extend far beyond these incidents. Like so many icons of the West—Jesse James, Wyatt Earp, Bill Hickok—the real things he did have been inextricably bound together with those he may not have. But the fact that he did everything he did out of faith, rather than personal enrichment, separates him from those other outlaws. He is the West's very own crusader, the closest thing it has to an avenging angel.

Whatever Rockwell may or may not have done in the name of his faith, the blood on his hands is decidedly light compared to the Mormons responsible for the Mountain Meadows Massacre of September 1857. On that day, an entire group of believers allowed themselves to indulge in the very evils that they ostensibly stood against in fleeing to the West. That day, the murderous and unreasoning mob was made up of Saints, rather than Gentiles. In perhaps the most terrible example of religious extremism on American soil before September 11, 2001, one hundred twenty pioneers died a horrible death at their hands on—ironically enough—September 11, 1857.

In the summer of 1857, a wagon train known as the Baker-Fancher party set out from Arkansas toward new opportunity in California. The party, made up of one hundred forty travelers, a thousand cattle, and two hundred horses, came largely from Arkansas, though along the way it had picked up a few apostate Mormons eager to head out of Utah for points West. It came well stocked for the journey; in addition to the regular horses they pulled along with them, they harbored at least one Thoroughbred racehorse, valued at three thousand dollars all by itself. The Fancher party cattle were all Texas longhorns, and rumor had it that the party carried thousands in gold among their wagons. For a Mormon population struggling lately with bad harvests and worse public relations, the bounty represented was hard to ignore.

It didn't take long for some in the party to become suspicious. The Mormons were generally known for their hospitality toward wagon trains headed to California; the Fanchers, however, met with hostility in Salt Lake City and in most of the other Mormon settlements they passed through. In fact, according to Sally Denton's *American Massacre*, the slaughter's definitive history, they were specifically told to break their camp and head to Mountain Meadow to water their livestock before crossing the punishing Mojave Desert.

They proceeded to head for the Meadow, not knowing of the area's other distinct feature besides water: its perfection as a death trap. From *American Massacre*:

> Surrounded by rocky outcroppings that provided cover for attackers, hills that afforded the enemy a bird's-eye view of the camp, and only two tapered exits at either end, it was strategically flawless for the site of an ambush. In fact, Mountain Meadows was known among Mormons as a 'preferred location for the quiet execution of unpleasant tasks,' according to one historian, and the site was the inspiration behind the infamous Mormon euphemism for blood-atonement killings—sending the victim 'over the rim of the basin.'

The Fancher party arrived at the Meadow on September 4, and promptly declared it the most beautiful place they had yet been. They enjoyed it for another two days.

On the morning of September 7, the trouble began. The initial barrage of gunfire left seven dead and twenty wounded, but the party kept their composure and circled the wagons quickly. From there, a standoff ensued, punctuated by periodic gunfire from both sides. Though the Fanchers weren't sure exactly who was shooting at them—after all, Indian raids were fairly common on the trail West—they soon found out: a pair of Fancher scouts had run into a group of Mormons who killed one of them and wounded the other. That surviving scout, known only as "the Dutchman," made it back to camp and told the party who was up there in the hills.

There were Indians involved; the Mormons had enlisted the help of the local Paiutes in exchange for a share of the booty the wagon train had in tow. The leaders of the attack, however, were high-ranking Mormon militiamen— among them John D. Lee, a favorite lieutenant of Brigham Young and hardened veteran of the Mormons' previous military struggles. The attackers continued to fire on the pinned wagon train until the morning of September 11, when Lee and a number of other Mormons went down into the meadow, ostensibly to negotiate a truce.

Lee told the party the Indians were angry with them, but that he and the other Mormons would lead them out of trouble. Over three or four hours, he persuaded the Arkansans to lay down their arms in surrender, though many fought to keep their rifles. In the end, however, even the apostate Mormons in the party disarmed and waited for sixty members of the Mormon infantry to lead them to safety.

The infantrymen quickly divided and organized the Fancher party, separating the smallest children from their mothers, fathers, and siblings, and dividing the rest into three groups. They proceeded to march the women and children first, with the men about a half-mile behind. After a while, once the party reached a long patch of open ground, one of the Mormon leaders yelled out, "Halt! Do your duty!" Upon these orders, every Mormon soldier shot the prisoner next to him in the head. The apostates then had their throats cut in blood atonement.

The women and children, hearing the shots, came running back to their men. They were shot as they ran, cut down along with the few men who survived the first volley. Then the assailants turned to their blades and gunstocks, smashing the skulls and slashing the throats of any survivors.

In terms of naked barbarism, it's difficult to imagine a bloodier, more nightmarish scene. A fourteen-year-old boy had his face crushed by a rifle butt; two young girls, ages fourteen and sixteen, were stripped, brutally raped, then killed after swearing to love and obey their killer (by some accounts, John D. Lee). Two adult women were run through with a sword at the same time as they held each other in fear. These are only some of the stories witnesses related in subsequent years; the others are no less horrible.

In all, the Mountain Meadows Massacre would leave more than one hundred twenty people dead, with only seventeen young children left alive.

Those children were taken into the homes of the very people who had killed their parents, though in 1859 they were all found, liberated from their captors, and returned to their relatives back in Arkansas. Debate still rages about the massacre's particulars; in fact, the LDS church maintained that the attack was in fact perpetrated by the Paiutes until 1999, when definitive archaeological evidence verified the contemporary accounts of Lee and the survivors.

≋ 𝖸̵ ≋

Perhaps nothing defines the development of the West, and its eventual taming, like the locomotive. Only this great carrier of goods and people made the large-scale colonization of the West possible; San Francisco, Los Angeles, and any number of other cities would have been impossible without it. As the trains steamed West, so civilization followed them; but when those trains crashed, the savagery of the accidents introduced an element of primal fear and power into even that most civilizing instrument.

The earliest train wrecks, as you might expect, took place in the East and Midwest, as it took some time for the rails to reach the West. And, once they did, five decades of rail travel had helped to work out most of the kinks. Still, minor accidents happened regularly throughout the region. In 1892, a head-on collision between two trains in Lander, California, left their massive locomotives stacked one on top of the other. Eight years later, a train in Oakland was accidentally switched onto a track with narrower gauge, curling the rails underneath it and flipping the locomotive over on top of the engineer and fireman riding inside. They died, though a quick-thinking engineer named Frank Shaw saved the passengers by shutting down the steam engine and averting a massive explosion.

While most of these wrecks killed only a few people each, some resulted in major casualties. In general, when the destruction spread from the locomotive itself to the cars behind it, a lot more people met their ends. One such accident, the 1904 disaster near Eden, Colorado, ended up killing close to one hundred passengers, and may have killed more if not for some extremely well-functioning Pullman cars.

Pullmans are sleeper cars that people stayed in during long cross-country journeys when train travel was at its pinnacle. Missouri Pacific's "Denver, Kansas City, and St. Louis Express" (or the St. Louis Express, for short) ran every day between Denver and St. Louis, stopping in Pueblo, Colorado, for an overnight. The Express clipped along at a healthy sixty miles per hour under the best circumstances, making it a fairly quick ride in those slower-paced days. On August 7, 1904, the train was en route from Denver to Pueblo, carrying a contingent of sightseers fresh from the wonders of Pike's Peak and the other mountains around Boulder and Denver, along with people heading for points east from Colorado. They expected a leisurely run—the route had that reputation—and as the train pulled out of Denver around 5:00 p.m., many of them made their way to the dining car to enjoy some good food during the smooth ride.

Heavy summertime rains had camped between Colorado Springs and Pueblo, and conditions were bad enough that the St. Louis Express's engineer, Henry Hinman, received warning to watch out for water and adjust his speed according to conditions. He did so, throttling the train down to around twenty miles per hour once he reached Colorado Springs. The rains were indeed heavy farther south, and local drizzles rendered visibility almost nil. The passengers weren't very happy with the delay, but everything seemed fine as the locomotive reached Hogan's Gulch, an arroyo seven and a half miles from where Fountain Creek meets the Arkansas River.

During heavy rains, torrents of floodwater blew through the gulch, as it was the only route for water draining into the Arkansas from higher elevations. The high stone walls channeled this runoff into a crushing wall, and on that rainy evening, it would exert enough force to destroy the only two things in its way: the road bridge running between Pueblo and Pinon, and Bridge 110-B, five or six hundred feet downstream, the single-track railroad bridge that carried the St. Louis Express on its journeys.

The road bridge went first. Thirty feet of floodwater smashed it to bits, which then washed downstream and damaged the foundations of Bridge 110-B. The St. Louis Express, its crew suspecting nothing, came to the bridge and began to traverse it. David Mayfield, the train's fireman and the only crewmember to survive the wreck, reported a strange swaying in the locomotive that caused them to increase speed in hopes of reaching the ground beyond the bridge. The locomotive did make it there, but as it did the timbers below gave way, dropping the baggage car, coach (otherwise known as the smoking car), and chair car down twenty feet to the torrent below. As they fell, the locomotive plummeted down with them, yanked backward by all the weight. The remaining cars—two Pullman sleeping cars and the dining car—came to a dead stop, thanks to an automatic braking system that halted them once their connections with the cars in front were severed. The people in those cars were thrown violently forward as they came to a screeching halt, but were otherwise unhurt.

Mayfield dove from the locomotive just as it fell, and landed in the raging water flowing underneath the ruined bridge. He tried to pull his friend Henry Hinman from the wreckage, but to no avail—the water pushed him back as the cars and locomotive hit the surface and generated massive waves. That plan dashed, he pulled himself up to the track and began running south toward the Eden depot one mile away. As for the survivors in the rear cars, they didn't know what was happening right away—the night was dark, after all, and all they heard was a loud crash from the forward quarters of the train. Only when a few of the men began moving forward on the track did they discover the horrible truth: there was no more track, and the noise they had heard was the rest of the train, and all its occupants, crashing down into the roiling waters below. Out of the one hundred fifty passengers on the St. Louis Express, those brakes saved more than fifty.

Those who perished probably did so quickly, though they most certainly suffered in their last seconds. The locomotive, being so heavy, simply sunk to the bottom of the arroyo; the other cars began rolling downstream, tumbling through the water until coming to rest a half-mile away. Passengers' bodies were thrown from the cars all during their journey, and in subsequent years skeletons from the wreck would be found downstream as far away as Holly, Kansas. In the end, ninety-seven people were confirmed dead, with fourteen never seen again.

The affair spelled dark days for Pueblo; after all, fifty-two of the victims were from that little town. Funeral after funeral moved through its streets, reinforcing the dark mood. One local family, the Thomases, lost three adult members, and four Thomas children were orphaned in the tragedy's wake. Perhaps because Pueblo was such a tight-knit, small community, the loss seemed particularly grave; David McHaffey, whose grandmother Nana Beck lost her husband in the crash, said that she had forbidden anyone "to even talk about the Eden wreck." Ultimately, the families of the dead all received two thousand dollars in restitution—about forty-five thousand dollars by current standards. Small compensation for such massive loss.

The Eden wreck was the worst of its kind in U.S. history up until that point. That record came close to being broken only six years later when, in 1910, a horrific accident in Wellington, Washington, nearly equaled the Eden in fatalities, and actually passed it in terms of pure destructive power. Two trains tumbled down Windy Mountain that day, thanks to what was probably the worst avalanche ever witnessed on North American soil.

Winter had been punishing across the region. Heavy snow held few surprises for the people who worked on and rode the trains of the Great Northern Railway, running through the Cascade Mountains and bringing goods and people to the Pacific coast. But February 1910 had been particularly harsh, dumping a foot of snow every hour during its worst storms. The end of the month hit particularly hard, with dozens of feet falling in the final nine days of the month, eleven of those feet in one single, snow-blinded day.

Two trains reached Wellington between massive snowfalls: the Spokane Local No. 25 carried people, while the Fast Mail No. 27 toted cargo and mail between the coast and the interior. Both were headed to Seattle, and both spent a few days waiting in Leavenworth before even reaching the Cascade Tunnel and King County. Now both were marooned in tiny Wellington, a burg almost completely populated with railroad workers. On February 23, snow covering the tracks ahead, both trains waited with diminishing patience.

The passengers and crews passed the time, hoping conditions would improve enough to let plows in to clear the tracks. Unfortunately, the incredible volume of snowfall made this impossible; the trains would simply have to wait until the snow slowed, and the route to nearby Stevens Pass could be cleared. Even the telegraph lines went down, making communication with the outside world impossible.

Over the following days a number of ideas for dealing with the situation were circulated. Some passengers, eager to reach Seattle, hiked through snow four or five feet deep toward Scenic Hot Springs four miles away. The railroad bosses thought it might be a good idea to back the trains into nearby Cascade Tunnel, but since an avalanche would seal them all into a confined, unventilated space with two trains belching noxious flumes, that plan was nixed. They eventually decided to simply sit tight and wait for the snows to abate. The passengers held a little prayer service, then talked nervously about their prospects before turning in for the night.

At about one in the morning on March 1, forty-three passengers and seventy-three railway workers were sleeping in the two trains that sat one hundred fifty feet above little Tye Creek. The weather conditions had abated somewhat in that rain began replacing the snows. The showers came down in great sheets, and lightning stained the skies every few minutes. The thunder echoing up and down the Cascades shuttered the snows and the mountains under them until something happened on Windy Mountain's peak, which reached up above the trains.

In the dead of night, the avalanche, its roar obscured by the thunder, came with almost no forewarning. "Relentlessly it advanced, exploding, roaring, rumbling, grinding, snapping—a crescendo of sound that might have been the crashing of ten thousand freight trains." This statement came from Charles Andrews, a Great Northern employee and one of the only people awake at the time. Not that it would have mattered much—the avalanche was huge, and avoiding it was next to impossible. The trains themselves had created the conditions for the avalanche; Windy Mountain's slopes were largely bare, thanks to fires started by the steam locomotive's cinders and sparks. The only thing left was a massive sloped field, on which blizzards could accumulate snows in astounding quantity.

Once they broke free, those drifts surged with apparent vengeance. The trains and everything around them swept forward under tsunamis of heavy, rain-soaked snow. Keep in mind that the typical steam locomotive of the period weighed in upwards of one hundred twenty tons; yet this avalanche tossed them off their tracks like toys. Along with those two big engines, the snow grabbed three or four additional electric and steam engines waiting in Wellington, as well as fifteen cars carrying both freight and people. Buildings too were torn up from their foundations as the snow rolled down, depositing everything below in Nye Creek. *(or Tye?)*

Rescue efforts began immediately, as the town of Wellington was largely spared. Soon more than one hundred people were combing through the snow, pulling out survivors and cataloging the dead. Some got lucky; one conductor sleeping in a mail car was bounced off the ceiling and floor of his car as it rolled, yet he was thrown clear as his vehicle smashed to splinters against a massive tree. Twenty-three people, in fact, survived the ordeal, though quite a few were injured. Of those that died, thirty-five were passengers and sixty-one were railroad employees, for a total death toll of ninety-six, including three railroad workers who slept in cabins swept under by the snow.

Because communications were cut off for so long, news from the accident site trickled out slowly; at different times, newspapers reported casualty counts of thirty, fifteen, and one hundred eighteen. In the wreckage, rescuers found macabre evidence that some survived the initial avalanche, only to perish in the subsequent live burial. One note, found in Sarah Jane Covington's handbag, read, "I trust in God to save us." Ms. Covington, sixty-nine, was headed to Seattle and her golden wedding celebration before she was killed. Of the survivors, four leapt clear of the carnage, while another six were able to dig themselves out. The locomotives' crews benefited from their location; the engines, though flung violently downhill, weren't crushed the way the wooden sleeping and freight cars were. They had a bit of breathing space, which gave them all the time they needed to be found or to dig out themselves.

Later train wrecks would mar the West's tracks, too. In 1956, twenty railroad employees died in New Mexico when two Santa Fe Express trains collided. That same year, the Santa Fe's *San Diegan* derailed outside of Los Angeles, killing thirty and injuring one hundred seventeen. More recently, an Amtrak passenger train derailed in Arizona thanks to the work of saboteurs who were never identified. That 1995 incident killed one crewmember and injured seventy-eight passengers. History shows that one hundred fifty ton blocks of steel gone out of control can make for horrible tragedy.

Plane crashes, too, have been rare in the West's history. East Coast states from Virginia to Massachusetts have seen seven of the top one hundred worst plane crashes in world history; the West, by contrast, has only seen two, both of which took place a fairly long time ago. In 1978, Pacific Southwest Airlines flight 182 collided with a Cessna midair, bursting the fuel in its wing tanks into a fireball that, according to one witness, baked apples and oranges still on the trees. One hundred forty-four passengers died, as did the two Cessna pilots and seven people on the ground, as wreckage scattered across four city blocks and destroyed twenty-two houses in the North Park neighborhood of San Diego.

Though it did not result in as much loss of life, the 1956 air collision over the Grand Canyon ranked as the worst air disaster of its time, killing everyone on board both planes and strewing wreckage across the iconic landscape. The accident brought about major changes in the way air traffic is controlled, and served as the impetus for the Federal Aviation Administration's creation.

In November 1955, another air disaster foreshadowed things to come when United Airlines flight 629, a Douglas DC-6B, exploded in the air seven minutes after taking off from Denver's Stapleton Airport. A bang deep in the aircraft preceded the force of the explosion, which tore the plane into bits before detonating its fuel tanks and engulfing the craft in a fiery burst. Forty-four people died as the plane simply disintegrated on its way to Earth, scattering across northern Colorado's Weld county, though much of it plummeted down to a sugar beet farm below the explosion's site.

The recovery scene, covered with twisted corpses, smoldering wreckage, and massive chunks of the plane, took on a hell-like glow as tiny fires burned up the remaining fuel. Flames shot back at the sky from a crater where one engine had landed, while body parts—feet with shoes still on them, unrecognizable pieces of scorched human flesh—were gathered and cataloged as best as they could be. Witnesses soon confirmed that the aircraft had exploded in the air, setting the stage for an investigation by the Civil Aeronautics Board, the organization responsible (at the time) for investigating aerial disasters.

Within a very short time, the investigators discovered that the explosion had erupted from something *on* the plane, rather than the plane itself. Sabotage seemed the likeliest possibility. Since the investigation had revealed a crime, an incredible cataloging of every stray bit of the plane began, eventually revealing, like a slowly forming jigsaw, a disturbing plot drawn straight from the movies.

It began with the smell of dynamite, or rather the discovery that some luggage recovered from the wreckage reeked of the stuff and had actually been burned differently than the other bags on board. Other suspicious discoveries followed: four little pieces of unusual sheet metal that couldn't have been part of the plane; a gray, sooty residue on that metal; and trace sodium carbonate, nitrates, and sulfates, chemicals associated with dynamite explosions. The evidence pointed to sabotage by bombing and the murder of forty-four people.

Though air sabotage has taken on a whole raft of connotations since September 11, 2001, it has always been around. Thirty-four planes have crashed as a result of mid-air bomb explosions, killing more than three hundred people.

Motives for these crimes run the typical gamut—financial gain, revenge, cold and simple desire to kill. The first recorded case of aerial sabotage in commercial aviation history happened in October 1933, over Chesterton, Indiana, and killed ten people. Two crashes in late 1959 and early 1960 killed another seventy-six people when bombs exploded and destroyed planes mid-air. There is some speculation that these explosions are somehow connected, as they happened so close together, though the link has never been proven; the second accident, in fact, may have had something to do with passenger Julian Frank, who bought one million dollars' worth of insurance before taking off that day. The bomb detonated directly under his seat, indicating a possible suicide. The fact is, however, that it will never be clear what happened on any of these flights, except that bombs destroyed them. No one was ever charged with a crime in any of these crashes.

The way people used to buy flight insurance may have had something to do with these bombings. Back in the day, it was common to purchase policies right before getting on a flight via coin-operated machines at the airport. You could get up to $62,000 in coverage, and six passengers on flight 629 had done just that; another four passengers had $50,000, while two more had purchased $37,500. Airport security wasn't as stringent as it is today, either—if you managed to get a bomb on the plane with the right insurance purchased, beneficiaries could collect on the policy quite easily. It was easy, that is, if you could live with the horrific, flaming death you'd be visiting on all the other passengers.Despite the inherent destruction of a plane crash, wreckage, along with tiny bits of evidence, still falls to the ground; some of it tells a story. Flight 629's investigators discovered wisps of suspicion in some newspaper clippings they had managed to recover belonging to Daisie King, a Denver businesswoman on her way to Alaska for a visit with her daughter. The clippings related to the woman's son, John Gilbert Graham, who was arrested for forgery in 1951 and, strangely enough, was listed as the sole beneficiary on his mother's $37,500 insurance policy.

In addition to that policy, John Graham, or Jack as everyone called him, stood to inherit a good-size estate, including a successful restaurant in Denver. (Though that same restaurant had burned earlier in 1955, resulting in an insurance claim paid to none other than Jack Graham.) That estate came as a result of Daisie's skill in business, as she'd run a few different companies and made some successful real estate investments. Jack, on the other hand, showed little promise; he joined the Coast Guard in 1948, and spent sixty-three days AWOL before receiving his discharge only a year later. Over the next few years he stole payroll checks and smashed into a police roadblock while trying to transport liquor across state lines, but eventually seemed to settle himself down, getting married and having two children by 1953. He managed the restaurant, a drive-in, and business seemed despite the rumors that Jack regularly stole from the family coffers.

Jack's deviant behavior didn't end there. In fact, by all indications Jack Graham was a bomb himself, simply waiting for the right circumstance to set him off. Graham's half-sister—the one his mother was heading to Alaska to visit—revealed that she'd never been comfortable around her brother, and that his temper often caused him to explode in anger. He had repeatedly struck both her and his wife. One day, Graham awoke from a nap and found his wife gone. He found her playing cards with his half-sister and mother and proceeded to fly into an uncontrolled rage, striking his wife repeatedly and threatening to strike his mother, too. The violent streak toward his mother, then, was no secret; his motive, quite obviously to the bombing's investigators, was well established.

He may have discovered insurance fraud in early 1955 when he left a Chevy truck he owned to be squashed by a train outside Denver. He submitted the insurance claim and collected a few grand, with which he paid back his mother for the payroll checks he'd stolen (she had made restitution for them). He wasn't very good at it, however; various policies that authorities found while searching his house totaled forty thousand dollars, but since his mother hadn't signed any of them, he could never have collected. In any case, he became a suspect once investigators found that he had given his mother a "Christmas present" right before she'd left on her trip. He'd deposited the "present" in her luggage without her knowledge, removing a bathrobe, some wedding pictures, and a couple antique flasks; he replaced them with twenty-five nicely bundled sticks of dynamite, two blasting caps, a battery, and timer, all nicely gift-wrapped. The same search that yielded the insurance policies uncovered wiring similar to some found at the crash site, and the pieces began falling into place. On November 13, nearly two weeks after the crash, Graham broke down and admitted he'd caused the explosion, sending his mother on the plane with that dynamite and a timer set for ninety minutes. He sent her off, then drank coffee and ate some some doughnuts at the airport coffee shop until he heard the plane went down.

His confession was textbook sociopath in its frankness, accuracy, and chilling disregard for other people. He told doctors that he "realized that there were about fifty or sixty people carried on a DCB, but the number of people to be killed made no difference to me; it could have been a thousand. When their time comes, there is nothing they can do about it." In fact, his confession, leaked to the press before his trial began, went into startling, minute detail of his acts, going so far as to describe the bomb itself. The leak may have resulted in the huge number of jurors who were examined for the trial before the final twelve were selected—231 in all, the state record at the time. The biggest objections to jurors: already holding an opinion on Graham's guilt, and opposition to the death penalty.

Forty-four counts of murder came down on Graham, and the press of the day sensationalized his beastly crime. His calm demeanor during confession gave the public a glimpse into his remorseless mind and indifference to the pain he caused. His trail moved forward quickly from there, with arraignment coming on December 9 and the death penalty on the table. The press, arguing that the case was big enough to allow for it, requested that TV cameras be present in the court room, which the judge agreed to provided they would not broadcast live. The case qualifies as the first trial of the TV age, as cameras had never been allowed to film a court proceeding before.

Graham, for his part, did his level best to squirm out of his predicament. On November 17, he claimed he'd been beaten and coerced into his confession and that he didn't even remember signing anything. He spent the balance of his trial looking pathetically thin and watching the prosecution sew him up in a burlap sack, presenting every sickening detail of the explosion including evidence of the actual bomb, bits of which they'd discovered among the wreckage. They also presented Graham's own twenty-page confession, which gave the exact time and method by which he placed the bomb. The defense lasted only two hours, versus fifteen days for the prosecution, and didn't stand a chance in the face of the mountains of evidence. The jury deliberated only for sixty-nine minutes, and came back with a resounding guilty, complete with a recommendation of death.

Graham's lawyers began appealing, but the man himself wanted to get things over with as soon as possible. On May 14, only weeks after the guilty verdict, he said in open court that he'd accepted the judgment and wanted to die. He tried suicide in September 1956 by attempting to strangle himself with two socks and his prison bars. In January 1957, the state took its shot, dropping a couple cyanide pills into a pail of sulfuric acid. Graham died on January 12, minutes after letting out a piercing scream and struggling against the leather straps that held him seated in the execution capsule.

≋ ⚰ ≋

No occupation, saving perhaps crab fishing in Alaska, is as fraught with danger as mining. That people die in mines is an irrefutable, terrible fact; the inconvenient truth that we need those mines and all the treasures they pull from the ground a lot more than we need Alaskan crabs lends a certain hue of heroism to the miners themselves. After all, they face those dangers so we can wire our houses, run our computers, and cook our food. Today, miners receive fairly good compensation for their toil and sacrifice. The average coal miner, according to the U.S. Bureau of Labor Statistics, made $21.57 per hour in 2004, versus $15.67 hourly for the average worker. Miners get a fair amount of vacation, and generally enjoy a fair shake, especially given the shoddy treatment they once received at the hands of mine owners.

In the early twentieth century, mining was positively lethal; fatalities exceeded two thousand every year from 1900 to 1910, when Congress created the Bureau of Mines to try and stem the bloodshed. This organization researched mine safety and tried to make those deep, dark places safer. Still, the mines continued to eat the men who worked them, and by 1969 more than one hundred thousand people had died in mining accidents since 1900. The century began, in fact, with one of the nation's worst underground disasters ever—a catastrophe that left two hundred miners dead and led to the slow, painful death of an entire community.

Located 115 miles southeast of Salt Lake City off a rutted dirt road is a locked gate, posted with "No Trespassing" signs. Beyond these signs lie a few walls and building foundations—the last remnants of Winter Quarters, a mining boomtown that saw nothing but bright horizons in the late nineteenth century. Though some early settlers had occupied the area—then known as Pleasant Valley—with their grazing cattle, the discovery of coal there in 1875 sealed the place's fate. A mining party journeyed into the nearby mountains, dug a hole in the ground, and began extracting the coal for use in nearby settlements. An early winter trapped the party up there, and they almost froze to death in the terminal Utah snows. Fortunately for them and their customers, they managed to survive, and named the site of their stand against nature Winter Quarters, for somewhat obvious reasons.

By 1877, enough miners had poured into the area to warrant a town—Utah's first built on a foundation of coal. The one-time village became a classic western boomtown, as big if not bigger than the capital itself. Hotels and saloons pocked the business district, said to be over a mile long and filled with sturdy stone buildings. As for the mines, a railroad line into the valley allowed the operation to continue apace. Over the next decade they grew into Utah's largest coal operation, with 1.1 million tons of coal coming from the ground in 1898, representing 88 percent of Utah's total coal production. The mines also earned a good reputation for safety, especially in comparison to other western mines; in Wyoming, for example, underground explosions in 1881, 1886, and 1895 drove scared miners to the relatively placid mines of Winter Quarters. Though there had been accidents—an 1890 explosion killed three miners at the Castle Gate mine, to cite one example—they were relatively rare, and the future of Winter Quarters looked pretty good as the century ended.

During the spring of 1900, about two thousand families lived in and around Scofield, a nearby town that held the majority of the miners' homes and families. Growth was still the order of the day, as new houses sprung up daily. A new contract with the U.S. Navy for two thousand tons of coal every day was to begin on the first of May, and no cases of smallpox or measles had been reported in recent weeks. In all, the miners of Winter Quarters were having a decent run as they set out to work on May 1, a Tuesday. Three hundred miners, some of them fathers training their sons in the art of coal mining, entered Winter Quarters' mines that day, many of them toting along twenty-five-pound powder kegs for blowing out new sections. The morning passed without much incident, until a shudder rolled up from deep inside mine number four just before 10:30 a.m.

The men working near number four's entrance knew immediately what had happened. A burning miasma of smoke, dust, and poisonous air seemed to propel mine cars and support timber out of the ground, blowing them with enough force to catapult the cars two hundred yards from the hole they came out of. John Wilson, who had been standing at the opening when the blast blew up at him, flew eight hundred twenty feet before coming to rest against a tree and—miraculously—surviving the experience. The force of the explosion even leveled buildings above ground, and completely blocked the entrance to the mine, delaying rescue efforts for vital dozens of minutes.

But the destruction up there was nothing compared to the almost instant carnage that had taken place below. Thankfully, death came relatively quickly for most; the explosion probably killed one hundred men immediately, with many others dying within minutes as the toxic gasses entered their lungs and choked them. Others, however, suffered horribly; of the first three men found during the rescue effort, two were burned beyond recognition—one even begged for his rescuers to kill him then and there. (He died the next day, after spending the intervening hours in unimaginable agony.)

As the rescuers made their way deeper, more bodies were discovered, and more families gathered at the mine entrance to verify the fates of their loved ones. In most cases, the result of their vigil was grief and pain, as one hundred, then two hundred bodies, variously burned and mostly unrecognizable, continued their grotesque parade back to the sunlight.

Only two men made it out of Winter Quarters' number four with their lives. The rest died, leaving behind 270 fatherless children and 107 widows. Like the Eden disaster in Colorado, this one took place in a small community that could hardly afford the loss of so many of its members. By some estimates, every family in town lost at least one member. There weren't even enough coffins locally available to bury all the dead—seventy-five had to be brought in from Denver, as Salt Lake City only had one hundred twenty-five available.

The U.S. Bureau of Mines continued to work for safer mines in the wake of tragedies like Scofield with varying degrees of success. In 1969, the government revisited mine safety once again, and passed the Federal Coal Mine Health and Safety Act of 1969. The act provided benefits for miners tortured by black lung disease, as well as the right of miners to call for federal inspection at their mine. Inspectors were given more power, and it seemed that the ghastly safety record the mining industry had amassed over the previous hundred might be altered.

Such a dream, however, wilted in the face of reality—more specifically, the reality that mine owners, even after decades of change and ostensible improvement, still had the capacity for nearly diabolical disregard for the people who made their stock prices climb. The Sunshine mine fire of 1972 reminded the country that even with vastly improved working conditions, mines are terribly dangerous places to work, and get even worse when the people in charge let them.

The Sunshine mine, located eight miles from Kellogg, Idaho, held more silver than any other mine in the U.S., and men have been pulling it from the ground there since the nineteenth century. They removed it in astounding quantities, too; from its inception until 2001, three hundred fifty million ounces have traveled to the surface from the hard rocks up to a mile below. Labyrinthine tunnels stretched in every direction from the mine's inception as miners searched deeper and farther for paydirt, until more than one hundred eighty miles of dug-out passages radiated from the mine's central areas. In 1972, those tunnels filled with smoke from an underground fire, producing the worst modern mining accident in U.S. history. Ninety-one men eventually succumbed to the black, choking smoke and incinerating flames, many of them hopelessly trapped below the point at which the fire started. And, as with so many industrial accidents of this magnitude, it didn't have to happen that way.

The Sunshine mine had already acquired a dubious reputation by the early 1970s. Mining is no picnic, to be sure; a 1977 congressional report estimated that miners were eight times more likely to die at work than someone working in a factory, and that nearly one hundred mining accidents since the turn of the century had killed five or more people. The Sunshine mine, however, exceeded even this threshold of danger; in fact, the place had a downright awful record in almost every way. In 1970, for example, Sunshine averaged five times more injuries than the average coal mine, and workers were three times more likely to die there than in any American metal mine. Fire drills were unheard of. Miners weren't sure about their escape routes back to the surface—not their locations, nor how soon they would have to evacuate in order to get up quickly and safely. Yet despite these violations, the U.S. Bureau of Mines never fined Sunshine, and never closed them down to ensure that safety requirements would be met.

Safety problems were legion at Sunshine, but the possibility of fire seemed fairly remote. After all, this mine was *wet*—standing water nearly a foot deep covered some paths through the mine, and dampness pervaded everywhere. Though temperatures reached more than one hundred degrees, the moist air calmed fears of fire down there, despite the mine's atrocious safety record. The humidity also rendered much of the emergency breathing equipment useless, as did the miners' continual monkeying around with the gear—breaking seals, stealing valuable items, and generally treating the safety gear just as disrespectfully as their superiors treated the safety codes. The unlikelihood of fire made determining exactly what caused the Sunshine fire largely fruitless. It could have been an errant cigarette or a welding job gone awry, but it could just as easily have been spontaneous combustion, or even—as was believed by a number of Sunshine employees—arson.

Whatever started it, the fire wasted no time in making conditions profoundly lethal. Mine fires, in case you had any doubt, mean big trouble to anyone caught down there when they start. Fire eats oxygen, first off, replacing it with carbon monoxide and smoke; in an environment already short on oxygen, miners caught in the fire's vicinity often have only a minute or two's worth of oxygen available before they pass out. If the deadly gasses make their way into the ventilation systems, this problem spreads throughout the mine, filling miners' lungs with poison hundreds of yards away from any point of escape. The Sunshine fire collapsed a vital bulkhead fairly quickly, which caused smoke and poisonous gas to run directly into the exhaust system and circulate throughout the entire mine. Men began dropping within minutes, and escape options dried up for anyone working below the level of the blaze.

The fire broke out around 12:40 p.m. There were one hundred seventy-three miners working at the time, and two electricians working nearby reported the blaze immediately. Within twenty minutes, eighty men had been evacuated, and the elevators were shut down. By that point most people aboveground knew that everyone still below ground would probably be dead already. Sadly, that was almost exactly the case; once the fire was out and the bodies started coming topside, seventy-seven widows were created, and three newborn babies would never get to meet their fathers.

Death came with horrific certainty as the toxic gasses of the fire tore through the miners' lungs. Blood poured from their noses and mouths; one miner, Casey Pena, dunked his head into a water trough "in a wasted attempt to escape the merciless air," according to Gregg Olsen in his account of the disaster, *The Deep Dark: Disaster and Redemption in America's Richest Silver Mine.* Many of the men died so quickly their faces didn't even register fear, so fast that they still held coffee cups and telephones.

Like any disaster, Sunshine had its survivors—namely Ron Flory and Tom Wilkinson, who survived down there for eight days until rescuers found them. When the fire broke out, they went lower into the ground and found a pocket of clean air. Over the next week, they ate their compatriots' lunches, talked about everything under the sun, and generally kept each other alive during their darkest moments. When they got back to the surface, the fact that they survived the ordeal was a complicated blessing; some survivors' families heaped scorn on them, claiming they were, according to Olsen, "embarrassed about living when so many had died."

The Sunshine mine closed down in 2001; silver was selling for around $4.50 per ounce then, and the Sunshine Mining and Refining Company just couldn't make enough money to keep the mine open. The disaster, still a painful memory for so many in the area, resurfaced in the news at the announcement. A year later, the National Institute for Occupational Safety & Health (NIOSH) released a documentary about the fire entitled *You Are My Sunshine*, in which numerous survivors recounted the day's horrific events. Though it was ostensibly a safety training video, *Sunshine* still reduced its audiences to tears when it was screened in Idaho's Silver Valley, amongst those who had lived it. Sunshine has since reopened, thanks to silver's price rebound to almost thirteen dollars today; in September 2006, it won the MSHA's Sentinels of Safety Award, marking it as one of Idaho's safest mines.

≋ ⚒ ≋

All of the natural disasters discussed in *Death in the West* resulted in their own particular brand of mayhem. Some killed more than others; some caused massive property damage but largely spared their human victims. The St. Francis Dam collapse of 1928, however, dwarfs them all, in terms of both property damage and human life lost. In fact, this little-known calamity killed almost as many people as the San Francisco earthquake, and more than just about every other natural disaster in American history. Its story, complete with tragic heroes, shows in one horrible stroke the overconfidence that defines so many human interactions with the natural forces of the West, as well as the consequences of such hubris when nature doesn't cooperate.

William Mulholland, more than any other man, birthed the modern city of Los Angeles. An Irish immigrant who came to San Francisco in 1877, he was a self-educated engineer who became head of L.A.'s Department of Water and Power in the late nineteenth century. As the city grew and boomed around them, Mulholland and a few other city fathers sensed a growing problem: Los Angeles didn't have enough water available to sustain its explosive growth. The Los Angeles River, a "beautiful, limpid little stream with willows on its banks," could only support a local population of about five hundred thousand. As the city pushed against that boundary in the early twentieth century,

Mulholland estimated a population of 390,000 by 1925. He, and those like him, contemplated ideas for expanding the water supply. (The actual growth of the city during the twenty years between 1905 and 1925 outpaced his estimate fourfold.)

The plan he arrived at: the Los Angeles Aqueduct, which ran from the Owens River to the City of Angels, 233 miles. The project was to be one of the biggest civil engineering feats of the twentieth century, perhaps one of the greatest in human history; five thousand men worked for five years to complete the project on time and within cost estimates. On November 5, 1913, the first cascade of crystalline mountain water flowed into Los Angeles, and Mulholland simply said, "There it is. Take it." Los Angeles, of course, has bloomed into America's second-largest city since then, and it could never have done so with Mulholland's hard work and vision.

Mulholland's great project didn't come without its share of intrigue. In fact, the ostensible reason for the aqueduct—to bring water to thirsty L.A.—might have been only half the story. The San Fernando Valley, through which the aqueduct runs on its way to the city, suddenly became a grower's paradise; those growers happened to be many of the people who'd put up the money for the aqueduct in the first place. Los Angeles, for its part, didn't even need the Owens' water. In fact, as the population continued to grow, its existing water supply seemed to hold up, much to the chagrin of Owens Valley farmers who saw their farms go dry not for city folk, but for other, better-connected farmers.

Sabotage commenced in May 1924, with the first of many attacks on the Los Angeles Aqueduct's structural soft points. The so-called Owens Valley War raged on for the next four years, resulting in more attacks on the aqueduct and hundreds of death threats to Mulholland. Eventually, the Owens Valley Bank folded, leaving Mulholland's rural opponents with no financial backing; his victory seemed assured.

Two years before this seemingly happy ending (at least from Mulholland's point of view), another of his building projects wrapped up to much less fanfare: the St. Francis Dam, more than two hundred feet high and nearly six hundred feet long, spanning the San Francisquito Canyon, close to where Six Flags Magic Mountain sits today. Mulholland had considered building a dam in the area as early as 1911, though his attention was at that point firmly devoted to the L.A. Aqueduct. By the 1920s, however, with the aqueduct bringing in all that water from the Owens Valley, Mulholland started considering alternative storage space in case of even further growth or some natural emergency that would somehow shut down the water flow and require a rainy day supply. He came again to San Francisquito Canyon and began building a dam there to store extra water for the City of Angels.

In 1924, construction began on the St. Francis, and though everything seemed to run well at the time, in hindsight problems were legion. First and most important was the dam's location—Mulholland had it built on an ancient landslide, something he could not possibly have known about at the time. There was some question, however, as to whether he knew about some of the other problems: mixing of clay with the dam's concrete, which would soak up water and eventually give way; failure to account for a twenty-foot increase in the dam's height, from one hundred eighty five feet to two hundred five; cracks that developed in the dam during 1926 and 1927, but were simply dismissed as routine (in Mulholland's view, concrete dams developed cracks over time, and they were of little consequence). In early March 1928, more leaks developed, but the engineer maintained that they were harmless. Even as damkeeper Tony Harnischfeger discovered a brand-new leak on March 12, the very morning of the disaster, Mulholland stuck to his guns and told him not to worry.

Three minutes before midnight, twelve hours after Mulholland's personal inspection, people nearby would feel rumbling in the ground, as if a minor earthquake were moving through. What they actually felt, however, were titanic chunks of concrete falling from the top of the dam as the water powered its way forward and out. Once the wave started, it would not be held. Tony Harnischfeger, his wife, and six-year-old son probably died first as the one hundred twenty-five-foot wave blasted forth from the shattering dam, carrying 12.5 billion gallons of water into the unsuspecting valley below.

The destruction was complete. The surging water scrubbed the landscape clean of human presence, including a massive concrete hydroelectric power plant. For sixty-five miles the water marched on, finally emptying everything and everyone it carried into the Pacific between Oxnard and Ventura. The wave's proportions were mythic: it's said that forty-two miles away, in Santa Paula, the water was still twenty-five feet deep. Twelve hundred homes were swept away, along with railroads, farms, orchards, and just about everything else. All told, damage estimates hit $20 million (about $228 million in current dollars). The water crashed forward at close to twenty miles per hour, and by morning the whole thing was over—the reservoir was empty and hundreds were crushed, swept out to sea, or simply drowned and left wherever the torrent deposited them.

The human toll: close to five hundred, though the exact number will never be known. Then, as today, vast numbers of undocumented immigrants worked the area's farms and orchards; the casualties they suffered may have bumped the death toll far beyond that. Stories of heroism abounded—Santa Paula police officer Thornton Edwards, along with another patrolman named Luther Williams, rode on motorcycles through the streets of their little town shouting for people to get to higher ground, not knowing exactly when the rushing waters might reach them. The officers, it was said, saved hundreds of lives that night.

The good deed also earned Edwards the chief of police's post in Santa Paula the very next year. (Though subsequent reports said that he was an arrogant bully of a chief, who was railroaded out of office by an angry city council.)

Telephone operators all over the area stayed at their posts—in those days, many local switchboards ran right out of operators' homes—and called all their neighbors to warn them. People fortunate enough to live on higher ground watched in horror as their low-lying neighbors were swept away, many of them never to be seen again. Back at the dam, nothing remained but a few stray chunks of concrete, which would end up pulverized a year later after a hapless explorer pitched off of one.

The migrant workers may have suffered most: many of them couldn't understand the shouted warnings of their white neighbors, or why they were throwing rocks at them to get their attention. Camped near where they worked on the valley floor, a huge number of them were swept up and away as the water surged. Others victims lost their entire families, though some were lucky enough to be "adopted" afterward. One particularly strange story in the aftermath of the disaster involved Bill Hart, a Newhall resident, legendary screen cowboy, and friend of Wyatt Earp. He took a particular interest in one victim: a three-year-old boy whose body went unclaimed after the flood. Hart, who volunteered in the makeshift morgue that held the boy's body, dressed him in a little cowboy outfit and made funeral arrangements for the boy in San Fernando. Just before the burial, the boy's last name was discovered— Prixler—though his first name still remains a mystery.

On March 12, 1928, Mulholland's apparent victory over his Owens Valley enemies took a back seat to something else: massive, horrific disaster. The nineteenth dam he'd built in his storied career had given out on him, and he took full responsibility for it. At first some talked of sabotage—after all, the Owens Valley rabble-rousers had made threats against the dam—but in the end Mulholland shouldered the weight of accountability. Investigators helped him do it, blaming Mulholland's faulty plans for the disaster only twelve days after it happened.

Predictably, it crushed him to dust; he allegedly said on a few occasions that he envied those who died in the tragedy. He retired from the Department of Water and Power in March 1929, and exiled himself from public life. He died in 1935, believing that he was directly responsible for the St. Francis collapse. In the 1990s, researchers discovered the prehistoric landslide under the dam, something Mulholland never could have seen given the technology of the time. In fact, two noted geologists gave the site their blessing before Mulholland began construction. Still, the corners he did cut in efforts to come in under budget—that clay-heavy concrete, the unwillingness to investigate known leaks—played a part in the collapse that will never be fully known.

The great things Mulholland did for California, Los Angeles, and American agriculture in general are beyond dispute. Also beyond dispute is his terrible treatment of the Owens Valley rebels who fought the theft of their water, and the fact that he could not have known what would happen at St. Francis thanks to both natural forces and, perhaps, his own hubris. Had he tempered his success with more attention to his fellow Californians, perhaps he would not have been forced to resign in humiliation, and left to die an obscure death.

Today exactly one memorial is dedicated to William Mulholland, titan of civil engineering: a fountain located near Los Feliz.

CHAPTER SEVEN

Just Enough Luck
They Shouldn't Be Alive

They were already black and purple and red. ... I tried to forget them.

—SNOWBOARDER ERIC LEMARQUE,

describing his feelings upon taking off his frozen socks
and watching the soles of his feet come off with them.

ometimes people just get lucky. Despite making all the worst mistakes, turning left all the places you should have turned right, and forgetting every one of the essentials you should have packed with you, sometimes you just can't screw up enough. In those cases you might get hurt— you might even end up losing a limb or two—but you'll still come out on the other side with your life intact.

The West will swallow up the unwary and unlucky with no compunction and spare them just as capriciously. More often than not, saving grace for those caught in dire circumstances rests within them; the will to live simply overcomes all adversity. The question as to why some people live and some don't under identical circumstances is worth answering, and some good people have taken a shot at it; Laurence Gonzales's *Deep Survival*, for example, lays out twelve rules of survival that nearly always apply to those who make it. The twelve rules all have to do with keeping your cool, making a plan and sticking to it, and even appreciating your situation a bit. After all, getting lost in the wilderness puts you in the middle of majestic backcountry that, chances are, you were looking for anyway. Might as well enjoy the ride as best you can.

Unfortunately, not everyone has the wherewithal to follow these steps. According to Gonzales, "Only 10 to 20 percent of people can stay calm and think in the midst of a survival emergency. They are the ones who can perceive their situation clearly; they can plan and take correct action, all of which are key elements of survival." Lots of people panic, give up, or go crazy. They end up making bad decisions, ones that—in a survival situation—are tough to undo without drastic action. In fact, another survivor's hallmark is that, in planning to live, he or she is often willing to do things that the rest of us simply can't or won't contemplate, whether it be crawling down a sheer cliff with no gear, swishing our own urine around in our mouths to stave off thirst, or taking a penknife to our own flesh, leaving it behind the way a trapped coyote gnaws off a leg.

Some survivors do have luck to thank. Those who experience a natural disaster often live because conditions favor them. Take this elderly gentleman, a Californian who found himself in the path of the St. Francis dam break:

> Old Man Koffer was saved. And the term old is not used lightly or slurringly, for he is seventy-four. He and his wife, also aged, lived on the Carter ranch above Fillmore. The waters caught them as they slept. And that is about all that Old Man Koffer remembers. For when he realized where he was, he was on his knees, clinging to the mattress, his old wife gone. A few awful moments and the mattress and its aged occupant swirled out to one side and landed in the Illharaguy lemon orchard, where help came to him.

Political correctness aside (the story was written in 1928), this was one lucky old guy—it's not every day that someone survives one of the great deluges of the twentieth century by riding out of it on a mattress. For every person that dies in one of these great calamities, there are survivors like these, providing some hope in the midst of terror and destruction.

But the ones who survive the elements thanks to their own grit provide by far the most interesting stories, the ones that force us to ask whether we would be able to do what it takes to come back and tell the story. Aron Ralston, who survived an ordeal most of us couldn't live through, is one such person.

Ralston, by his own admission, made some questionable decisions on April 26, 2003, when he headed into Utah's Blue John Canyon. The slot canyon is in the San Rafael desert, making it some of the most remote wilderness in the lower forty-eight. Ralston set off into that wilderness alone—nothing strange in and of itself, as he often hiked by himself in his native Colorado. In fact, he'd climbed forty-five of Colorado's fifty-nine "fourteeners" (mountains over fourteen thousand feet) in the winter and alone, and he planned to solo Mt. McKinley once he was done warming up in Utah. Perhaps worse, Ralston set off without telling anyone where he was going, committing the crucial error so many other skilled outdoorsmen make just before they disappear.

But there were real differences between Ralston and those who found themselves in similar situations and didn't live to write books about it. First off, he didn't sustain injury to his head at any time, an eventuality that makes recovery a lot less likely. Take Jeff Christensen, the Rocky Mountain National Park ranger discussed in Chapter One—he had a ton of outdoor experience, but his head injury probably rendered him unable to deal as effectively with his predicament as he might have otherwise. Perhaps more importantly, Ralston decided very quickly that dying was simply not an option he would accept.

Ralston's physical conditioning also helped—after all, he spent a lot of time outdoors, often without the benefit of a safety net. He clearly had some advanced fitness going for him. On the same note, he had a wealth of backcountry experience to draw on, and he had been a mountain rescue volunteer for four years. He and two friends had been caught in an avalanche before, an incident that by Ralston's own admission "should have killed us." Obviously, the man had dealt with adversity before, even if it could not possibly have compared with what he faced in the dark moments to come at Blue John.

The disaster went down like this: Ralston biked two and a half hours to the canyon, and began his descent into the crevasse. All around him were boulders that canyon floods had lodged between the narrow walls, one of which he grabbed as he negotiated a ten-foot drop in the canyon bottom. Somehow the boulder—an eight-hundred-pound monster—dislodged and fell down toward Ralston. He managed to jerk his left hand out as the chockstone was still moving, but he wasn't so lucky with his right—that hand stayed pinched between the massive stone and the wall of the canyon. The pain was intense, but that wasn't his biggest problem; the main problem was that he was stuck to a slot canyon wall, alone, with no one in the world knowing exactly where he was.

The next six days have been the subject of hundreds of articles and interviews. Ralston stayed pinned to that wall that long, waiting for help, contemplating his fate, and otherwise marking time before acting on the idea that came to him within an hour of becoming trapped. Inside that first hour, he came up with four solutions: get rescued by someone happening by; chip away at the rock until his hand was free; rig a pulley up to the boulder using his climbing equipment and lift the rock up and off him; or, use his multitool to cut through his arm, then stay conscious enough to get himself out of the canyon. Notably, none of these options involved dying, which might explain more than anything else why Aron is still with us today.

Another factor in his survival might be the preternatural calmness he exhibited after some understandable initial panic. Within a very short period of time, he actively contemplated self-amputation. Yet he remained calm enough to think through his options, take inventory of his supplies, and otherwise figure out how to make the best of the situation.

In fact, reading about the routine Ralston established for himself down there during his ordeal is nothing short of astounding; it got downright mundane at times. To take pressure off his legs, he managed to get his climbing gear attached to the canyon wall and took twenty-minute sit breaks—religiously, the same amount of time each time—so the harness wouldn't cut the blood off from his legs. He rigged a system to move the boulder, using the bag of climbing gear he'd brought along. Though it didn't work, the idea kept him occupied for a while. He set small tasks for himself, a mark of the survivor's mindset according to Gonazales, and proceeded to carry them out with regular, strict precision.

Then there's the amputation idea, which he first tried putting into action on the second day. He simply couldn't do it. According to a 2004 *Outside* magazine article: "I picture my blood spilled on the canyon walls, the torn flesh and ripped muscles of my arm dangling in gory strands from two white bones pockmarked with divots ..." You get the idea. In addition, the knife he tried to use—the longest one on his multitool—was barely sharp enough to puncture his skin.

But the thought never left him, and as more time passed the bloodiest course came to seem more and more necessary. Finally, at about eight o'clock in the morning on the fourth day, Ralston sunk his knife into his arm for the first time; he found that the shorter blade, measuring all of an inch and a half, had enough edge to penetrate his flesh. It took him another two days before an epiphany helped solve the riddle of the bones. Ironically, he came to the final conclusion by sticking himself again with the knife, this time poking at his trapped hand. Again, from *Outside* magazine:

> Out of curiosity, I poke my thumb with my knife blade twice. On the second prodding, the blade punctures the epidermis, like it is dipping into a stick of room-temperature butter, and releases a telltale hissing...
> I don't want it.
> It's not a part of me.
> It's garbage.
> *Throw it away, Aron. Be rid of it.*

And with that, he broke his own arm, sitting down until his weight snapped the bones, and sawed through his flesh until free. The action, the fact that he was doing something to affect his fate, reinvigorated him; he rappelled sixty feet down to the canyon floor, hiked five miles downstream, and eventually encountered three Dutch hikers who helped him get back to civilization.

Subsequent years have made Ralston famous, a notoriety culminating in his fascinating book *Between a Rock and a Hard Place*. Some outdoorspeople were highly critical of Ralston as his star rose; as he himself has admitted, he made some big-time mistakes out there, and making a hero out of the guy who made them carries the risk of downplaying those errors. Still, as a pure specimen of human willpower, you'd be hard-pressed to find someone with more guts—more will to live—than Aron Ralston.

That's not to say other people haven't matched his true grit. In fact, self-amputation is, while rare, certainly a recurring theme in wilderness survival stories. William Jeracki, a Colorado anesthetist, found himself on a considerably shorter timeline than Ralston when a massive boulder crushed his left leg in October 1993. He had been fishing in the backcountry near St. Mary's Glacier, and weather reports were calling for snow that night. Given his light clothes and lack of supplies, surviving such a storm would have been nearly impossible, so he proceeded to tie fishing line around his leg, saw through it at the knee, and pull his femur out of the socket. He used fishing gear to stem the various arteries and veins that lay exposed. Jeracki then crawled back to his truck, got in, and drove himself to the hospital—with a stick shift, no less, making him perhaps the best driver in history. Other recent examples from points East include the Maine fisherman who cut off his arm after catching it up in a winch, and Donald Wyman, who was cutting down trees in Punxsutawney, Pennsylvania, when a giant oak pinned his left leg against his bulldozer. Using a shoestring for a tourniquet, he cut off his leg below the knee and lived to tell about it.

Of course, the willingness to go as far as humanly possible—up to and including self-amputation—isn't necessarily the foremost requirement for great survival stories. Wily ingenuity in the face of long odds rates pretty high on the scale, too. Snowboarder Eric LeMarque certainly exhibited this trait in spades when he got lost on California's Mammoth Mountain back in February 2004—along with a will to live that definitely places him within the ten or twenty percent mentally built to survive backcountry calamity.

LeMarque, like Ralston, did some things he shouldn't have. He left Mammoth's boundaries in search of new powder, neglecting to let anyone know about his detour. He did so with a dead cell phone on him, as well as a food supply consisting of four pieces of gum. Of course, he didn't have much reason to carry emergency supplies, seeing as how he was boarding at a well-known ski area. Only leaving the beaten path without exact knowledge of where that path led made the otherwise unremarkable lack of gear a glaring problem. (However, one might make the case that backcountry skiing is an activity in which bringing at least the barest backcountry basics—some water or a whistle just in case—is a wise thing.)

Even so, he also had many of the same things going for him that Aron Ralston had. First off, he was in superb physical shape—in fact, LeMarque was a former professional hockey player who had suited up for Team France back in 1994 and got drafted by the Bruins out of college. In addition, he had an outdoorsman's ingenuity. He knew the basics of backcountry survival, and he kept his head about him even as his situation got worse and worse. In fact, on the first night, he didn't mind being lost very much at all. "I figured it was an adventure," he said, perhaps indicating some of what got him through that subzero night along with the subsequent ones.

As he got further off-track that first day, the errant boarder knew things were getting worse. The sun kept dropping as he kept getting deeper and deeper into the woods, with no sign of the civilization he'd left behind. He tried to light a fire but couldn't get his matches to spark up. So, not knowing what else to do, he kept going downhill and moving farther away from anyone who might have been able to help him. The next day he kept at it, continually moving down and away from the resort. He eventually reached a fast-moving creek and tried traveling along it by jumping on the rocks, since the twelve-foot-deep snow was decidedly slow going. He promptly fell into the water, got pulled downstream when the flow grabbed his snowboard, and nearly coasted off an eight-foot waterfall. He managed to get himself clear, but the damage was done.

He was soaked through and freezing to the point that the soles of his feet peeled off along with his frozen socks when he took them off. Still, he used his head, and followed the rules of winter wilderness survival—not eating the ample snow to stay hydrated (it lowers body temperature profoundly); making a pine-bough bed each night to keep himself off the cold pack; even engaging in a little MacGyver-esque backcountry problem solving by rigging up a compass with some wood, a metal needle, and water. He also used his MP3 player to find the direction in which he should travel, realizing that a Mammoth Mountain station seemed to come in clearer when he was pointed in a certain direction (which happened to be north).

Despite his ingenuity, things were looking bad by the fifth day. Out of steam, he sunk into a snow shelter for two nights, barely moving. By Friday, February 13, he was about spent, no longer able to walk or stand on his ruined, frostbitten feet. He was thirty-five pounds lighter and hadn't eaten anything but pine seeds and bark for eight days. His body temperature: eighty-eight degrees. Hallucinations started to overtake him to the point that he thought he was playing a video game about dying instead of actually doing it.

LeMarque had disappeared from a well-known spot, and rescue personnel would have some idea of where he was once they were looking for him. But no one knew he was missing for a few crucial days—his friends had already returned to L.A. the morning he went missing, and his parents didn't worry too much about their thirty-four-year-old son not calling for a couple days. But after a while, they got worried enough to head over to his house, where they noticed a few things missing, most notably his board and Mammoth season pass. They called attention to his disappearance, and searchers were on the ground and in the air within hours.

The search began on Thursday, February 12, and produced quick results—within a day the ski patrol found LeMarque's tracks and his aborted attempt at a fire. Later in the afternoon on Friday they found him, barely conscious and waving up at a National Guard helicopter. They picked him up and quickly discovered his survival came with a serious price: LeMarque eventually lost both his feet to profound frostbite. They were blackened and sloughing, the water in the cells frozen and bursting just like soda cans in a freezer. Doctors amputated his feet at the shin, though he—like so many athletes facing adversity—vowed to be back on his board the very next year.

Perhaps the most important trait Eric LeMarque shared with Aron Ralston—and all the survivors here, for that matter—was his willingness to take responsibility. After his rescue, he said, "I wasn't going to sit around and wait for anybody. ... This was an adventure I'd put myself in, and I just had to get myself out." That thinking falls right into line with Laurence Gonzales's take on why some people survive out there; of his twelve rules of survival, the first one is admitting "you're really in trouble and you're going to have to get yourself out." He goes on to elaborate, citing action and honesty as the best defenses against death in extreme circumstances. "Survivors don't candy-coat the truth, but they also don't give in to hopelessness in the face of it." In all of these inspiring—if terrible—stories, the one constant is adherence to this first rule.

Another rule Eric LeMarque might have benefited from is this one: *bring a map*. When you get right down to it, he got into a bad situation because he ended up not knowing where he was. Losing one's way in the wilderness is always a possibility. Eventually, all forests or deserts or mountains start to look the same no matter how good your sense of direction, how detailed your map, or how extensive your outdoor savvy might be.

Lauren Elder had no idea where she was when the Cessna she was riding in crashed somewhere in the Sierra Nevada in April 1976. Her boyfriend's boss had set out with her and his own girlfriend for a little picnic in Death

Valley; unfortunately, he didn't have much time in the cockpit and wasn't quite equipped to make the passage from San Francisco across the high mountains. Had the weather been good, he probably would have been all right, but he chose not to heed a high wind warning, and things simply went downhill from there. Complications forced them to crash at about 12,360 feet in altitude, well above the snowline at that time of year (though, to be fair, crashing in the mountains provided a slightly better chance for survival than if he'd crashed in the middle of Death Valley).

The couple died almost immediately, leaving Elder solo. Unfortunately, she was wearing high-heeled boots, a little skirt, and nothing resembling a warm garment. She could see the San Joaquin Valley spread out in front of her, beyond several miles of ice and snow. Amazingly, she managed a thirty-six-hour hike down the frozen mountain, along with a little side trip thrown in: she went skinny dipping in a chilly pool she found in the untracked wilderness. In the midst of her dire situation, she found time for a little fun. She wasn't wearing underwear, either, which provided a little more amusement for her as she worried someone might see up her skirt as she slogged through the snow. A better example of the survivor's ability to make the best of the situation, I have not yet seen.

Faced with this daunting situation, Elder got angry, started helping herself, and eventually made it back to civilization without any assistance from anyone, despite the fact that she suffered a broken arm in the crash. Like Ralston and LeMarque, she attacked rather than sitting back; what's more, she, unlike them, had little outdoor experience, being something of a bohemian city dweller from San Francisco. She simply decided to live, and then did so regardless of her apparent limitations in health, experience, and wardrobe. She devised a method of moving down the icy cliffs she faced, spider-walking down on all fours and punching herself hand- and toeholds through the sheet of surface ice. Lauren Elder simply concentrated on the task at-hand, only thinking ahead to the next job, and made it as far as she needed to go.

Peter DeLeo had some outdoor experience, as well as discipline acquired through years of martial arts. He suffered the same kind of accident Elder did—he was piloting his single-engine Maule M-5 over the Sierra on a little photographic expedition when he experienced some difficulties and crashed on Kern Peak, an 11,510-foot mountain only seven minutes by air from the Kern Valley Airport near Lake Isabella. He'd taken off from Long Beach with two friends on November 27, but didn't make it back to civilization until almost two weeks later, after trudging through the rugged Sierra with a lot of broken bones and frostbite too horrible to imagine.

DeLeo, Waverly Hatch, and Lloyd Matsumoto were snapping a few shots as they flew over the high Sierra, having a good old time. Sudden turbulence intervened in the proceedings, however, slapping the plane down about three thousand feet in one shot. DeLeo couldn't get things back on track, and the plane went down at about eighty-five hundred feet elevation in the middle of a box canyon.

All three men suffered profound injuries. Matsumoto's chest was crushed by the instrument panel; he couldn't be moved from the plane. Hatch had a broken back, which would eventually cause him to collapse in the snow and freeze to death after DeLeo set out. For his part, Peter DeLeo suffered seven broken ribs, seven fractures in his ankle, a right arm broken in four places, a torn rotator cuff in the same arm, and blindness in his left eye. Still, he managed to head-butt his way out of the plane's skylight, as he couldn't get through the press of the men and wreckage behind him.

DeLeo and Hatch came up with a plan: DeLeo, the younger of the two, would attempt to hike out and get help. Loyalty to the two men left behind would help drive DeLeo through the rest of his ordeal; unfortunately, they died soon after his departure, Matsumoto succumbing to his injuries and Hatch collapsing, probably in excruciating pain, out in the snow. In DeLeo's mind, though, their presence remained, giving him something to push for through the pain and deprivation.

Over the next thirteen days, DeLeo fell into a vital routine. He barely slept because his injuries may have pushed him into shock if he did. According to his account, real sleep only came twice, in an abandoned cabin and a fetid old outhouse. He also didn't have much to eat beyond the bugs he could find under bark and logs as he trudged. (He eventually lost forty-five pounds, the same number of miles he would traverse.) Every step drove pain deep into his ankle, and the snows deadened his extremities to the point that they barely looked human by the end.

Still, he continued, heading toward Highway 395. And given his desperate circumstances, he did just about everything right. He lived, mostly because he followed another one of Laurence Gonzales's twelve rules with slavish devotion: "Think, Analyze, and Plan." He came up with little routines and carried them out religiously each day. He dried out his clothes during the day to make sure he wouldn't turn into a popsicle when the nighttime temperatures dropped. He rested on logs and inside trees when the snows fell, staying away from caves and other rock formations as their freezing temperatures would leech vital warmth from his body.

When he stumbled from the wilderness, his dire condition didn't stop him from getting help out to his friends. Their deaths made his survival seem a bit empty; he called his success "a hollow victory" in light of what happened to them. It didn't end when he escaped the forest, either. He weighed only one hundred fifteen pounds by the end of his trek, and it would take him a year to get all the weight back. Doctors debated amputating his hands and feet for a month before deciding he could keep them. And the surgeries to repair his body took place every two months for a year. No wonder it took him a few more years to so much as talk to reporters, then to write his own account of his ordeal, appropriately titled *Survive!* (Actually, there's some question as to what really happened in the plane crash—evidence indicates DeLeo might have been flying a bit low, taking unnecessary chances. He may have been negligent in his flying, and thus culpable for the deaths of Hatch and Matsumoto. The final point, however—and the one most relevant here—is that the guy survived for two weeks on his own in the Sierra Nevada.)

≋ 🦴 ≋

Wilderness survival usually depends on the person lost—their attitude, what they're willing to do, and their general handling of a bad situation. Only rarely do those people owe their survival to someone other than the rescue personnel who find them. These facts make John Donovan's case—and the events that followed it—particularly singular, tragic, and stirring, all at the same time.

Donovan disappeared near Palm Springs, California, in May 2005. The retired social worker knew his way around a hiking trail; in fact, he probably spent more time hiking in the wilderness than most people spend walking at all. He'd covered about ten thousand miles of trail in the years before he disappeared, including the Appalachian Trail, the Colorado Trail, much of the Pacific Crest Trail (PCT), and countless lesser routes. Friends called him "El Burro" in honor of his stubborn streak (and, probably, his steadiness on the trail). In April, to celebrate his retirement, he'd begun a thru-hike of the PCT at the Mexican border, planning to cover eighteen hundred miles clear up to Oregon by the time he finished.

Once he reached the San Jacinto Wilderness, however, he was feeling a bit worried; he hadn't really prepared for the snow and ice he found up there, or for the snowstorm that dumped three feet on the area just as he reached it. Somehow he became trapped in an isolated ravine, found no means to escape, and burned through his supplies. As he was hiking such a massive distance alone, no one would know exactly where he was, at least not until he'd been missing for quite some time. In his diary he wrote of resignation, of knowing that he would die in that gorge. He wrote about his regrets, his fear, and the fact that at the end he only had three crackers left to eat. Then he died, and his body stayed missing for a year.

This story is in this chapter given one additional fact: in death, John Donovan saved two people. Two people, in fact, who just happened to be the polar opposite of the consummate outdoorsman he was. They ended up in his former camp not because they too were hiking the PCT, but because they'd separated from a tour group taking a one-hour nature hike and stumbled blind into the wilderness. That they lived had everything to do with John Donovan's skills and preparedness.

Brandon Day, a financial adviser, brought his girlfriend Gina Allen with him to Palm Desert for Securian Financial Group's sales convention in May 2006. As conventions will often do, this one put together a tour of the local sights—specifically one involving the Palm Springs Aerial Tramway, an engineering marvel located on the slopes of Mount San Jacinto. With forty-one other attendees, the couple set out on the tour and promptly got lost. Not to worry, they thought, as they could still hear the rest of the group; at least they could for a while. The voices vanished with startling abruptness, though, and in a few short minutes they were on their own with absolutely no supplies, heavy clothes, or other means to survive. A very quick word on the San Jacinto area: it's cold, even in May, even with sunny Palm Springs right down the road. The temperature drops like a rock at night, and snowfall—as poor John Donovan found out—isn't uncommon even in mid-spring. Day and Allen, in their unprepared state and with their clear lack of outdoor experience, seemed on the brink of disaster.

They spent their first night in a cave, huddled together and trying to figure out what to do next. In the process of getting there they'd banged themselves up a bit but were otherwise in the right frame of mind. They simply wouldn't concede that they were going to die on the mountain after getting lost during a measly tourist hike. The next morning they began following a nearby river, thinking that the best thing would be to head downhill. (They were wrong; if you go uphill, rescuers have a better chance of spotting you.) After another freezing night and another day of walking, their journey brought them into a little gorge, where a campsite—weathered, yet organized as if by a skilled outdoorsman—caught their attention.

The couple began yelling for help but no one answered, and the closer they got, the stranger the scene. They soon discovered that the camp was deserted; but a green tarp shelter remained, as did a pair of tennis shoes, a sleeping mat, a jacket, and a backpack, soaked in the late-snow-season melt. They opened the pack and found their salvation: matches in a waterproof bag, as well as a sweater and socks. Once the clothes dried, Allen put on the sweater and Day commandeered the socks. Then they lit a fire and got warm. They also found Donovan's diary, kept in twelve entries along the blank edges of his maps, with the last entry written on May 8, 2005—a year to the day before they found the abandoned camp. They knew that they'd stumbled into a tomb, albeit a highly scenic one.

That night—their third in the wilderness—a helicopter flew over them without stopping or looking back. They resolved to get attention the next time someone flew by, and started a forest fire with John Donovan's matches. The burning acreage caught rescuers' eyes, and they were picked up by 9:30 that morning. (The fire almost ended up dosing the story with a little more tragedy—it burned for a couple of days before firefighters could get it under control.) Day and Allen emerged from their incident largely unscathed, and they had Donovan to thank for it. The experienced outdoorsman got one last chance to show the newbies how it's done.

This story is even more fascinating because exactly what that diary revealed is unknown. Allen and Day kept its contents to themselves, mostly; they said that he wrote of impending death, and that he was "preparing for the end, and had some regrets," but nothing much more out of respect for their savior. Day said he didn't even want to know what happened to Donovan. The man's situation, he said, was too close to the one he and Allen were facing. They kept his secrets, in any case.

Area rescue workers found John Donovan's remains in June 2006, about one hundred yards away from his last campsite. He was sitting on a log. The temperature was around a hundred degrees, only a month after Allen and Day couldn't sleep because they were shivering so hard.

※ 豐 ※

All of these stories involve a fair span of time. For Aron Ralston, it was five days; Lauren Elder hung on for a day and a half. Peter DeLeo wins the prize for longest ordeal, at nearly two weeks. And each ordeal happened in a place that, while not completely hospitable, wasn't the pinnacle of environmental hostility. After all, most of them had food of some kind available; they all had water or some form of it, though Ralston in particular exhausted his supply before escaping his predicament. And as punishing as all those far-off places were, they still provided some basics, like the aforementioned nourishment, as well as shelter, fuel, and tools.

The southwestern desert, by and large, doesn't throw such bones to people lost in it. The absence of the most important element of survival—water—fundamentally alters the equation; after all, Peter DeLeo and Eric LeMarque both suffered terrible injuries en route to rescue. Their ability to stay hydrated kept them at a baseline of health despite those wounds. On the other hand, Raffi Kodikian and David Coughlin were in the desert for four days before Eric begged for death. Granted, those two exhibited few of the survival impulses that drove the survivors above, but they were still young, healthy, and out there for a shorter time. Had they been hopelessly lost in the mountains or forest, they would have at least had something to drink.

Stories of people lost in the desert and coming back to tell the tale are rare for one simple reason: most people who get lost out there don't live through the ordeal. Instead, they succumb to the sun and thirst, dying in as little as two days. There are a few stories, however, of people surviving in blazing conditions, with little or no water available. They come from all over the world; possibly the most famous involves Mauro Prosperi, an Italian police officer and triathlete who survived ten days in the Sahara. He got lost while running the Marathon des Sables, a stunning display of human psychosis in which victims choose voluntarily to run one hundred forty-five miles across the desert in an effort to prove...something, surely. In any case, a massive dust storm threw off Prosperi's sense of direction and sent him careening into the desert with only a little water left in his bottle. He survived by sheer luck, stumbling first upon an abandoned desert shrine after three days. Inside he found a few bats, tore two of their heads off, and drank their insides. (He also tried to kill himself by cutting his wrists, but his sludgy blood would no longer flow out of him.) He happened on a puddle a few days later, which he also drank as best he could given that extreme dehydration paradoxically closes the throat, making it nearly impossible to drink anything. By the time he reached the tiny desert town that would mean his salvation, he had lost thirty-three pounds, nearly destroyed his liver, and looked like a zombie. Incidentally, he also ran in the Marathon des Sables six more times, making him a far better— or nuttier—man than I am.

In the American Southwest, the most famous such story involves one Pablo Valencia, a prospector from Mexico who was searching the desert for riches back in 1905. He was sixty-five years old, and apparently not very smart— two things that make his ordeal all the more unbelievable. What he did have, though, was a driving purpose that would eventually save him from death in the Arizona desert: vengeance.

Valencia, luckily for us, crossed paths with a man named W. J. McGee somewhere along the *El Camino del Diablo*, the "Route of the Devil," well-known to settlers moving out to California. McGee, a naturalist and director of the St. Louis Museum, was best-known as a geologist, and would go on to hold a number of important posts including president of the American Association of the Advancement of Science. He was also among the first scientists to explore the Arizona territory, and his presence there when Pablo Valencia passed through his camp would be the only reason posterity managed to capture the man's struggle.

But that came after Valencia's ordeal, which began on August 14 at the height of the desert summer. He and his guide Jesus Rios came into McGee's camp that day on their way to some mines they'd found a few months before. They were fairly well equipped, and spent the day eating with the scientist and his guide. The prospectors left around five that evening, then returned after a short while to wait out the heat. They set out again at 3:45 a.m., August 15.

Jesus turned up again at seven in the morning with a confounding report: Valencia had requested that Jesus turn around and water the horses back at McGee's camp. Valencia, for his part, would take a two-gallon container of water and keep going through the desert on foot, and Jesus would catch up with him down the trail. McGee, amazed, called the plan "an inane if not insane one in desert life." Nevertheless, he lent Jesus one of his own canteens and watched him leave again early on the sixteenth.

At this point, Valencia had been out there for an entire day; by the rules of desert survival, that's how far his two gallons of water should have gone, since an adult walking in the desert requires that much every day just to stay fully hydrated. So McGee was concerned when Jesus came back again in a few hours, claiming that he couldn't find Valencia. Another search by McGee's guide Jose—an expert tracker—would prove just as fruitless, leading the scientist to expect the worst. On August 18, he packed Jesus up, watching him head off to Yuma where he would have to break the news that Valencia was lost. McGee, for his part, went about his business. That is, he did so until dawn on Wednesday, August 23, when an "ear-piercing bellow of challenge and defiance" ripped him out of sleep.

Jose thought it might have been a lion. McGee, however, instantly instructed his guide to grab the water, somehow believing it was the lost prospector. They ran outside and found the man a complete wreck:

> Pablo was stark naked; his formerly full-muscled legs and arms were shrunken and scrawny; his ribs ridged out like those of a starving horse; his habitually plethoric abdomen was drawn in almost against his vertebral column; his lips had disappeared as if amputated, leaving low edges of blackened tissue; his teeth and gums projected like those of a skinned animal, but the flesh was black and dry as a hank of jerky; his nose was withered and shrunken to half its length; the nostril-lining showing black; his eyes were set in a winkless stare, with surrounding skin so contracted as to expose the conjunctiva, itself black as the gums … his skin generally turned a ghastly purplish yet ashen gray, with great livid blotches and streaks. …

And it goes on—think textbook undead, freshly risen from the dirt, and you've got it. His cuts would not bleed, and he weighed, by McGee's estimation, around one hundred fifteen to one hundred twenty pounds. He could barely hear or see, and his pulse all but fluttered it was so weak. McGee rubbed water all over Valencia, and soon his leathery skin was greedily drinking it in. He also gave the man some whiskey as a curative, along with nitroglycerin to get his heart pumping harder. The change he describes is quite amazing; within just a few hours, during which Valencia "ingested and retained about two and a half ounces of whisky, with five ounces of water, and two or three ounces of food," his skin began to soften and his many scratches and abrasions began to bleed. Eventually the wounds swelled alarmingly with infection as his body, long out of the fight, began again to combat the troubles brewing within it.

Over the next few days Pablo continued to recover, and he soon told his story. Things had begun quietly enough; he'd simply walked to where he said he would, drinking a little of his water each day and eating some pinole he'd brought with him. (Pinole is a corn-based gruel eaten by the Indians and Mexicans of the Southwest.) But by his second day things were already getting urgent—that night he was "filling his mouth and gargling his throat with urine" to stave off thirst. He'd also ditched his gold and the pinole, along with his coat.

As one might imagine, things simply degenerated into a circus of horrors from there. He saved every drop of urine in his canteen, and couldn't swallow any more by the third day. On the fourth, he found a bit of mescal and chewed it for a small bit of moisture; he also started eating the flies and spiders he could catch. He shed all his clothes, and became convinced that Jesus had sold him out, sending him into the desert on a trail that didn't exist. He began fantasizing about killing his former guide, reliving the scenario again and again, creating—in McGee's words—"a potent incentive which carried him miles and doubtless saved his life."

He found a massive scorpion, crushed off its stinger with a rock, and ate it; he dreamed of finding the well called Tule, and throwing himself in to die in the mud thirty-seven feet down. He used the urine he carried to abate "mouth thirst," never swallowing it but instead swishing it around his cheeks. (By the fifth day or so, you can imagine how that tasted.) The last three days of his ordeal involved a lot of crawling around, wishing for death, thinking about killing that bastard Jesus, and otherwise watching his body disintegrate before his eyes. Valencia did, however, manage to keep to trails and he knew where he was; throughout McGee's description of the ordeal in his seminal article, "Desert Thirst as Disease," he describes Valencia's location and position, which he could have known only if the old man had told him. The old prospector always knew his location, but where he was held no water or fellow travelers who might supply it.

By the time it ended, he'd stumbled and crawled between one hundred and one hundred fifty miles, gone without good water for one hundred sixty hours—about six and a half days—and lost twenty-five percent of his body weight. His kidneys had ceased functioning for about two whole days. But the things that stayed functional are worth noting, too; though he'd experienced hallucinations during his trek, he never lapsed into "wholly insane delirium ... he never lost his trail-sense, and apparently squandered little vitality in those aimless movements that commonly hasten and harden the end of the thirst-victim." That focus—along with his blind hatred of Jesus—got him through the desert for twice as long as the best desert survivors, and fixed him in the annals of survivors as one of the champs.

≋ 𝌆 ≋

Though the Loma Prieta quake killed almost seventy people, a million people survived it. Those 2003 forest fires might have decimated hundreds of thousands of acres, but for all this fury, only a few dozen people lost their lives in the conflagration. It seems that when natural disasters happen, no matter how bad they are, we can always take solace in this: far more people survive them than die in them.

We can also rest easy knowing that in every disaster, whether it be natural or man-made, some people always rise up to follow the better angels of their nature. No calamity ever passes without at least a few stories of heroism from its survivors. Whether jumping into freezing water to pull victims out or leading the injured to safety through burn-scorched forest, dramatic rescue is as common a theme during disasters as death and destruction. Most often, these incredible rescues are the work of the professionals who make it their business to get the rest of us out of any trouble we might find ourselves in.

The legendary Yosemite Search and Rescue (YOSAR) works in a class all its own. This elite team has saved hundreds, if not thousands, from the worst backcountry messes you can imagine. They answer an average of one hundred ninety-three calls every year—everything from people stranded up on El Capitan's big walls, to hikers lost in the park's remote backcountry. What's more, many of YOSAR's personnel are volunteers—that is, they don't get paid for doing that dangerous work. Actually, they do get paid a little—according to Friends of Yosemite Search and Rescue, volunteers make around four thousand dollars a year, despite being on call every second of every day.

And they do manage to save a *lot* of people. The year 2006 was a light one—with only 146 incidents—but 2005 saw 231 calls of every type and description. In February, for example, the team rescued a woman who'd been caught skiing in a blizzard and eventually collapsed from hypothermia. When they found her, she was barely conscious, and her clothes were completely soaked through. Had they been much longer, she certainly would have died.

The same might be said for the pair of rock climbers who stranded themselves on the Royal Arches climbing route in June 2005; they'd set out believing their chosen route was "relatively easy," though neither had ever climbed it before. They proved themselves wrong, as the climb took longer than expected; in fact, they were still on the rock as night began falling. Even worse, rain started falling just after dark, and the climbers had no rain or camping gear at all. What began as a simple daylong climb was starting to look like something a lot more high-stakes. That is, it was until YOSAR personnel rescued the climbers during the night and got them down safely via North Dome Gully, the descent they thought they would reach hours ago.

Today, hapless climbers like these are YOSAR's bread and butter. In the fifties and sixties, as rock climbing became more popular and Yosemite became the sport's premier destination, area climbers began helping out the park's rangers, many of whom couldn't climb themselves, in rescuing people who managed to get themselves hung up. Today, of course, many park rangers can climb, too; still, YOSAR provides indispensable help in pulling errant, hapless climbers down when things go bad for them.

A few lucky ones get pulled off the rock before they fall; others fare worse, despite YOSAR's and the park rangers' best efforts. In October 2004, a freak snowstorm rolled into Yosemite, turning the weather from temperate and sunny to a roiling, freezing mess. As conditions turned, everyone climbing on El Capitan saw their adventure turn into a dangerous gamble, exemplified by the two Japanese climbers who died while climbing the "Nose," one of El Cap's most-traveled routes. They had bivouacked on a ledge known as Camp Six, about six hundred feet beneath the summit. Their position there wasn't good, but they stood a chance of survival; they had decent sleeping bags as well as a tarp to hold off the weather. As it happened, however, they decided to try and summit during the height of the storm—clearly an act of desperation and fear—and froze to death as they hung from the rock.

The other three climbing parties on El Capitan still needed saving, though. In fact, a lot of people needed saving; no less than nineteen people had gone missing throughout the area in the freak storm, many of them with little on them but cool weather (rather than *cold* weather) gear. Without quick thinking and quicker rescuing, the consequences could have been very bad indeed all across California's national parks. Luckily, between the hikers themselves and the rescue personnel, things worked out for most everyone.

As it was, the only people to lose their lives were the unfortunate Japanese climbers. All nineteen of the other climbers and hikers were saved, though some of them experienced pretty serious privations on the way. Like Richard and Sandra Smith, ages seventy and sixty-six, respectively, who turned up in an air search after spending an extra two days stuck out on the snow on top of their original weeklong trip. Another group, four members of a well-known Santa Cruz wine family, had no gloves between them, and used their wool socks to keep their hands warm. They had brought enough food for three people to eat for one day, and had only one tent that didn't leak. They ended up spending four days struggling to keep warm and rationing their meager supplies; according to the group, they ate five peanuts each morning for breakfast and a scoop of peanut butter for dinner.

Over the course of that storm, personnel across the national park belt saved seventeen people, many of whom very well would have died without the assist. And those rescues represent only one storm, about five days or so; national park rescue teams manage to do it year in, year out, with an incredibly high rate of success. And they do it for little money, little real recognition, and at great risk to their own safety. If you don't believe in saints, maybe you should.

≋ 𝖄 ≋

On March 27, 1964, seismologists recorded the third-largest earthquake seen since scientists began measuring, and the strongest ever in North America. The quake's epicenter was in north Prince William Sound, about seventy-five miles east of Anchorage, Alaska, and fourteen miles beneath the surface of the Earth. On the Richter scale, it came in at 8.4 to 8.6; the quake's moment magnitude—a measure introduced in 1979 as a successor to the Richter— measured 9.2. The quake lasted four or five minutes, an eternity for such an event, and generated towering tsunamis that built up speeds of four hundred miles per hour as they raced outward from the quake's genesis.

The Good Friday earthquake ultimately killed only 131 people, owing to the fact that Alaska in 1964 was even more sparsely populated than it is today. In fact, only 115 people died in Alaska; the others died hundreds of miles away in Oregon and California, where massive tidal waves slammed into the coast. These waves, the worst tsunamis in U.S. history, hit a number of spots up and down the coast, but did their worst damage in little Crescent City, up in California's northern reaches. While eleven people died there, a lot more lived, and saved each other, as the waters crashed into their quiet little haven. The whole affair demonstrates that even during the worst natural disasters, ones that unleash the whole fury of the planet on us, you don't have to be a rescue professional to show all the best qualities of human nature.

The first tsunami warnings came about three and a half hours after the quake hit. Crescent City, a town of fishermen and loggers, had seen a particularly pleasant Good Friday by the time that warning brought news of impending disaster. Not that the residents hadn't seen their share; sunken ships littered the nearby Pacific, thanks to the angry storms that periodically visited the area. In addition, the town had experienced tidal wave scares before, most of which amounted to nothing. Compared to the disaster to come, those warnings, even the storms and their towering waves, would amount to nothing but exaggerated swells.

The Good Friday quake unleashed force equivalent to about twelve thousand Hiroshimas. Parts of the ground in Alaska liquefied as it shook, turning into a sucking slurry of sand and rock. Again, had the area been as well populated as the California coast, for example, the loss of life and property would have been disastrous. As it was, Anchorage and its outlying towns suffered terribly, with whole suburban areas detaching from their geological moorings and sliding off into the sea.

In the ocean, this incredible force generated a shock wave running miles down into the depths. A few billion tons of seawater suddenly shot forward, displaced by the moving plates and extending over thousands of square miles. Quite literally, the whole Pacific was moving, from the surface to the black bottom. In deep water, waves move incredibly fast, reaching four hundred miles per hour in water twelve thousand feet deep. As the waves reach shallower water, they slow down, but with a terrible consequence: they grow in height. The biggest eventually reach hundreds of feet, though a tsunami-style wave—that is, one generated by seismic disturbance—moves enough water fast enough at five feet of height to knock down and kill non-swimmers.

The water jetting down toward the Canadian and American coasts traveled invisibly, sweeping along the deep bottom. It reached British Columbia first, killing no one but causing about ten million dollars in damage. It then shot down into Oregon, reaching that coast around midnight (instead of at rush hour or midday, when things could have been much worse). Four people died there, and every beachfront town in the state saw some damage. An entire fleet of fishing and recreational boats was effectively destroyed, as it was washed down the coast and inland.

Crescent City took the mean hit it did for a few reasons. It lay in a direct line from the epicenter; no islands or other land stood in the way to blunt the force and speed of the waves. In addition, a number of rivers empty into the Pacific nearby. Rivers serve as conduits for tsunamis, bringing their force inland as the waves travel up through the freshwater. Underwater geography didn't help either, as the area's features served to redirect the wave toward town. In fact, during the infamous 1960 Chilean earthquake—the strongest ever recorded—Crescent City recorded tsunamis eight and half feet high, which grew to eleven feet as they surged closer to the beach. And that quake happened six thousand miles away—the one comparatively around the corner in Alaska was bound to hit even harder.

The initial wave measured fourteen feet in height. It crashed into town around midnight, immediately followed by a host of other waves that buffeted the town into submission. (The first two, high as they were—fourteen and eleven feet, respectively—actually caused no fatalities.) The fourth wave, about twenty-one feet high, commenced the real destruction, pulling cars and even entire houses in its wake. It also took a number of people by surprise, as most thought the worst had come and gone with the initial waves.

In some residents, that fourth wave's rude awakening also awakened the same instinct for preservation that saved Pablo Valencia, Eric LeMarque, and the rest of the individuals described above. The difference: many of Crescent City's survivors ended up saving their neighbors along with themselves. A teenager named Guy Ames, cast adrift on a van with his brother Brad and four friends, pulled another boy onto their "boat" as he drifted by clinging to a refrigerator; as they drifted, the boys caught sight of an elderly couple trapped in their Volkswagen, windows up but sinking fast. The boys eventually got to safety on the roof of a car port, and once they did the same car crashed into the building below them as the water level dropped. They leapt down into the maelstrom and tore off a door, freeing the couple. Once they did, they administered CPR and kept the couple alive, no small feat for a crew of teenagers with little experience in such high-stress situations.

After the second wave, Joe Snow remembered that his friend Dan's three children were at home alone. He sped to the house, his Jeep occasionally floating on the cresting waters, and hustled the three kids, ages eight, nine, and fifteen, into his car. He managed to drive off just as the third wave was rolling in, and just before Dan Bunting himself came storming home to save his kids. He barely saved himself; the massive fourth wave crushed the Bunting house into oblivion, forcing Dan to leap over to the next house in line. When the water destroyed that place, he leapt again, where a man driving a grader rescued him. All three children, along with Joe and Dan, survived.

Charles Laklin saved his landlady after a log came smashing through the front of her house and pinned her against the wall. (Massive logs rammed their way through town all night, thanks to the numerous trucks and boats that spilled their lumber.) He then spent the next day helping the National Guard patrol for looters. Patrolman Harold Evans carried elderly Maude Kincaid one hundred feet in chest-deep, freezing water on the way to their being rescued.

Things got worse as the waves' effects became known. One big problem: downed electrical wires threatening electrocution, along with massive fires. One fire, the worst of them, started half a mile out of town when a Texaco bulk-tank station, its tanks smashed open by careening logs and cars, spewed gasoline into the water. Nearby, an exploding transformer had started a few buildings on fire; the traveling fuel ignited and eventually brought the conflagration back to the tanks, which promptly exploded.

Al Stockman, the Texaco attendant that night, was in the garage when the first waters hit. His boss Sonny, Sonny's wife, and a customer waiting for his car to be done were also there as the water began running into the garage. Thinking quickly, Stockman raised his boss's car up on one of the grease racks, keeping the couple out of harm's way. As the fourth wave hit and more water poured in, Stockman grabbed his customer and got to the higher ground himself. They all survived and escaped just before the station's tanks went up in flames.

After that night, Crescent City brushed itself off with relatively little fanfare. The disaster couldn't have been constructed better for minimizing fatalities; the first two smaller waves warned people, preparing them for the serious water to come. Had that massive fourth wave come first, the cost in lives would certainly have been worse. As it was, the initial tsunamis helped to prepare the people of Crescent City, warning them as to the potential danger to come (even if some thought the worst had already come and gone). Then, when that danger came to pass, they were able to rise up and meet it.

Without question, every disaster produces stories and heroes like these; it speaks to our benefit as a species that they do. Perhaps the actions of the Crescent City heroes, like New York City's 9/11 firefighters and the Good Samaritans who pulled so many out of Oakland's Cypress Parkway back in 1989, demonstrate a fundamental goodness and charity in the human race that, all too often, goes unseen.

The instinct for survival, it seems, is programmed not only for self-preservation, but also with the willingness to tempt death in saving others. What does it say about human nature that, when faced with such terrible circumstances, when reduced to our basest impulse—simple, pure survival—so many still find it within themselves to protect and save others, even complete strangers?

Quite a lot of good, actually.

Afterword

We love it, but it doesn't necessarily love us.

—LOU WHITTAKER,

mountaineer, on Mount Rainier

n writing this book, I struggled at times to come up with a reason for doing so. There was the instructional angle—so "it," in all its varieties, wouldn't happen again, or to demonstrate the consequences of being ill prepared, or to highlight where inane ideas will get you, etc. Ultimately I couldn't motivate myself with any of these ideas, particularly as I came across those stories with no incompetence involved, or when someone else was doing the killing—attacking another person who could only be called a victim, rather than a careless participant. *Death in the West* just didn't work as a cautionary tale collection. How could a story about someone killing someone else be called a cautionary tale? How can you warn someone against coming to rest in a river of freezing snowmelt after someone else tumbles down the mountain and into you?

By the same token, the book's theme could not be the complete capriciousness of the natural world, us included. The case can be made that every outdoor accident is the fault of the person who headed out there in the first place.

I settled on this: *Death in the West* is a brief history of rarity, the rare victories of calamity over humanity. Even the murderers might be seen as some form of the primitive triumphing over the civilized—the sinister and ancient over the innocent and unprepared.

If these stories do manage to impart any lesson at all, it is that the western United States can, in very specific and often unique ways, kill you. But that lesson didn't push me through these fascinating, terrible stories. After a time, I came to see this book as a chronicle of the balance between what the West could *do*, and what it mostly *did*. Yes, it can kill, and that's what this book is most concerned with. But it doesn't kill a majority of the time, which could be a testament to our incredible, hard-earned respect for the natural world at large or to that world's general benevolence. Whether the story entails a Malibu highway at midnight or a water-filled, thousand-foot-deep cave, the fact is that no matter where you go in the American West, you're most likely going to be OK. You probably won't end up in a book like this no matter how vacuous you become in your worst moments, how far you push yourself into the untamed wild, or how late at night you decide to take a stroll. Even profoundly high-risk activities work out for the best a huge majority of the time. Consider this: 451 people died trying to cross the U.S.–Mexico border illegally in 2005. About half a *million* made it. Even walking for days across a blazing hot desert ends up working out for the best a surprising majority of the time.

However, there is logic in the idea that if one participates in high-risk activities long enough, eventually something is bound to go wrong. This is true for even the most experienced and careful outdoorspeople. In October 2006, for example, legendary rock climber Todd Skinner fell five hundred feet to his death while rappelling down Leaning Tower in Yosemite. He had spent much of his climbing career creating routes on sheer rock walls that extended hundreds of feet into the air. What happened to cause Skinner's fatal fall is still under investigation—he was using standard climbing equipment during this particular climb—but it seems likely that the odds just caught up with him. Skinner's climbing achievements are countless, and he was inarguably a meticulously safe climber; but this time, his skill and experience ran headlong into the circumstances of the day, and he lost.

These musings are in no way meant to downplay the tragedies that befell the people mentioned in these chapters. In fact, it may be that all of them, even the ones who died through their own foolish acts, were more unlucky than responsible. After all, how many stupid people do stupid things every day, without dying as a result? The answer, in case you didn't know, is quite a lot. Take Larry Walters, for instance—in 1982, he tied forty-five weather balloons to a patio chair and filled them with helium. He figured that he would float up about thirty feet, pop a couple of balloons with the pellet gun he'd brought along, and float back down. Instead, he flew up like a shot, hitting a maximum altitude of *sixteen thousand feet*. The first people to notice the stunt were airline pilots headed into Long Beach airport.

Larry lived. Yet Steve Donathan, who didn't run a line when he went wreck diving on a ship he'd been on numerous times before, died. On the continuum of mindless acts, which one rates higher?

The human race is capable of a lot of things, but maybe the thing we're best at is moving on and forward, even to uncertain destinations. Despite the terrible things that sometimes happen to us along the way—even those things that spell the end of the line—we manage to proceed. People keep climbing mountains, exploring caves, and skiing avalanche-prone slopes. And they keep going into the desert with too little water, wandering into the backcountry without a map, and flying higher than their license gives them permission to. And most of them come back to tell the rest of us all about it.

May the rarity of the worst-case scenario inspire the rest of us to take on the unknown more often—with compass (and a few other things) in tow, of course.

CHRIS BECKER lives in Arizona with his wife Danielle and daughter Evelyn. A Pennsylvania native, he moved to the Phoenix area in 1997 and began his writing career soon thereafter. He has written dozens of articles on recreation in Arizona and the West in general, working as a columnist, editor, bookseller, construction worker, bartender, and restaurant industry analyst in between real jobs. *Death in the West* is his fourth book; previous works include *52 Great Weekend Escapes in Arizona*, as well as two more books in that series for northern and southern California. He graduated from Arizona State University's prestigious creative writing program in 2005.

Chris occasionally entertains political ambitions but thinks that maybe the skeletons are just fine in their closets after all. He also longs for a place in rural Europe somewhere, maybe Bavaria, if anyone's selling. And contrary to what he says when Phoenix temperatures hit triple digits, he does not miss "those gorgeous winter drives on the Schuylkill Expressway" all that much.